Praise for *First SEALs*

"Well researched and very well told, . . . a rousing tale of wartime derring-do . . . An absolute must-read."
—STEPHEN HARDING, bestselling author of *The Last Battle*

"Beautifully written, original and compelling from first page to last"
—JOHN C. MCMANUS, author of *The Dead and Those About to Die*

"A terrific, unforgettable narrative of the forerunners of today's amazing Navy SEALs—that puts the reader right in the watery battlefield with them."
—FLINT WHITLOCK, Editor, *WWII Quarterly* magazine

"O'Donnell sets the scene for today's SEALs and provides the reader with the history of the inception of Navy special operations."
—*Naval Institute Proceedings*

"Much of the history of the MU was buried in classified archives until unearthed by this author."
—*Seapower*

"Extensive research and interviews have now brought this story back to light. The author is an established authority on special operations forces and his new book sheds light on the origin of the SEALs."
—*Military Heritage*

"[A] well-written chronicle [and] . . . engrossing account of previously unknown World War II history"
—*Library Journal*

Praise for Patrick K. O'Donnell

"A great American writer"
—CLIVE CUSSLER, *New York Times* best-selling author

"Remarkable and very readable . . . vivid"
—RICK ATKINSON, author of *Day of Battle*

"Patrick O'Donnell has a rare talent for isolating and burrowing into the great military stories of recent history."
—HAMPTON SIDES, author of *Ghost Soldiers*

FIRST

SEALS

THE UNTOLD STORY OF THE
FORGING OF AMERICA'S
MOST ELITE UNIT

PATRICK K. O'DONNELL

DA CAPO PRESS

A Member of the Perseus Books Group

Book design by Cynthia Young

Library of Congress Cataloging-in-Publication Data
O'Donnell, Patrick K., 1969–
First SEALs : the untold story of the forging of America's most elite unit / Patrick K. O'Donnell. — First edition.
    pages cm
Includes bibliographical references and index.
ISBN 978-0-306-82172-1 (hardback) — ISBN 978-0-306-82173-8 (e-book)
1. World War, 1939–1945—Commando operations—United States. 2. United States. Navy—Commando troops—History. 3. United States. Navy. SEALs—History.
4. United States. Navy. Underwater Demolition Teams—History. 5. United States. Office of Strategic Services—History. 6. World War, 1939–1945—Campaigns— Mediterranean Region. 7. World War, 1939–1945—Campaigns—Italy.
8. World War, 1939-1945—Campaigns—Austria. 9. World War, 1939–1945— Amphibious operations. I. Title. II. Title: First SEALs, the untold story.
    D794.5.O37 2014
    940.54'8673—dc23
    2014026097

First Da Capo Press edition 2014
First Da Capo Press paperback edition 2015

ISBN 978-0-306-82414-2 (paperback)

Published by Da Capo Press
A Member of the Perseus Books Group
www.dacapopress.com

Da Capo Press books are available at special discounts for bulk purchases in the U.S. by corporations, institutions, and other organizations. For more information, please contact the Special Markets Department at the Perseus Books Group, 2300 Chestnut Street, Suite 200, Philadelphia, PA 19103, or call (800) 810-4145, ext. 5000, or e-mail special.markets@perseusbooks.com.

10 9 8 7 6 5 4 3 2 1

To Jack Taylor
and the renaissance men
of the Maritime Unit

—m—

To Lily

To Dawn

CONTENTS

Photos following page 148.

LIST OF MAPS

PREFACE

BEGINNING IN THE SUMMER OF 1942, an extraordinary group of men embarked on an experiment that would alter the course of modern warfare. A dentist, a Hollywood star, a British World War I veteran, an archaeologist, California surfers, a medical student, and even former enemies of America united to pioneer U.S. Sea, Air, and Land operations. They combined intelligence gathering with special operations, much like today's Navy SEALs. Known as the Maritime Unit, these were America's first swimmer commandos, an elite breed of warrior-spies decades ahead of their time. Technically, there were no SEALs in World War II, as the unit officially formed in 1962. But the Maritime Unit bent the norm to create tactics, technology, and a philosophy that live on in the modern U.S. Navy SEALs and shape the battlefield of today. No other American World War II unit was quite like it.

The men of the Maritime Unit maintained their vows of silence. Their story was classified, lost, and buried in miles of warehoused government records. Now, the World War II generation is in its twilight, and the last of these extraordinary men are slowly fading away.

This is their story.

PROLOGUE

NOVEMBER 1942, SHOREHAM HOTEL, WASHINGTON, D.C.

At the intersection of Connecticut Avenue and Calvert Street in Washington, D.C., stands the well-appointed Shoreham Hotel. Built in 1930, the impressive art deco structure boasts 832 luxurious guest rooms, several elegantly furnished ballrooms, high-ceilinged dining rooms, and a sumptuous lobby illuminated by a host of glittering chandeliers. The hotel features nearly every amenity a discerning traveler or even a president could desire. At the behest of Franklin D. Roosevelt's staff, the hotel quietly added a special ramp and elevator to accommodate the president's wheelchair, allowing the Shoreham to serve as the venue for FDR's first inaugural ball and host inauguration galas for every subsequent president throughout the twentieth century.

The Shoreham has had more guests and hosted more functions than history has recorded, but on the evening of November 18, 1942, a small group of men gathered at the hotel to engage in an activity that would directly and substantially influence the evolution of America's military. They came not to stay in one of the suites or to eat in the dining room or even to relax with a drink in one of its lobbies. Instead, they gathered around the hotel's expansive indoor pool, which at the time was one of the largest in Washington, D.C.

On that cold November night, Jack Taylor was gearing up for the evening's demonstration while guards posted at the pool doors turned away any guests who came down to enjoy a swim. A renowned Hollywood dentist, Taylor put his livelihood on hold

1

during World War II to serve his country. He was an avid swimmer and lifelong adventurer who had a penchant for racing yachts, sailing solo halfway around the world, and flying airplanes. An ultimate survivor, he once escaped from an Alaska gold mine after being trapped for two days following an earthquake. After Pearl Harbor, Taylor volunteered for the U.S. Navy, which initially relegated him to a dull dental position on a ship. Later, the highly secretive Office of Strategic Services (OSS) sought to recruit him, and Jack enthusiastically volunteered to join its ranks.

This swim was unlike any other in Taylor's lifetime. He dipped his toes into the 60-plus degree water and put on a face mask, carefully checking the hoses and buckles of the newly invented Lambertsen Amphibious Respiratory Unit (LARU), a breakthrough underwater breathing device that was a precursor to SCUBA (self-contained underwater breathing apparatus). Initially constructed in the inventor's garage from an old World War I gas mask and a bicycle pump, the LARU was the first closed-circuit rebreathing device that would be used in American military underwater operations. That night at the Shoreham pool, America would finally have a device that would enable it to compete with the Axis powers' much more advanced and sophisticated underwater military operations. The LARU provided the technology America needed to pioneer the formation of an elite and highly effective American commando unit that would ultimately do it all: sea, air, and land operations.

Taylor secured the oxygen tank and scrubber, then plunged into the pool. The water enveloped his body as he remained submerged, breathing with the assistance of the LARU, swimming one lap after another. Normally exhalation underwater would cause a stream of air bubbles—a telltale trace that could reveal the presence of any diver. Any sign of bubbles remained absent as Taylor's audience watched him swim without coming up for air.

The small retinue of men present for the testing included the device's inventor, twenty-five-year-old Christian Lambertsen, a medical student. In the coming months, Lambertsen would covertly engage in testing and development of the LARU, traveling back and forth to Washington, D.C., from Philadelphia, where he attended the University of Pennsylvania's Medical School. Sworn to secrecy, he couldn't tell anyone—not even the school dean—the true reason for his trips.

Standing next to Lambertsen was British officer Commander H. G. A. Woolley of the Royal Navy, on loan to the OSS. Recently Woolley had been serving on the personal staff of the British Chief of Combined Operations and the British Joint Staff Mission in Washington, D.C. General William J. Donovan personally chose him to "assist in the study of British methods of training operatives and raiding forces." Prior to the war, Woolley lived in Hollywood, where he was a successful scriptwriter for several major studios. It is likely Taylor and Wooley ran in the same circles and were friends before the war. The bearded World War I veteran possessed the dynamic transformative leadership capabilities that could take an idea and develop it into a new form of warfare. With very few resources, he quickly built a new organization that would reshape intelligence gathering and warfare for generations to come.

On that cold November night, Taylor, Woolley, and Lambertsen made history. Their successful experiment in the Shoreham's pool spawned the beginnings of one of America's most elite military units—the U.S. Navy SEALs.*

---

*U.S. Army Special Forces, the Green Berets, also trace their combat swimmer program to the OSS Maritime Unit.

1

"CAVITIES IN THE LION'S MOUTH": THE BIRTH OF UNDERWATER COMBAT SWIMMING

DECEMBER 19, 1941, THE WATERS OUTSIDE ALEXANDRIA HARBOR

Resting silently in the dark, cold waters of the Mediterranean at a depth of forty-five feet below the surface, the *Scirè* released three lethal *maiali* (pigs) that would change the balance of power in the region. Frogman Luigi Durand de la Penne and his five other confederates riding the *maiali* were part of a special undersea Italian commando group known as *Decima Flottiglia Mezzi d'Assalto*, or, simply, *Decima MAS*. Created more than a year earlier, the unit consisted of Gamma men (frogmen specially trained in affixing underwater explosives), a parachute battalion, and the San Marco Battalion, a group of highly trained operatives and boat handlers.

Early in the war, the Italian Navy had modified the 709-ton *Auda*-class Italian submarine to deliver the twenty-four-foot, 1.6-ton torpedoes as well as the specialized SEAL-like teams trained to maneuver the warheads and affix them to their intended targets. An electric motor powered the submersibles, which were guided by two frogmen who rode atop them. This daring mission called for the men and their pigs to travel over a mile underwater and stealthily enter the lion's den: Alexandria Harbor, one of the most heavily defended Allied harbors in the world and where many of the prized ships of the Royal Navy were berthed. To reach their objectives, the divers would have to carefully and covertly navigate the maze of torpedo nets and other defenses that ringed the harbor.

The Gamma men wolfed down a quick meal and took stimulants before being discharged from the submarine. On their way to the deck from which they would be launched, the commanding officer of the submarine, Prince Junio Valerio Scipione Borghese, also the leader of *Decima MAS* and known as the "Black Prince," gave each of them a ceremonial kick in the ass for good luck. The Black Prince was largely responsible for pioneering and directing Italy's underwater combat operations.

Surreptitiously, the commandos rode through the water, quickly advancing on their intended targets. Patiently, de la Penne and the others riding the pigs waited for the Allies to open up their defenses to let three British destroyers exit the harbor. The massive hulls of the Royal Navy ships loomed in front of them when a small British motorboat appeared suddenly from the night's gloom and randomly dropped a series of depth charges in the harbor. The crude tactic was meant to repel Axis underwater operatives, who the British had encountered several months earlier.

Booming underwater concussions began wreaking havoc on the men's bodies, "painfully constricting [their] legs." Undaunted, de la Penne and his partner were closing in on the HMS *Valiant* when everything began to go wrong. As he was maneuvering around the many underwater obstacles that littered the harbor, de la Penne ripped his wetsuit and icy seawater hit his skin. Despite months of training to condition his body to withstand the elements, hypothermia began to take its toll. Increasing the likelihood of detection, his partner's underwater breathing device failed, and he had to surface. De la Penne was now swimming solo atop the gigantic torpedo when suddenly the propeller stopped after snagging a cable. Unable to disentangle it, he was forced to transport the huge underwater explosive manually. As de la Penne recalled, "[I had] to drag the torpedo along in the mud by [my] strength until directly beneath the ship. The mud was extremely gooey and cut out all visibility, but I guided my pig by the noise of one of the pumps on board the enemy ship. . . . Seawater seeped into my mask, and I had to drink it to avoid drowning."

Despite all the adversity, he somehow managed to attach a 230-kilogram explosive charge of TNT under the centerline of the hull of the *Valiant* and set the time-activated detonator. The pigs were the pinnacle of high technology for the time, one of Italy's most classified secrets. Naturally, they didn't want the crafts to fall into enemy hands. They were equipped with self-destruct mechanisms, but de la Penne knew he didn't need it on this occasion because the explosion would destroy the submersible. Though his teammates failed to locate their primary target, a British aircraft carrier, they were able to attach their mines to the battleship HMS *Queen Elizabeth* and to a large Norwegian tanker known as the *Sagona*. The Gamma men also carried with them incendiary devices to ignite oil from the destroyed tanker with the goal of wreaking further havoc in the harbor following the explosions.

Out of air and exhausted, de la Penne surfaced. When a crewman aboard the *Valiant* spotted him, the ship sent a hail of machine-gun fire his way, forcing him and his partner to surrender. Ironically, both men were taken aboard the *Valiant* and placed in a compartment near the location of the explosive charge they had just planted. Fifteen minutes before the explosives were scheduled to detonate, de la Penne made an urgent request to speak to the ship's commanding officer (CO), Captain Charles Morgan. After approving the request, the CO listened intently as the Gamma man informed him of the imminent explosion on his ship. However, the cagey Italian frogmen refused to reveal the location of the mine. Morgan, in no mood for games, ordered the Italians to be placed in the hold. Before they reached their destination, a tremendous blast ripped apart the *Valiant*'s hull.

Simultaneous explosions echoed across the harbor as the limpets affixed to the other ships detonated. The *Sagona* lost her entire stern. A destroyer, the HMS *Jarvis*, berthed alongside the Norwegian tanker, was also badly damaged, as were many other craft in the area. The two battleships, *Valiant* and *Queen Elizabeth*, sank in a few feet of water, effectively putting them out of action for nearly a year. One historian has noted, "Overnight, [the eastern Mediterranean] had become an Axis lake, and the Italian Navy held the dominating power." Although the Italians succeeded in their mission, they failed to escape capture. Ultimately, the British arrested all of the Gamma men involved in the attack, though two nearly escaped by disguising themselves as French sailors. En route to rendezvous with the *Scirè*, the "French sailors" attempted to exchange British currency outside Alexandria and blew their cover, leading to their rapid arrest.

The *Scirè*'s crew observed the devastation the explosions caused as they waited at the rendezvous point. Time passed. Eventually it became clear to everyone on the ship that the Gamma men would not be returning. Borghese ordered his vessel to depart the area. He had reasons to be pleased, as he had seen his prophecy become a reality. In a coded message to headquarters prior to the attack he predicted, "Foresee cavities developing in Lion's mouth."

This innovative, highly trained group of Italian Gamma men had changed the course of underwater combat forever.

* * *

FOLLOWING THE ITALIANS' successful underwater attack on the British Navy, an intense race ensued among the powers of the world to replicate *Decima MAS*. At the time the United States was the furthest behind. The federal agency in charge of developing special operations units and gathering foreign intelligence was the newly formed office of the Coordinator of Information (COI), later known as the Office of Strategic Services (OSS).

Prior to World War II, no national intelligence agency existed, and America lagged far behind the world's major powers. Several departments within the U.S. federal government each collected intelligence separately and sent reports on to the White House as they saw fit. Rather than sharing, agencies hoarded what they knew, and the president received a hodgepodge of reports that may or may not have been important enough to warrant his attention. As one intelligence officer lamented, "Our intelligence organization in 1940 was primitive and inadequate . . . operating strictly in the tradition of the Spanish-American War."

To help integrate the stove-piped organizations, Franklin Delano Roosevelt established the COI to aggregate the intelligence reports, making them available to various departments and the White House as necessary. According to the organization's official history, "through COI and its successor, the Office of Strategic Services (OSS), the United States was beginning its first organized venture into the fields of espionage, propaganda, subversion and related activities under the aegis of a centralized intelligence agency." Although the concepts of spies, sabotage, and propaganda were as old as warfare itself, "the significance of the COI/OSS was in the concept of the relationship between these varied activities and their combined effect as one of the most potent weapons in modern warfare."

To head the new intelligence agency, FDR chose a dynamic Wall Street lawyer, William J. Donovan. In his past, Donovan had been an assistant attorney general of the United States under Calvin Coolidge, a personal political adviser to Herbert Hoover, and commander of a battalion of the 165th Infantry Regiment, better known as the "Fighting 69th." A true war hero, Donovan had received the Medal of Honor, a Distinguished Service Cross, and two Purple Hearts. Nicknamed "Wild Bill," which referred to his prowess on the college gridiron, he "knew everybody" and had important connections at all levels of American society.

Prior to his assignment as COI chief, Roosevelt had tapped Donovan to make two overseas fact-finding trips. The first took place in 1940. Donovan went to the UK to determine whether England, at the time under threat of invasion from Germany, would survive the war. During this trip the Brits showed Donovan the workings of their intelligence services. Nearly a year later Roosevelt asked Donovan to return and analyze the Mediterranean. Donovan "accepted [the mission] with alacrity, for one of the concrete ideas which had developed in his mind was the importance of the Mediterranean in World War II." Whereas many military thinkers viewed the Mediterranean merely as a shipping channel, Donovan saw it as a crucial battle line—one that the Axis controlled. He believed the Allies needed to reclaim this front in order to prevail in the war. His firm belief would guide OSS action during the war.

Donovan's activities for the president helped him to recognize another major problem with the country's intelligence system. FDR and his cabinet were being deluged with a stream of fragmentary information. They had no time to analyze the pieces of data and make the necessary decisions. In a memo sent to Roosevelt, Donovan wrote, "It is essential that we set up a central enemy intelligence organization which would itself collect either directly or through existing departments of the government, at home and abroad, pertinent information." He went on to call for the analysis of the data by "specialized trained research officials in the relative scientific fields, including technological, economic, financial and psychological scholars." His argument convinced Roosevelt of this need, and FDR appointed Donovan to the top job at the newly formed organization. Donovan would prove to be the ideal COI chief.

Before accepting the position, Donovan made three requests: "that he should report directly to the President; that the President's secret funds would be made available for some of the work of COI; and that all departments of the Government be instructed to give him such materials as he might need." Roosevelt agreed to all three and further directed Donovan to "carry out, when requested by the President, such supplementary activities as may facilitate the securing of information."

As America's top spymaster, Donovan spearheaded a new approach to combat: a combined arms shadow warfare. He saw espionage, propaganda, sabotage, and other covert operations as the "modern counterparts of sapping and mining in the siege warfare of former days." Donovan's office would not only gather intelligence; it would also serve to soften up the enemy before ground forces invaded. He combined intelligence analysis, special operations, psychological operations, and counter-intelligence all under one roof. All the other major powers of World War II had these functions largely siloed, which hindered needed collaboration and integration. To do this, Donovan needed an extraordinary team of covert agents and analysts to be able to compete with the Germans, whom he considered "big league professionals in shadow warfare, while America lagged behind as the bush league club." He had studied the German psychological warfare in detail and noted that "they were making the fullest use of threats and promises, of subversion and sabotage, and of special intelligence. They sowed dissension, confusion, and despair among their victims and aggravated any lack of faith and hope." The Americans, by contrast, were doing almost nothing in this arena and, as a result, were unable to compete in this new form of shadow warfare. Donovan would opine that the only way to catch up would be to "kill the umpire and steal the ball." Practically overnight he would have to create a national intelligence agency, and in so doing, he would birth America's modern special operations and the first SEALs. Donovan became the father of America's special operations.

Making good use of his connections at every level, Donovan recruited people from all walks of life. Safecrackers recently paroled from prison joined Ivy League graduates from the country's leading law firms and corporations. Tough, battle-hardened Marines worked alongside the most elegant of debutantes. Donovan considered an ideal candidate someone with a "Ph.D. who could win a bar fight." According to one expert, "The OSS undertook and carried out more different types of enterprises, calling for more varied skills than any other single organization of its size in the history of our country."

Donovan possessed an uncanny ability to pick the right person for the right job, a skill that enabled him to build the new agency in record time. One operative captured the vibe within the new agency: "All the services were represented, and everyone was working up a scheme. Everything shimmered in secrecy, and it was a rare man who knew what his fellows were doing. Brooks Brothers was the unofficial costume-maker, while Abercrombie and Fitch functioned as an uptown Quartermaster Corps, supplying air mattresses and sleeping bags and paraphernalia so dear to the heart of small boys and civilians turned semi-guerrillas."

Donovan organized the new agency into several departments: Research and Analysis (R&A), Research and Development (R&D), Counterintelligence (X-2), Secret Intelligence (SI), Special Operations (SO), Psychological Operations or Morale Operations (MO), and, eventually, the Maritime Unit (MU). But developing a combat swimming group was a complex project that would have to wait while the COI concentrated on more pressing needs. In its infancy, the COI was primarily concerned with getting its agents into enemy territory, a key task for any intelligence organization. In Europe, organizations typically inserted agents by parachute, but they also occasionally needed to bring agents in by sea. According to OSS history, "To get from ship to shore in secrecy and in stealth is a special operation with a technique akin to no other. It belongs, strictly speaking, to neither Army nor Navy, yet is needed by both. It is the vital link in any combined operation. Approaching enemy shores, either for the purpose of depositing personnel or equipment or merely for reconnaissance, can ably be accomplished by submarines, fast surface craft, or disguised fishing vessels." In World War II, the difficulty lay in getting from a submarine or a large boat to shore, which often meant utilizing smaller craft such as rubber boats, folbots (foldable boats), and kayaks. The handling of these small craft required highly specialized training and fell under the COI's Special Operations branch. Initially the maritime group functioned as a servicing unit to support the other branches within the OSS with their naval needs as they related to espionage and sabotage. Originally known as the Maritime Authority, the pioneering group gave rise to a branch within the OSS known as the Maritime Unit (MU).

With the ability to see a tree where there was an acorn and select the ideal person for the right job, Donovan turned to a British officer, Commander Herbert George Arthur "H. G. A." Woolley. Dashing and brave, Woolley was a veteran of World War I, where he earned the Distinguished Service Cross at Gallipoli and was recognized for tending to wounded sailors at sea. Later he had participated as an adviser on numerous combined amphibious operations. Donovan met Woolley in Washington, D.C., where he was a member of the British Joint Staff Commission.

Woolley fit Donovan's ideal for a partner—an out-of-the-box thinker and risk taker. Woolley's additional gifts included consensus building, leadership, and, most importantly, the ability to take an innovative idea and turn it into reality. A veteran of war and the politics of service, he had the presence of a grandfatherly figure who wisely delegated authority to his subordinates. Woolley's concept of underwater combat swimming broke from the Italian methods of underwater attacks. Instead of riding most of the way to the target on the surface of the water, as the Italians did on their missions, Woolley suggested using combat swimmers who would swim under the water most of the way to conduct an operation. The OSS needed the technology to enable these kinds of missions, so they developed it from scratch.

On April 9, 1942, Donovan requested that the Special Operations branch establish the Maritime School to train its agents and operatives in covert insertion into enemy territory. On that day the

COI officially requested an allotment of personnel from the U.S. Navy. COI needed experienced seamen to train its agents and to set up a school. Nearly a month would pass before the Navy would approve three officers and twenty enlisted men. The Navy also sent three officers and fourteen enlisted men from the Marines.

The men, including Lieutenant J. H. "Jack" Taylor, slowly began to trickle in. Tall, with striking good looks, slate blue eyes, and brown hair with natural highlights from the perpetual southern California sunshine, thirty-four-year-old Taylor was a master of the sea who brought with him a lifetime of experience and adventure. Some would argue Taylor was hooked on the rush of adrenalin, continuously craving more—a man of action who preferred doing over talking. One operative remembered him as "a daredevil, bent on having his own show." Taylor exuded confidence, earned from countless brushes with death, and he had a habit of engaging in extreme sports, which was so far removed from his professional life of fixing teeth.

Taylor also tended to be laconic, a bit of a loner, and his tough outer shell masked a tempestuous inner side. A fellow officer recalled, "[He was] perpetually tense, with a remoteness in his eyes, forever flicking his tongue over dry lips."

As the half-dozen or so officers joined Woolley's staff, they began the hard task of building an organization and its training facility. To keep pace with the Italians, it would have to be built practically overnight.

2

AREA D

As the *Maribel* slowly rocked back and forth in its mooring at the Washington Yacht Club, Jack Taylor closely inspected the white and wood-stained planking of the aging sixty-seven-foot cabin cruiser. The search for a boat for training missions had gone on for months. Under the auspices of the OSS's Special Operations branch, the Maritime Authority, later known as the Maritime Unit, had little in the way of funds with which to acquire boats for training. With the Americans gearing up for war, the Coast Guard and the Navy had already pressed most of the private craft into service. Commander Woolley had joined the prestigious Washington Yacht Club in the hope of helping them find vessels, but there weren't many options. Taylor, Woolley, and the small group of men who made up OSS's Maritime Authority got what was left—the worst of the worst.

The official report on the *Maribel* noted, "She is, of course, a rather old boat, and her general condition reflects this." Before the craft would be fit for duty, she needed replacements for much of her decking as well as a complete overhaul of the engines.

Unfortunately the company that had built the engines had gone out of business, making it all but impossible to find replacement parts.

The other boat the Maritime Authority acquired for training purposes was in even worse shape than the *Maribel*. By all accounts the *Marsyl* was a rotting tub. According to the inspection report, "General appearance and condition of boat is poor with the following conditions existing: A. Hull structure would not stand survey as to soundness. B. Evidence of dry rot in bilges amidships and in frames in the stern. C. Deck will not hold fastenings for stanchions, davits, etc. D. Bad leak or leaks mainly from region of large butt-block on port side amidships." And the *Marsyl's* engine was in greater disrepair than her hull. In fact, they couldn't even get it started during the inspection.

Despite their deplorable condition, the two decrepit boats were towed from their berths at the yacht club and, after an extensive overhaul, were put to work on the Potomac, often operating at night, "blacked out" in a secret training area. Through constant maintenance, major repairs, and countless quick fixes, the boats served the OSS as transports and makeshift "submarines" for training purposes.

* * *

WOOLLEY AND TAYLOR had their work cut out for them. They had a mission, but they lacked the necessary supplies and equipment to accomplish it. Finding an area suitable for training was just as difficult as finding boats. Practically overnight they had to build facilities for OSS operatives being trained in maritime operations and sabotage. "It was necessary for Commander Woolley to beg, borrow, and almost steal" in order to be ready in time for the first class of OSS covert operations trainees.

Somehow Woolley found the funds, and the OSS took out a lease on April 1, 1942, for frontage of approximately ten thousand feet on the Maryland side of the Potomac River, several miles south of

Quantico, known as Smith Point. Because the land had no buildings to house the men or future supplies, they shipped in structures from an old Civilian Conservation Corps (CCC) camp at St. Stephens Church, Virginia. But the buildings were far from complete. Taylor and a small group of OSS men had to lend a hand erecting the structures. With hard work and dogged determination, they transformed 1,230 acres of mosquito-infested, waterlogged territory into a top-secret training facility codenamed "Area D."

"D" was in the middle of nowhere. There was no place for those constructing the facility to sit comfortably at night. According to one OSS officer, "The barracks were too hot and the mosquitoes and ticks will eat [people] alive if they sit outdoors." Initially OSS tightly controlled the use of the small fleet of Jeeps the men were issued, so no one could readily escape Area D. Compounding the misery, the nearest store was miles away, so they couldn't easily buy cigarettes to feed the nicotine habit that was pervasive among the American military at the time. One OSS officer opined, "There is an argument that the men on Guadalcanal [the battle in the Solomon Islands that was raging at this time] and other places have a tougher life than my men but they are in the U.S.A., and are human enough to want a life for which they are fighting for." Gradually, as the buildings were constructed and the government restriction on travel eased, life improved.

As the buildings went up, someone needed to guard the secret facility, but the OSS faced a severe shortage of military security personnel due to the war efforts. The Army unit assigned for security around Area D did not arrive in time for the first class of operatives, so the OSS improvised. In its habit of doing much with whatever resources it had, "[f]our elderly and reliable local men were hired to act as watchmen and four [African Americans] were engaged to carry out mess duties." Area D was finally ready to receive its first class of recruits to engage in covert OSS maritime training.

In addition to building the Area D facilities, the men also went to work repairing the rotting hulks that would serve as their

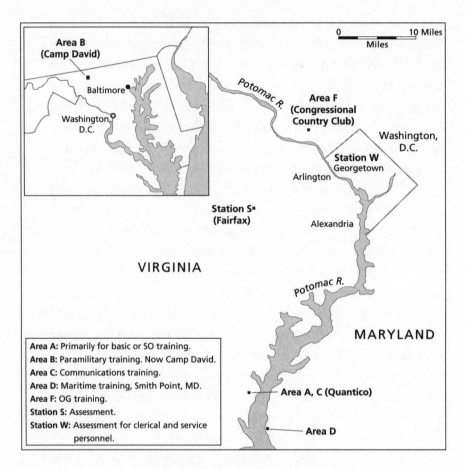

0   10 Miles
         Miles

Area B
(Camp David)

Baltimore

Washington,
D.C.

Potomac R.

Area F
(Congressional
Country Club)

Washington,
D.C.

Station W
Georgetown

Arlington

Station S
(Fairfax)

Alexandria

VIRGINIA

Potomac R.

MARYLAND

Area A: Primarily for basic or SO training.
Area B: Paramilitary training. Now Camp David.
Area C: Communications training.
Area D: Maritime training, Smith Point, MD.
Area F: OG training.
Station S: Assessment.
Station W: Assessment for clerical and service
          personnel.

Area A, C (Quantico)

Area D

OSS TRAINING GROUNDS
IN THE WASHINGTON AREA

training boats. Taylor not only helped with repairs but also acted as a scrappy supply sergeant, borrowing from Peter to pay Paul and doing everything from ordering sparkplugs to consulting with marine architects on ways to improve the vessels. Taylor rolled up his sleeves and got out his hand tools to make the continuous repairs the boats sorely needed. According to a note handwritten by Taylor, "I can't recall but presume that it [the part for one of the boats] was paid. It was for *Marsyl*, just before we took her down the river for good. We have the putty knife for the *Maribel*," which he knew how to put to ample good use.

An expert sailor, Jack Taylor had taken his own boat solo across much of the Pacific. With his incredibly well-honed boat-handling and nautical skills, Jack was a natural choice to become the chief instructor at Area D.

Joining Taylor as an instructor at D was Lieutenant Ward Evelyn Ellen. Dark-haired and well-built, Ellen had previously served with the Merchant Marine and the Navy, where he obtained the nautical skills that made him invaluable to the OSS. But unlike many of the other men recruited for the MU, Ellen was just an "average Joe" and didn't share Taylor's gung-ho spirit about entering into the thick of the action, though he served his country well. His service record notes his excellent practical intelligence, stability, ability to work well with others, leadership capabilities, courage, integrity, and diligent work record as well as his "picturesque language," which the OSS perceived as a potential weakness. However, Ellen never felt he belonged in the OSS and longed for a less exciting assignment. One of Ellen's personal evaluations noted, "Considerably disgruntled by a series of assignments for which he feels he was not fitted by training, experience, or interest, he wishe[d] to leave OSS and return to the Merchant Marine or Navy. He was assigned to OSS involuntarily and without any knowledge of the objectives or functions of the organization, and perhaps for this reason found the operations too 'dramatic,' the duties too varied, and the periods of inactivity too frequent." Despite some perceived shortcomings, Ellen proved to be an excellent operator who would be integral to many of the MU's early activities.

* * *

BY EARLY SEPTEMBER 1942, the first class of students arrived at Area D. The objective of the school was "to teach each student how to penetrate an enemy-occupied territory by sea." The course lasted two weeks and covered small-boat handling (including kayaks and canoes), navigation, tides, currents, charts, landing operations, and how to use explosives to sabotage shipping targets, such as ships, docks, warehouses, and other facilities. Each OSS student also left knowing how to crew and sail an antiquated sailboat that was moored alongside the *Maribel* and the *Marsyl*.

Many of the trainees' covert exercises carried a real element of danger. For example, in one session, "Under the direction of the leader, the operatives go on to throttle the sentry and demolish the central station, about a half mile inland." The mock exercise even included "killing the enemy sentry with a hand grenade, which noise immediately raised the alarm." Two Maritime trainees actually died in one of the exercises after their boat capsized; they drowned in the churning, dirty waters of the Potomac.

As chief instructor, Taylor did everything to make the night training as realistic as possible. It was wartime 1942, and in order to succeed the students needed to avoid detection by roving bands of armed shore patrols. In the frenzy of the burgeoning war efforts and after the attack on Pearl Harbor, national security was on high alert, and the military set up a series of security detachments along the Potomac to guard against enemy infiltration via U-boat. Instructors informed the students that the shore patrol was there to apprehend them and that they were amply supplied with "live ammunition." The Maritime Authority documents noted, "The students got small comfort from the rumor that [the shore patrol] were poor shots." Little did they know at the time, the "live" ammunition was actually blank rounds.

The backbone of the course was a covert night-landing operation at the end of the first week. Teams of students would attempt to make a clandestine insertion under the cover of darkness. Typically a four-man crew of trainees would set out in a small rubber or folding boat. Working in pairs, they attempted to land with the utmost of stealth at a very specific prescribed point. The trainees completed scores of exercises. A typical assignment read, "1) You are to land within . . . a strip of beach in front of the camp about 2,600 yards in length. 2) Hide your boat effectively." Throughout the exercises "the instructors encouraged students to take risks." Unsurprisingly, most of the candidates were "of a daring type."

After—hopefully—avoiding the shore patrols, the candidates were to "rendezvous at an abandoned house bearing 152°." On other occasions they were sometimes directed to a small graveyard, which lent an eerie aura to the proceedings. One set of instructions read, "POSITION OF CONCEALED RUBBER BOAT: In brush 10 yards directly east of tombstone marked 'William Mitchell,' which is in center of clump of trees approximately 150 yards north of camp and 50 yards east of beach."

In these high-stakes, clandestine scavenger hunts, candidates had to gather a specific piece of intelligence. In the early training exercises the OSS began blending special operations insertion with intelligence gathering, which was groundbreaking by World War II standards. After collecting the information, the trainees had to once again avoid the dreaded shore patrol, quietly launch their craft, and vigorously row to meet their "submarine," a role played by the aging and venerable *Marsyl,* which sat anchored in the river, awaiting their return.

3

THE RACE TO DESIGN
A REBREATHER

INSPIRED—AND ALARMED—by the feats of the Italian frogmen, the Americans raced to catch up. Woolley, Taylor, Ellen, and the first men of the Maritime Authority anxiously pored over their enemy counterparts' accomplishments. "Almost weekly reports come to OSS recounting exploits of maritime sabotage that constitute one of the most intriguing chapters of this war. They have served as a constant guide and incentive to the Maritime Unit." The Italian frogmen had the expertise and technology to achieve spectacular success, and the major powers all formed underwater swimmer programs. What Woolley needed was a device for breathing underwater.

Woolley went to the Washington Navy Yard during the summer of 1942 to investigate the possibility of underwater swimming for the United States—through the OSS. Woolley, ever the visionary, saw the powerful potential of underwater combat:

> With the possibilities of carrying out operations using the underwater swimming apparatus, what might be called a new field is opened up. Using the apparatus, it would be possible to carry or tow a much larger limpet [a magnetic mine] as would be preferable from a destructive point of view. A number of limpets would be placed against the hull of a ship to go off simultaneously. For this type of operations,

men specifically trained in the use of the equipment and good swimmers in practice would be desirable. I believe that using a submarine
or a fast boat under cover of darkness, an approach could be made
within a few miles of certain Axis-held harbors. From this point, a
few miles out, operatives and explosives would be transferred to a
new type of eight-man kayak. It would be carried in the vessel for that
purpose. The eight-man kayak could then proceed using an on-board
silent motor and paddling when necessary to avoid the question of
noise to the harbor.

In order to make Woolley's vision a reality, the United States
would need as-yet-undeveloped equipment that would allow swimmers to breathe underwater without releasing telltale bubbles. The
race was on to create a closed-circuit device related to SCUBA
(self-contained underwater breathing apparatus)* that would allow
swimmers to "rebreathe" their exhaled air underwater.

An innovative two-hose breathing device (the Italian device had
a single hose that only worked for short distances) that enabled the
swimmers to remain underwater for long periods of time was critical for a successful underwater swimmer program. The apparatus
needed to be lightweight and maneuverable so the swimmers could
adroitly move through the water, set charges, and accomplish other
tasks. Most importantly it needed to help the swimmers avoid detection by eliminating the usual bubbles that accompany underwater swimming. And because lives would be on the line, the device
had to be totally dependable.

---

*Christian Lambertsen may have been the first to coin the term SCUBA.
In 1943 underwater pioneer and explorer Jacques Cousteau improved
an aqua-lung design, developing an open-circuit demand regulator that
refreshed air when the diver breathed. But the open-circuit design left a
stream of bubbles. The Italians developed a rebreather, manufactured by
Pirelli, for the Gamma men to use.

Woolley first began his efforts to develop a new underwater breathing apparatus by inspecting the equipment the Navy already had on hand. He recalled, "Soon after I was put in charge of maritime training, I came across [a] diving mask. I found this could be used as a self-contained unit and arranged with the Navy department so that I could carry out tests with it at the diving school and at the [Washington, D.C.] Navy Yard. This unit did not last very long and showed [a] considerable amount of bubbles. The diving school put me in contact with Mr. Browne of Diving Equipment and Salvage Company (DESCO). I explained to him the requirement and he produced a mock-up unit."

Jack Browne, a young, pioneering underwater diver, had an extraordinary gift for innovation. He fabricated his first diving helmet from tin cans. Browne later designed a diving suit to be used for salvaging the *Lusitania*, a passenger ship sunk in the Irish Channel by a German U-boat in 1915 during World War I, killing nearly all aboard. In 1937 he had formed DESCO, based in Milwaukee; however, he had to put off formally incorporating the company until 1938, when he would reach twenty-one years of age.

The OSS conducted the first official test of Browne's "lung" at the Washington Navy Yard's diving tank on October 20, 1942. Commander Woolley and Lieutenant Jack Taylor stood around the tank as Browne remained underwater "for thirty minutes, swimming leisurely in the confined area of the tank at an average depth of eight to ten feet." However, the mask leaked, causing more bubbles than would be expected.

Browne tested the equipment again at the Annapolis Natatorium on October 21, 1942. "The apparatus was demonstrated by Mr. Browne and one of the divers [from the Navy diving school]. Very few bubbles appeared [in the swimming pool], and the dive was entirely successful, except for some water getting into the canisters, making it slightly more difficult to breathe," recalled Taylor. While the canisters used as CO_2 scrubbers were being dried, Jack Taylor donned the standard Navy diving mask with a hose connected to a cylinder at the edge of the pool and swam underwater with ease for several minutes. Taylor suggested that the mask "might possibly be incorporated into the apparatus." Once the canisters were ready to go, Browne then strapped the lung back on and transported two limpet mines underwater, demonstrating an important technique of covert underwater sabotage. Woolley succinctly summed up the trial, saying Browne's lung "appeared to have good possibilities of being satisfactory for underwater swimming."

Woolley then approached the OSS chief of the Research and Development (R&D) branch, Dr. Stanley Lovell. A natural inventor renowned for his sometimes wacky yet ingenious ideas, Lovell and his team developed everything from a "truth drug" made from marijuana to a special project using bats as miniature drones to carry tiny incendiary bombs to ignite Japanese wooden houses. After Lovell scrutinized and ultimately blessed the breathing device, the OSS issued a contract to Jack Browne, paying him $400 for delivery of a refined lung. Browne returned to Milwaukee and continued to make modifications to his device based on the trials, including adding a luminous compass that the swimmer could see underwater. Though commonly found on diving equipment today, this useful feature was a very novel idea at that time.

Despite the promise of Browne's lung, the OSS wisely did not put all its eggs in one basket. As Browne continued development of his lung, another breathing device caught the attention of the OSS. On November 17, Christian Lambertsen, a young medical student from the University of Pennsylvania, arrived at the OSS office in the Q Building, located in downtown Washington, DC, and presented a rebreather of his own design to Woolley and Taylor. The next day, the three men tested Lambertsen's rebreather at the Shoreham Hotel and made history.

Lambertsen had grown up in New Jersey during the Great Depression, and he spent many summers at the Jersey Shore with his uncle. In 1939 he entered the medical school at the University of Pennsylvania, where one of his first classes covered respiratory physiology. "To learn about oxygen (O_2) and carbon dioxide (CO_2), the students breathed hypoxic gas to unconsciousness, hyperventilated to become hypocapnic, and conducted breath-holding contests to feel the effects of hypoxia and hypercapnia." Given his experience at the shore, "Chris was impressed by ten-minute breath-hold times after hyperventilation with O_2, and found O_2 and CO_2 particularly interesting for their control of ventilation."

Soon thereafter he began experimenting with rebreathing devices at the Jersey Shore. His first model relied on a couple of cousins to operate a bicycle pump, but he soon discovered the benefits of compressed oxygen. That still left the problem of expelled carbon dioxide, which made breathing underwater uncomfortable, but Lambertsen soon found a solution in the form of a scrubber made from a material used in anesthesia.

Impressed by Lambertsen's inventions, his mentor, University of Pennsylvania physiology professor Henry Bazett, brought the young student to the attention of the Ohio Chemical and Manufacturing Company. They offered him a job for $30 a week, which he gladly accepted. Lambertsen and the company set out to produce an underwater breathing apparatus for use in lifesaving situations. Ironically, in one of the device's first tests Lambertsen nearly needed lifesaving himself when he began to notice strange twitches in his eyes and legs as well as catches in his breath. He attempted to tug on the emergency rope to receive assistance but found he had forgotten to attach it to the boat. Amazingly, he managed to surface safely.

That wasn't Lambertsen's last brush with death. He and the company thought the unit might also be useful to rescue miners from potentially deadly situations. To test their theory, Lambertsen, wearing the rebreather, along with a dog and a canary, entered an air-tight chamber, which was then filled with cyclopropane, a highly flammable anesthetic gas. "The demonstration was filmed, with the local press and fire department in attendance. The canary fell off its perch; the dog fell off its shelf. When [Lambertsen] leaned over to check the dog, he, too, fell over. Something was wrong, and fire axes quickly dismantled the chamber where [the young medical student] was found unconscious. No one had realized that cyclopropane would penetrate the latex breathing bags and be inhaled. Mr. Sholes [the president of the Ohio Chemical and Manufacturing Company] issued a stern reprimand, 'Chris, you shouldn't have done that.'"

Soon after that disastrous encounter, England entered World War II. Lambertsen's mentor, Professor Bazett, immediately saw the military implications of his student's invention and wrote about it to the British Admiralty and the U.S. military. Soon Lambertsen was involved in talks with the U.S. military, and he adapted his device into the model that would become the Lambertsen Amphibious Respiratory Unit (LARU). He continued his dangerous practice of testing the device himself, diving ever deeper underwater in an attempt to ascertain the pressure limits of the rebreather. After one such test he reported, "My pressure tests went very well. CO_2 absorption was fine but O_2 poisoning came on at 80 feet. I was almost a goner."

In 1940 Lambertsen patented the device and continued his studies at medical school. He also worked steadily on the rebreather, making it his top priority. He noted in one letter, "As one of my professors put it, I do not intend to let my medical course interfere with my education." He continued to perfect the LARU, making minor modifications that improved its operation.

By the time the OSS became interested in the LARU, Lambertsen's rebreather was more refined than Browne's, which Woolley noted. The day after the youthful medical student arrived in Washington, "tests were carried out . . . at the Shoreham Hotel. Mr. Lambertsen remained underwater for forty-eight minutes, during most of which time he was swimming across the deep end of the pool. The apparatus appeared to be satisfactory. Lieutenant Taylor, who had never used this apparatus before, then put it on and appeared to have no difficulty swimming underwater with it."

★ ★ ★

THE LARU WAS A CLOSED-CIRCUIT rebreathing carbon dioxide–absorbing system, similar to Browne's lung. It consisted of a face mask, breathing tubes, soda-lime canisters, breathing bag, and several valves of special function. A canvas vest held the main parts of the "apparatus in a proper position relative to the diver's body; an oxygen supply; and the respiratory system. The oxygen supply system comprises a small oxygen cylinder, which when full, contains pure oxygen at a pressure of two thousand pounds per square inch. Oxygen is breathed and the carbon dioxide formed is absorbed in the soda-lime canister, permitting rebreathing of expired gases. Oxygen is added to the breathing system from the oxygen cylinder as needed as to replace that used by the diver." The use of pure oxygen is quite different from today's modern SCUBA gear, which contains air from the natural atmosphere. In addition, an internal Maritime Unit memo noted, "The Diving Unit is so designed that the wearer retains his natural balance and buoyancy equilibrium underwater. This permits him to work or swim in any conceivable position without interfering with respiration."

The main difference between Lambertsen's and Browne's devices was that the LARU outperformed Browne's lung in the trials. Accordingly, OSS requested that the young medical student produce additional devices and issued a contract to Lambertsen and the Ohio Chemical and Manufacturing Company to develop several more of his rebreathers.

News of the LARU spread. The British—particularly a high-ranking officer in the Special Operations Executive (SOE), Colonel John Frank, who knew Woolley—also expressed their interest in the device. The SOE was OSS's experienced British equivalent that conducted espionage, sabotage, and reconnaissance in Europe. "[When Frank] had heard about this apparatus . . . [he] asked about it and the Browne apparatus and was anxious that he could obtain two of the apparatus as quickly as possible." He then stated "that cash would be paid for them." The orders were placed.

For months, Lambertsen and Browne would be competitors. Both worked on improving their equipment with additional trials. Ultimately the OSS recognized the genius of both men. Keenly aware that collaborative efforts could exponentially increase the potential for innovation, Woolley encouraged the inventors to partner together.

4

COMBAT SWIMMERS

With some anxiety, lifeguard George Peterson put on Browne's lung and held on to the side of the boat. Slowly he submerged into the Pacific under the watchful eyes of Lieutenant Jack Taylor, inventor Jack Browne, and Fred Wadley, who was a former national champion swimmer, a member of the Santa Monica Sheriff's Department, and Browne's close friend. Peterson swam around the boat under the surface of the water for about twenty minutes, relying solely on the lung to breathe. He could have remained underwater, except the frigid 53-degree water "made it impossible to stay in longer."

Taylor, visiting his hometown of Santa Monica on personal leave, wanted to test Browne's lung in the open water of the Pacific Ocean. He had been a lifeguard stationed on these beautiful beaches throughout his high school years, during which time he broke numerous swimming records. Teeming with hard-core "beach rats," Santa Monica was home to some of the most experienced ocean swimmers in the world. Many of them were ahead of their time, already donning swim fins and face masks as they swam in the often turbulent ocean. Eventually the OSS would return to recruit from this extraordinary pool of aquatic talent. Santa Monica

31

was also the perfect place for Jack to simulate a real underwater combat mission, which he knew would likely take place against Axis forces operating in the Pacific, the Atlantic, and/or the Mediterranean. The ocean testing was necessary to ascertain the durability of the device because the rebreather had not yet been used in saltwater, which could have corrosive effects on the equipment.

Continuing to act as a sort of guinea pig, Peterson next attempted to swim from a mile and a half out in open water back to the Santa Monica beach. But just as he was donning the breathing apparatus, "the regulator in the oxygen line stuck, allowing the full charge of the cylinder (1,800 pounds) to go into the rubber connecting tube, causing it to burst." The equipment malfunction spelled the end of the trial.

With the equipment out of commission and his leave expired, Taylor transported the lung on a train back to the East Coast, where additional trials of both Browne's and Lambertsen's devices were scheduled to be conducted in the renowned natatorium at the U.S. Naval Academy in Annapolis, Maryland.

* * *

WEARING LAMBERTSEN'S LARU, Jack Taylor dove into the deep end of the natatorium pool. He and a comrade carefully carried limpet mines across the bottom of the pool, from one end to the other. They were vigorously testing the equipment, and before they could put it into use in combat situations, they had to determine precisely how long the rebreather would allow them to remain underwater, what were the best ways to maneuver while wearing the equipment, and the limitations of the device.

Extensive testing of the competing rebreathers went on through the winter and into the early spring. Eventually the OSS determined that the LARU was superior to Browne's lung. However, Woolley also recognized the genius of Browne's invention, valued his expertise, and attempted to enlist the pioneering diver on a full-time basis in OSS's underwater swimmer program. Woolley estimated he needed at least six months of Browne's time. But Browne was busy running DESCO, and his schedule didn't permit him to work full time for the intelligence agency. As a compromise, the OSS requested and Browne accepted that he would consult on a part-time basis with Lambertsen.

* * *

THE MARITIME AUTHORITY and combat swimming took a huge leap forward when, on February 18, 1943, Donovan himself granted approval of an Underwater Swimmer Group (USG). Until this time the men of the Maritime Authority trained Special Operations men in maritime sabotage and boat handling; the USG were the first operators for this unit—and America's first underwater combat swimmers.

At Annapolis, Jack Taylor was joined by the much younger Lieutenant Robert J. H. Duncan of the U.S. Naval Reserve, whom the OSS designated to help lead the organizational development and training efforts. A former swimming coach, Duncan was a tall, square-jawed, determined man with a thick crop of black hair and very strong opinions. Taylor and Duncan instructed the OSS's combat swimmers; five swimmers were split into two groups, with Taylor and Duncan each taking command of a unit. Three other men were part of the initial group: Gunner's Mate Second Class John P. Spence and Gunner's Mate Third Class Norman W. Wicker were both former Navy divers who had volunteered for the OSS. Jack's fellow "beach rat," Fred Wadley, who was designated "Operative #1," rounded out the group.

The group had placed an order for twenty-five LARUs. During combat swimming training the five-man training team tested the equipment on a regular basis, usually in late afternoons. Getting adequate pool time and maintaining secrecy was incredibly difficult due to the hundreds of midshipmen vying for time in the natatorium. Working around the limited access to the pool, the men also engaged in other commando-like activities to prepare for their future missions. A typical day's schedule read as follows:

8 a.m. Rifle range, armory, pistols

9 a.m. Rifles/carbines

10 a.m. Sailing/seamanship/knockabout (On Saturdays this was substituted with wrestling.)

11:30 a.m. Swimming

12:30 p.m. Noon hour (chow)

1:30 p.m. Boxing

2:30 p.m. Obstacle course

3:30 p.m. Swimming and lifesaving

4:30 p.m. Use of equipment in pool (On some days the pool would be freed up so the men could have a two-hour block in the pool)

5:30 p.m. Military drills and hand-to-hand combat on alternating days, sometimes with wrestling thrown in for good measure

As the training program launched into full swing, Duncan and Taylor obtained the support and cooperation of the Naval Academy's Henry Ourtland, whom they recruited as a "coach and advisor" for $50 per week. "It is obvious how valuable his services are since he has served in a similar capacity for the Navy Dep," wrote Duncan in a letter to Commander Woolley. The gung-ho lieutenant optimistically stated, "We will need four to six weeks training here and will have every facility, and we will be ready for the field at that time."

Duncan then went on to propose a novel, some would say harebrained concept: the "Aqua-Marines." Duncan saw the Aqua-Marines as a "specially trained force of men . . . created for the purpose of [pre-invasion] work." Essentially Duncan believed a team of swimmers could sneak onto enemy beaches and soften up the enemy before the main force arrived. In order to minimize losses he proposed towing "submarine rafts" to coastal areas prior to attack: "From these submarine rafts . . . the men can be disgorged from the rafts twenty feet beneath the surface of the water." Once in the water the men would float to shore on "surf boards whose decks are flush with the water," and these boards would also transport "machine guns and trench mortars."

From there, Duncan's imagination really got carried away, and he proposed that "the boards can be enlarged to accommodate five men and complete equipment with sail and auxiliary electric motor. Another added attraction of the paddle board is that it has many air chambers enabling the operator to deflate several chambers and submerge the board and carry out operations. After leaving the beach and returning to the board it can be re-inflated through the use of carbon dioxide chambers." He even believed these surfboards could tow floating mines into the harbors and concluded, "There is no question but what a beach-head could be established without arousing the fire of defensive fortifications. . . . Locations and obstructions to harbors could be easily blown apart without telegraphing the approach of surface vessels which were still miles at sea."

The entire concept didn't sit well with Jack Taylor, who told Duncan, "In general, I can see no advantage to the submarine rafts nor to disgorging the men from twenty feet beneath the surface. For ferrying operations, I can see no advantage of paddleboards over folbots and the disadvantage that the operator and equipment will be wet when arriving at the beach." Although he did see using the surfboards to transport underwater combat teams, he could not "visualize armed boards and forced landings from boards." Eventually the Navy SEALs did utilize underwater submersible craft—not to lead an invasion, but for covert work.

But not all of Duncan's ideas were pie in the sky. In fact, it was Duncan who advocated the importance of the combat swimmers working in teams, which is also a practice today's SEALs utilize. Likely smarting from Taylor's rebuke on the Aqua-Marine

concept, Duncan admonished Taylor, "With reference to our recent conversation, I cannot emphasize too much the importance
of requesting a team instead of individuals when there is a need
for a diving unit in a particular area. A team is composed of six
men who work in pairs. They each understand the other's charac-
teristics and ability." Duncan recognized the inherently dangerous nature of combat swimming, stating, "It is easy to visualize
the many hazardous possibilities which may eliminate two men
on any one assignment." Both Taylor and Duncan were highly
invested in the nascent combat swimming program, and each of
them had definite opinions. A rift began to grow between the
two men, and they found themselves frequently at odds over the
development of the program and the training of the swimmers.

* * *

DUE TO THEIR LIMITED access to the Annapolis pool, Taylor
and Duncan moved the combat swim training to the indoor pool
of the posh Ambassador Hotel in Washington, D.C. But for more
realistic training, the group swam in the grimy waters of the Potomac at Area D.

The OSS ordered Duncan, Spence, Wicker, Wadley, and a
Marine named Charles N. Koulias to engage in high-level training and hone their maritime intelligence gathering and sabotage
skills at Area D. Most of the men received good marks. Lieutenant
Duncan, for instance, was described as "a good man, extremely
well versed in small boat craft. Most cooperative and anxious to
take in the entire course, including all the hardships that go with
it. Navigation and such subjects were new to him, and naturally,
he was not as proficient as some of the class who were old hands
at the game."

Wadley's report was similar: "A very good man. Knows small
boating extremely well. Tries extremely hard and learns better and
faster than the average."

July 27 through August 7, 1943, proved ideal for the swimmers. There was no moon and "enough wind to make small waves on the beach, which in turn made enough noise to deaden the noise of approaching folbots." Taylor and Duncan devised simulated limpet attacks against mock German freighters—using the *Marsyl,* of course. All the men passed the training at Area D and would go on to form the core leadership of the swimmer program, but Koulias chose to stay behind at Area D rather than continue as a swimmer.

* * *

As the training progressed, the OSS developed a number of specialized and innovative pieces of equipment. Going back to the Ohio Chemical and Manufacturing Company, which had fabricated the rebreather, the OSS designed an inflatable surfboard that ran silently on a battery-powered motor. The board could plow through the waves and accommodate two men or a total of eighteen hundred pounds of equipment, grenades, and ammunition. The "boat" had a cruising speed of five knots and a maximum range of fifteen miles. But its low silhouette allowed men to approach ships at anchor covertly and to land operatives. Commander Woolley was extremely keen on the use of these devices, which could be rolled up into a small portable size when not inflated. "I believe that great use can be made of surfboards," he stated, "especially for landing through surf which cannot be crossed by any type of boat without serious danger." Woolley further explained, "The inflatable surfboard . . . will roll into a small package and weigh very little." At the conclusion of the trials the OSS contracted with the Ohio Chemical and Manufacturing Company to make two full-size prototype boards at a total cost of $500.

To protect the men's bodies from hypothermia in the cold waters of the Potomac, the OSS developed and enhanced a wetsuit. One of the first swimmers to wear the suit was John P. Spence, who fondly recalled how the term "frogmen" may have come about. He was climbing out of the water one day in his green waterproof suit when someone yelled, "Hey Frogman," and the name "stuck for all of us."

The OSS had also developed a number of kayaks, including two- and eight-man versions that could be broken down and quickly assembled on the deck of a submarine or small boat. In addition they began experimenting with underwater submersible craft, something today's SEALs often use when they exit submarines to conduct covert operations. The OSS first took a look at an invention known as "the Toy." During the summer of 1943 a Frenchman named Jean de Valdène contacted the agency about a one-man submersible that he had designed. Both the British Navy and the Italians had constructed underwater submersibles that their combat swimmers utilized. Made of balsa wood in the "shape of a large cigar," Valdène's Toy was "steadied by horizontal and vertical fins." Like the surfboard, it was powered by a silent electric motor, and it could achieve a speed of six knots underwater.

Commander Woolley immediately saw the possibilities that the Toy offered his swimmers: the ability to enter enemy ports covertly and attach limpet mines to ships. He convinced Donovan to earmark $1,000 for the project. But a string of unfortunate events plagued the development of the device. They trucked a mock-up of the Toy to Area D on July 20. There Duncan and the swimmers participated in tests with the submersible. The craft dipped a few feet beneath the murky Potomac, but once again the dirt and pollution got in the way of finalizing the test. So the Toy was "transferred in great secrecy" to the David Taylor Model Basin at Glen Echo, Maryland, a large U.S. Navy facility used to test ships and smaller craft.

Ultimately, the Toy proved to be a flop. In final tests in January 1944, the electric motors broke down repeatedly and "other flaws developed." They abandoned the project and later replaced it with another submersible known as the "Sleeping Beauty."

Over the spring and summer of 1943, development of underwater gear proceeded at a breakneck pace: wristwatches with luminous dials, depth gauges, a waterproof swimsuit, and swim fins ("both hand and foot"). The Ohio Chemical and Manufacturing Company once again provided its expertise in manufacturing waterproof flashlights and underwater containers as well as other equipment that would allow swimmers to transport explosive devices without detection. The OSS accordingly created and tested limpet mines that the swimmers could affix magnetically to the metal hulls of enemy ships and then detonate.

But the polluted Potomac once again became a problem. At one LARU trial, Taylor swam for more than a mile in the river. Visibility was terrible, making the test difficult. Moreover, in combat, either in the Pacific or near Europe, the swimmers and equipment would be in saltwater, and it was unknown how well the unit would perform in the sea. They needed clear water—clear ocean water—to conduct realistic tests. Duncan proposed that they take the team to Florida.

* * *

THE SUMMER OF 1943 BROUGHT great change to the "Maritime Activity," as it was known. Some called it the "Marine Section," leading to confusion that it was associated somehow with the Marine Corps. But General Order Number 9, issued by General Donovan, clarified and effectively led to the establishment of the Maritime Unit as a full branch within the OSS. Instead of training agents and operators for the special operations branch of the OSS, the Maritime Unit was gaining its own independence as an organization. "The significance of the order was for the first time the Maritime Unit had authority to send its own personnel into the field," recalled an officer within the unit. Prior to that, the Maritime Activity was relegated to just training OSS personnel from other branches. This would lead to a drastic enlargement of the unit's activities, including the establishment of field stations overseas in far-flung outposts around the world, such as Burma and Egypt.

Lieutenant Taylor was by nature a patriot and a man of action. Eager to enter the war, he asked to be one of the first Maritime Unit officers to deploy overseas. Taylor, determined to obtain an assignment in the field, made it clear to the OSS that "if he was not deployed overseas he would request a transfer back to the U.S. Navy." Woolley and the OSS placed tremendous value on Taylor and approved his request. But before heading into the field, OSS's fledgling combat swimmers headed south to Florida for additional training.

5

SILVER SPRINGS

IN THE FIRST WEEK OF SEPTEMBER 1943, Lieutenant Duncan and the underwater swimmer group departed Washington, D.C., aboard the *Tamiami Champion*, a fast, full-service passenger train also known as "The Champ." The men were to undergo further amphibious warfare and diving training at a naval facility in Fort Pierce, Florida, where they would study demolition techniques, test the LARU in seawater, and make a demonstration film. A motion picture crew from the OSS would come down near the end of their time in Florida. Their film would demonstrate the Maritime Unit's capabilities to the theater commanders and serve as a training film for future OSS swimmer recruits.

Nearly twenty-four hours after leaving Union Station, the men arrived at Fort Pierce, where they proceeded to the Navy's amphibious training school on a small, secluded isle off the Atlantic coast. The training school had been up and running since June, but the facilities were Spartan. When the first groups of trainees arrived, the camp had no buildings. For shelter they pitched tents on the sand, right on top of the sand fleas, whose bites left itchy welts. Later recruits enjoyed the "luxury" of wooden floors and sides for the tents, but the conditions remained tough. The heat was oppressive, and mosquitoes and flies constantly swarmed the men. With no mess hall to prepare meals, the food was consistently subpar. To top it off, the training was extremely rigorous, with the instructors putting the men through workouts and drills eight to twelve hours per day—the origins of what the SEALs now call Basic Underwater Demolition/SEAL (BUD/S) training.

Duncan reported to Lieutenant Commander Draper Kauffman, who led the facility and training program. A pioneer of Navy demolitions, Kauffman later participated in numerous amphibious assaults in the Pacific. But Kauffman was an unusual choice to lead the school that would train the Navy's underwater demolitions team. He had graduated from the Naval Academy but hadn't received a commission because of his poor eyesight. Instead, he volunteered as a driver with France's American Volunteers Ambulance Corps. Captured by the Germans, he spent time in a prison camp. In 1940 he served on a mine disposal team with the British Royal Navy Volunteer Reserve during the London Blitz before finally receiving a commission in the U.S. Naval Reserve in 1941. Although his experience with demolitions made him extremely qualified as an explosives instructor, Kauffman allegedly wasn't particularly fond of the water. Many years later, OSS swimmer John Spence reportedly said, "I remember showing him the fins and face plate. This 'Father of the Navy SEALs' looked me square in the eye and said, 'Swimming is not one of my favorite things!'"

Duncan and his OSS swimmers introduced Kauffman to their latest equipment, which was far ahead of anything he and his men possessed. They demonstrated the Lambertsen unit and "exchanged ideas with Commander Kauffman as regards to the use of underwater equipment." Duncan also trotted out the innovative surfboard the OSS developed. The groundbreaking OSS technology initially awed the Navy and Kauffman. "Every man [present] was enthusiastic about its potential use," recalled Duncan. At the time the Navy was using only face masks and no fins (they often swam in sneakers) and had nothing remotely comparable to the Lambertsen rebreather. The LARU signaled a new era in underwater diving technology that would render Kauffman's practices obsolete and potentially threaten his command authority.

The next couple of days started out cordially. On September 12, Duncan's group, along with Lieutenant Commander Kauffman and other Navy representatives, anchored off North Island and once again demonstrated their unique surfboard and the Lambertsen rebreathers. Even Kauffman tested the equipment underwater. The devices performed superbly, and afterward, the OSS men and Navy demolition trainees conducted a highly successful joint underwater exercise, with both groups using the rebreathers.

Buoyed by the powerful potential of an OSS collaboration with Kauffman's program, Lieutenant Duncan inadvertently ignited a political firestorm by foolishly engaging in "a discussion with Lieutenant Commander Kauffman regarding the possibility of using men who were trained by the demolition unit," without first consulting OSS leadership. Duncan pointed out to Kauffman that "the training of these men is closely parallel to that proposed for our [Maritime] Unit, and to open up another training camp seemed to be at the time duplicating effort." Duncan believed the Underwater Demolition Team's (UDT) training would qualify Kauffman's men for recruitment into the OSS's underwater swimming groups.

As Duncan and the MU swimmers were leaving Fort Pierce, one of Kauffman's officers relayed to them just exactly what the Navy really thought of the OSS. "I received one of the most severe criticisms expressed in the vernacular, all because the lieutenant in charge, Lieutenant Kirby, had allowed us to proceed to the [UDT training school] on what the commanding officer considered useless orders," said Duncan. Kauffman's sound rejection of Duncan's emboldened overture and the OSS's rebreather doomed the UDT to lesser technology for years. It would be long after World War II before the Navy would finally utilize the groundbreaking LARU device.

Stunned by the tongue lashing, Duncan and his men proceeded to Silver Springs, Florida, where they holed up in a group of cottages. There they conducted additional tests with one of Stanley Lovell's Research and Development (R&D) scientists, Lieutenant Alexander. Seemingly in an attempt to keep the overly ambitious lieutenant in line, OSS headquarters had dispatched a hulking, taciturn, combat-hardened Marine captain by the name of Alfred Lichtman to supervise the team and keep the top-secret equipment secure. A Jewish company commander from the 1st Marine Division, Lichtman had earned a Silver Star repelling a Japanese tank attack on Guadalcanal's Matanikau River. In a letter to Lichtman, OSS leadership emphasized the importance of this mission: "As I have discussed with you, security [of the devices] may have to be achieved by whatever means are at your disposal, for it will undoubtedly be impossible to maintain a 500 yard isolation area around the equipment area where it is stored. Nevertheless, when it is not in use, it should, of course, be kept in one place under guard."

With security firmly in place, Duncan reported, "Experimentation under Lieutenant Alexander started yesterday and will continue until all of his prospective work has been completed. That should be by Wednesday of next week at the latest [mid-September 1943]. Conditions are good for this work. The water is clear; the weather so far has been clear and warm; the management of Silver Springs has loaned us an electric boat and has been most cooperative in all matters." This would be the last report Lieutenant Duncan wrote for the OSS; shortly after the training concluded he returned to the fleet due to the flap with Kauffman.

As the training was winding down in the pristine, crystal waters of Silver Springs, an OSS camera crew began capturing on film the remarkable exploits of the LARU-equipped underwater combat team. After the war, the footage would be classified top secret and locked away in a vault for decades before the Navy SEALs would again view it in the 1960s.

SEA

6

CRAZY YANKS:
THE MARITIME UNIT'S
BEACHHEAD IN EGYPT

LIEUTENANT JACK TAYLOR WAS ON his own in Cairo. As he wandered through the maze of the city's bazaar, a colorful, exotic scene played out before him. Even though the direct threat from Rommel, the German field marshal who made *blitzkrieg* assaults across the deserts of North Africa, and his *Afrika Korps* had since passed, Egypt's capital teemed with spies, danger, and intrigue. Carts filled with an array of fresh fruits, other foods, and various sundries lined the winding, narrow streets. The sweltering heat of the summer air was heavy with pungent odors, and thick smoke from burning hookahs swirled amidst the crowds and filth. Flies blanketed the vendors' succulent offerings, relentlessly assaulting man and beast alike. The first OSS Maritime Unit officer to be deployed overseas, Taylor sauntered through the ancient metropolis, grappling with the massive responsibilities that lay before him. With no staff and only the lowly rank of lieutenant, Jack Taylor was charged with building the infrastructure of the Maritime Unit's first foreign base and training center.

★ ★ ★

In August 1943, the Cairo headquarters fit into Donovan's greater obsession with the Mediterranean, stemming from his earlier travels and fact-finding mission in 1941. Based in Egypt, the Cairo OSS focused most of its missions on intelligence gathering against German-occupied Greece and the Greek islands of the Aegean Sea. Colonel C. B. Guenther, OSS's station chief in Cairo, directed OSS's Secret Intelligence (SI) branch through a program known as "The Greek Desk." Getting the SI agents in and out of Axis-occupied areas and ferrying supplies by sea were operations ideally suited for the Maritime Unit.

At the Cairo headquarters of the OSS, Taylor would meet some of the agency's most interesting characters—Indiana Jones–like individuals who crossed the line between academia and international intrigue. Most of the secret intelligence staff were classical archaeologists—men and women who had spent decades unearthing the history of ancient Greece. These scholars-cum-spies possessed an astute understanding of the culture and nuances of Greek politics, and most were fluent in the language. The agents of the Cairo Desk risked their lives by using their scholarly profession as a cover for covert activities. Many considered archaeology to be an overused veil, as the Germans and British commonly used it as a cover throughout World War I. But rather than a classical archaeologist turned spy, one of the first special operators Taylor met in Cairo was a famous Hollywood leading man, Sterling Hayden. Together they would undertake some of the most daring missions of the war.

Hayden cut quite a magnificent figure. He stood "six foot five in his leather jumping boots and weighed close to two hundred and thirty pounds. A British parachute emblem and a small American flag were neatly stitched to the sleeves of his combat jacket. There was also the conventional military insignia, and a .357 Magnum revolver strapped to his thigh." Hayden attempted to downplay his Hollywood past, even legally changing his name to John Hamilton. Still, the former star remained recognizable.

"'Haven't [I] seen you somewhere before?' Taylor asked.

"'I don't know, sir.'

"'Your face is familiar, did you play football in college?'

"'No sir, I never went to college.'

"'Oh.'"

On entering the not-exactly-covert OSS headquarters in Cairo, visitors walked into a luxurious stone mansion in the heart of the city. Observing the opulent scenery surrounding him for the first time, Hayden dryly noted that "the chiefs of the various OSS headquarters overseas had a spectacular talent for living in style. The Cairo villa looked like a bastard version of the Taj Mahal. The high wall around it was pierced by a tall iron gate; there were broad verandahs of inlaid tile and a profusion of shade trees above vast stretches of lawn. A young platoon of servants glided in endless circles, the punkahs [fans] revolved overhead, and through a leafy crevasse you could gaze each dawn on a pair of Egyptian girls as they combed each other's hair."

Hayden soon met Taylor and found him an "oddly chilling guy." Nevertheless, the two men formed a bond and worked together well. Because the Maritime Unit (MU) and Special Operations (SO) spawned from the same branch and Taylor was the only MU personnel in Cairo, it was natural for him to work with Hayden and the other SO men in the theater.

Hayden was a true adventurer cut from the same cloth as Taylor. He had spent years at sea, sailing schooners and piloting boats on transoceanic voyages. The two men also shared a connection to Hollywood. In 1940 and 1941 Hayden was one of the silver screen's leading men. Paramount, with whom he had a contract, called him "The Most Beautiful Man in the Movies" and "The Beautiful Blond Viking God." But Hayden was no shallow movie star; he possessed a profound depth of character and understanding of life. In his autobiography, he wrote,

To be truly challenging, a voyage, like a life, must rest on a firm foundation of financial unrest. Otherwise, you are doomed to a routine traverse, the kind known to yachtsmen who play with their boats at sea . . . cruising, it is called. Voyaging belongs to seamen, and to the wanderers of the world who cannot, or will not, fit in. If you are contemplating a voyage and you have the means, abandon the venture until your fortunes change. Only then will you know what the sea is all about. I've always wanted to sail to the south seas, but I can't afford it. What these men can't afford is not to go. They are enmeshed in the cancerous discipline of security. And in the worship of security we fling our lives beneath the wheels of routine—and before we know it our lives are gone. What does a man need—really need? A few pounds of food each day, heat and shelter, six feet to lie down in—and some form of working activity that will yield a sense of accomplishment. That's all—in the material sense, and we know it. But we are brainwashed by our economic system until we end up in a tomb beneath a pyramid of time payments, mortgages, preposterous gadgetry, playthings that divert our attention for the sheer idiocy of the charade. The years thunder by. The dreams of youth grow dim where they lie caked in dust on the shelves of patience. Before we know it, the tomb is sealed. Where, then, lies the answer? In choice. Which shall it be: bankruptcy of purse or bankruptcy of life?

Hayden took an interesting path to the OSS. Prior to America's entry into World War II, Hayden wanted to serve. He knew Donovan's son through their shared interest in sailing, and Donovan offered the former movie star a cryptic invitation to go to Scotland for commando training. Hayden seized the opportunity with alacrity and was soon parachuting out of airplanes, learning hand-to-hand combat, and mastering small arms. One instructor noted that Hayden took to commando operations "like a duck to water." As part of his training, he successfully made ten parachute jumps, but on the eleventh he broke his ankle, dislocated his knee, and sustained spinal injuries. That effectively ended his commando days, and he returned to the United States.

There he tried to join the U.S. Navy, but they rejected him due to the extent of his many injuries. Dejected, he took off alone in a schooner for the West Indies, where he proceeded to get thoroughly intoxicated with a group of Marines. The entire group ended up in jail, but Hayden was so taken with his drinking buddies that after his agent bailed him out, he returned to New York and enlisted as a private in the Marine Corps.

After passing through boot camp just as easily as he breezed through commando training, Hayden received orders to transfer to the OSS on Donovan's orders. He shed his Hollywood past and even his name, legally changing it to John Hamilton. "To complete my metamorphosis and cut my last tie with Hollywood, Madeleine [his wife] went to court and obtained legal permission for a change of name. Henceforth I was John Hamilton," he recalled.

Hayden made the transatlantic journey to Cairo with a taciturn, tough former State College wrestler, Captain Lloyd Smith. Stocky, with a mind for numbers, the blond-haired, blue-eyed operative was a former wrestler at Penn State.*

* * *

CAIRO WAS AN ICONIC STEW of one-of-a-kind personalities, including Captain Hans V. Tofte. Born in Denmark, Tofte had played an active role in resisting the Nazi takeover of his country. When the Gestapo learned of his involvement and began closing in, he escaped and fled to the United States. Almost immediately he began fighting for the Allies as a British Army major in command of a guerrilla team fighting in Burma and China that ran a supply line between the two areas. He later returned to the United

---

*I interviewed Lloyd Smith in 2002, and we immediately connected because we were both college wrestlers. On a snow-filled January day, Smith fondly pulled out Hayden's .357 Magnum, which he had won in a poker game.

States and enlisted as a private in the U.S. Army, where he swiftly rose through the ranks and volunteered for the OSS.

Originally the OSS assigned Tofte to their training facility designated Area F, the Congressional Country Club in Bethesda, Maryland. Lacking revenue to pay its debts, the club leased its posh grounds to the OSS. There they turned raw recruits into special operators and Operational Groups—twenty- to thirty-man commando teams with language and cultural skills. Trained in everything from demolitions to guerrilla warfare, these groups were the forerunners to the U.S. Army Green Berets.

An expert on hand-to-hand combat, Tofte instructed OSS agents, as well as Marines and FBI agents who came to the facility, on the deadly art of "gutterfighting," such as using a single karate chop to an opponent's neck or face to kill or cripple him. In his day Tofte earned a reputation as "the world's second best killer"—the "best killer" being Tofte's mentor, Captain William Ewart "Dan" Fairbairn, the inventor of gutterfighting. Fairbairn was known as the "Shanghai Buster" for all the skulls he cracked while organizing riot squads for the Shanghai police. He summed up the black art simply: "I developed a system that got results . . . there's no fair play; no rules except one: kill or be killed."

Fairbairn and Tofte taught recruits the finer points of the "Tiger's Claw," a clenched hand whose forceful upward swing was designed to gouge out an opponent's eyes. Along with offensive moves, Fairbairn had a number of counters, including how to get out of a bear hug: "To break a bear hug . . . go limp . . . grab his testicles. Ruin him."

Fearless and highly skilled, Tofte didn't hesitate to put a snarky recruit in line. On one occasion, a hulking, famous professional wrestler named "Jumping Joe" Silvaldi, who was going through training at Area F, challenged Tofte. Tofte drily recalled, "Unfortunately, his insults went a bit over hand and I broke one of his arms."

The training program turned many Ph.D.s into bar fighters. But Fairbairn remained realistic on the bounds of his training, noting, "In a sense, this is for fools, because you should never be without a pistol or a knife. However in case you are caught unarmed, foolishly or otherwise, the tactics shown here will increase your chances of coming out alive."

Tofte trained women as well, teaching them to use an umbrella as a weapon "every bit as dangerous as a bayonet." However, Tofte longed to take a more active part in the war, and recognizing the value of his skills, the Army eventually sent him to Cairo with a mission to destroy the Italian oil industry in Albania. As soon as he arrived, that mission was canceled, but Tofte would soon tackle an equally formidable challenge with the assistance of the MU. Taylor, Tofte, Smith, and Hayden initially went about their own missions but would come back together as a team and thrust themselves into the heart of combat and Allied operations as they moved into continental Europe.

* * *

SINCE JANUARY 1943, when Churchill and Roosevelt met at the Casablanca Conference to plot their war strategy, the two Allied leaders had faced mounting pressure from the Soviet Union to open a western front. Roosevelt and Churchill disagreed on the best approach. The Americans preferred to use their existing forces in North Africa to invade Europe. Churchill, with an eye on postwar Europe and keeping the Soviet Union in check, favored launching an invasion of southwest Europe through Greece and the Balkans and persuading neutral Turkey and its large army to align with the Allies. But the Turks refused to budge and maintained neutrality. Despite Churchill's protestations regarding Greece and the Balkans, the Allies decided to first attack Sicily in July 1943 and then advance up the spine of Italy as they prepared for the Normandy landings and the invasion of France. Throughout the remainder of the war Churchill remained obsessed with the Mediterranean. With limited men and shipping to spare, Eisenhower and Roosevelt agreed to only a small increase in guerrilla activity in the area. British General Henry Maitland "Jumbo" Wilson proposed occupying some of the Greek islands by "means of a piratical war," using small bands of commandos and other specially trained troops to raid German and Italian garrisons. One of the first such raids was on the Greek island of Kos. Swept up in these island buccaneering efforts was the OSS, which provided intelligence services independent of the British and took part in special ops and intelligence operations.

In the summer of 1943, the Allies went to great lengths to inflate the size and strength of their forces in the eastern Aegean. Through deception operations they attempted to convince the Germans that they planned to land in Greece. One elaborate disinformation operation, code-named "Mincemeat," involved a dead body from a London morgue dressed in a high-ranking officer's uniform and handcuffed to a suitcase full of "top secret" plans for a fake invasion of Greece and Sardinia. They cast the body into the sea so it would wash up on an Axis shore. The Germans fell for the canard and bought the fake invasion plans. Double agents working for the Allies fed troves of disinformation to the Germans. The deception plan had a measure of success, and the Axis shifted reinforcements to Greece, Sardinia, and Corsica instead of Sicily, where the Allies eventually landed on July 9.

★ ★ ★

GRAND STRATEGY ASIDE, Taylor's first priority involved setting up MU's base camp to train operatives and house vessels. He handled everything from obtaining vessels and office supplies to developing the training curriculum. To his dismay, Taylor discovered that OSS headquarters had already selected a site in Ras el Kenayis, Egypt, which was located on the Mediterranean coast about 140 miles from Alexandria. He found the location undesirable because it lacked "protection from the elements, and the outlying reefs made it a nightmare to navigate in and out of the base camp." Taylor spent the next several weeks traveling throughout the Middle East trying to find a suitable spot for the base camp, but his efforts to set up operations were in vain. He identified a potential site in Palestine and yet another in Mersa Matruh, Egypt, a city ten miles west of the Ras el Kenayis. However, Colonel Guenther did not approve either location, and the Maritime Unit ultimately abandoned plans for a training facility in Egypt. Lieutenant Taylor's lowly rank undoubtedly played a role in his inability to win the approvals he needed from colonels and majors. He also faced extreme challenges in building consensus and recognition of the Maritime Unit from the other branches within the OSS, which were reluctant to recognize the nascent unit that had recently broken away from the Special Operations Branch. For months, Taylor and the small team of extraordinary men focused on the mission and, as a result of their sheer determination, overcame the barriers of rank and branch.

After his failure to establish the MU training base, Taylor thrust himself into an area he knew well—the sea. To conduct maritime covert operations and missions in the Aegean, Taylor urged Commander Woolley to send him high-speed PT boats. He cabled headquarters that "it was absolutely urgent that a fast surface craft approximately 85-ft. in length, with speed in excess of 15 knots, be assigned to his area in the Middle East." Taylor pestered anyone who would listen, but the acute shortage of Allied surface craft in the Aegean forced the OSS to resort to extreme alternatives.

The first craft Taylor managed to employ looked more like a pirate ship than a covert craft for inserting agents. Known as the *Samothrace,* the 90-foot, 150-ton high-masted luxury yacht was most definitely not the fast boat Taylor had requested. The flashy craft stuck out like a sore thumb among the other boats in the Aegean. The ostentatious schooner was owned by cotton tycoon George McFadden. Fittingly code-named "Daffy," McFadden was an old Princeton classmate of one of the archaeologists at the Greek Desk.

Tired of waiting for vessels from Washington, the OSS leased the schooner from McFadden, who continued to entertain guests on the yacht—even while it was on convert missions! One OSS staffer acidly wrote, "Daffy intolerable. . . . Tell him we are at war. He hasn't heard."

But using a luxury yacht for covert operations wasn't just fool-hardy; the cost was exorbitant. Because the *Samothrace* was de-ployed in a war zone, the insurance premium topped a whopping $1,500 per month, more than $20,000 in today's dollars. The OSS had to invest even more money before Taylor could undertake the mission—the boat required a total engine overhaul that "was com-pleted two days later after many exasperating delays."

It's likely Hayden also piloted the *Samothrace*. While waiting for his mission orders, the movie star once "borrowed a Jeep from the motor pool and cruised alone down to Alexandria, where I pro-moted a fast cruising sloop from the Royal Egyptian Yacht Club and had myself some sailing."

* * *

THE OSS'S OTHER OPTION for sea-going transportation seemed better-suited to covert missions. They began utilizing Greek boats known as caïques, small, wooden-hulled vessels that weighed ten to forty tons. The boats had auxiliary sails, but most were pow-ered by gasoline engines. Two to six men crewed the small boats. Generally the captain was the boat owner, and most of the crew members knew each other or were from the same island. "Some of these men showed great loyalty and daring in their operations under OSS; others (occasionally the same ones) were masters of smuggling, thievery, and goldbricking," noted one OSS operative. Money motivated the men, as did patriotism fueled by the German occupation of their country.

Taylor's first battle was to wrestle control of the caïques from the Secret Intelligence branch, which had previously taken re-sponsibility for inserting its agents into occupied areas within the

Aegean. The thirty-four-year-old Hollywood dentist used his well-tuned social skills to convince SI and Guenther to place the caïque service under control of the Maritime Unit. To pry the control of the boats out of SI hands, Taylor used the argument that "they were wasting good intelligence men on maritime matters" better left to the MU.

Ultimately the Maritime Unit's caïque fleet would swell to thirty-six boats, although not all of them operated at the same time. A maintenance nightmare, the boats cost OSS headquarters $3,000 per week to maintain, operate, and compensate their Greek crews. However, these native craft were very valuable and effective because they easily blended in, helping to avoid detection by German patrols.

After assembling the MU's ragtag fleet, Taylor, working with Hayden, Tofte, and other OSS officers, began planning for future missions to set up a supply line to bring food, medicine, and weapons to Yugoslav partisans fighting against the Germans. Despising desk work, Taylor, a man of action, immediately started inspecting the existing fleet of caïques and, acting in his customary hands-on style, prepared his first operation.

7

PIRATE YACHTS AND
SPIES OF THE CLOTH

THE WIND AND SPRAY OF THE WESTERN Mediterranean pelted Jack Taylor as he piloted the 150-ton *Samothrace* across the turbulent blue-green water. Controlled by the Axis, the Aegean Sea was swarming with roving patrols of enemy ships and planes, which provided a formidable challenge to the MU's first mission. A master sailor, Taylor felt at home at the helm of the 90-foot sloop. Years of experience on solo cruises across the Pacific, yacht races in the Caribbean, and a narrow escape from being buried alive in a gold mine in the Yukon had given Jack Taylor skills and mental toughness few men possessed.

In September 1943, Taylor set off on one of the most dangerous voyages in the eastern Mediterranean. His orders were to deliver critical supplies to the Greek island of Samos, located less than a mile off the coast of Turkey. Samos was the birthplace of several ancient Greeks, including Pythagoras, Epicurus, and the astronomer Aristarchus, but at this time it was part of a tiny pocket of Allied occupied islands surrounded by Axis garrisons. Taking the helm of the *Samothrace*—now serving as a cargo vessel—Taylor departed Cairo with two tons of food, TNT, Tommy guns, ammunition, and camp equipment. The expert sailor adroitly navigated the ostentatious schooner and dropped anchor at the OSS's caïque base at Pissouri, Cyprus, code-named "Cincinnati." The OSS had several of these hidden coves, all code-named for prominent American cities, and they used them to refuel, make repairs, and even hide agents. As the war dragged on, the OSS established nearly a dozen of such covert marine bases across the Aegean.

Jack and his team unloaded the supplies and ammunition onto the *Irene,* a fifteen-ton caïque awaiting their arrival. They saved space for fifteen hundred pounds of "urgently needed medical supplies for Samos arriving by air from Cairo." Little more than a rotting tub, the *Irene* had a breakneck top speed of only two knots in calm water. Like many of the boats, it carried sails as a secondary means of propulsion. But with "Samos being dead to windward, sails could not assist. It was an impossible situation," Taylor reported. In desperation, Taylor sailed to another port in Cyprus known as Famagusta to "grab any fast caïque and talk about it later." Though the Greek government was holding two "very suitable caïques for size and speed" for no apparent reason, the local officials refused to allow Taylor to put them to "good use."

It was then that Taylor, in his own words, "blew a fuse." He enlisted the help of OSS operative Captain John Franklin "Pete" Daniel III to make an urgent plea to the Greeks. Captain Daniel, code-named "Duck," was the Cyprus chief of the Greek Desk for Secret Intelligence and spoke the language fluently. As a former professor of archaeology at the University of Pennsylvania who had conducted extensive digs in areas around the Mediterranean, Duck was extremely knowledgeable about the culture and government. Jack asked Daniel to explain that the "U.S. was not interested politically or economically in post-war Greece; that [the U.S.] wanted nothing in return for helping them; that the money and resources expended were for the sole purpose of aiding their people; that [the OSS] was not begging for the loan of a caïque to deliver humanitarian supplies which [they had] every right to do but wanted only to charter the transportation from them, and it seemed that [the Greek officials] were very unappreciative." Their impassioned entreaties ultimately persuaded the Greeks to lease

**EASTERN MEDITERRANEAN
AREA OF OPERATIONS**

the Americans three capable boats: the *Mary B.*, the *Kleni*, and the *Angelike*.

The OSS crew transported the much-needed supplies and medicine onto the new boats. Taylor, along with two secret intelligence agents and their equipment, sailed aboard the *Mary B.* On October 1, 1943, the three caïques set out at dawn. The occasional British patrol planes and low-flying German surveillance planes passed over the small flotilla as they headed to Samos.

En route, the caïques docked briefly at another of the OSS's forward operating bases, a secret harbor code-named "Miami." Then, on October 3, at 8:15 a.m., Taylor got his first taste of the grim realities of war. After the caïques left the relative safety of their base, eight German Junker JU-88s "dive-bombed and strafed a destroyer close under the south coast of Kos. Plenty of ack-ack [anti-aircraft fire] and one shot down, crashing and burning on the hillside." The German dive bombers sank the British destroyer. According to Taylor, "One of the Junkers came out of his dive in our direction and gave us a long burst with cannon and machine guns. The Greek crew, with the exception of the helmsman, were so busy diving for the hold . . . that I was not able to accompany them. . . . One bomb burst fifty yards to the starboard." With the crew badly shaken by the attack, Taylor then changed course, and the small fleet hugged the Turkish coast to avoid German planes. Taylor then witnessed another battle on the island of Kos around 12:30 p.m.: "Nine Junkers circling easily just above the ack-ack. Absolutely no fighter defense. Several warships, the largest probably a light cruiser . . . were counted through the glasses. Float planes directed the fire. Airfield and ammunition dump were bombed, sending up a huge smoke and debris column."

At 7 p.m., Taylor and his crew departed from the coast of Samos for Kos. Taylor then reduced speed to ensure that the island hadn't fallen to the Germans. Over the next several months the islands around Samos would be the scenes of some of the most intense fighting in the Aegean. The strategic location of the islands made them a valuable prize to both the Allied and Axis forces. Later, a daring German airborne and amphibious attack would assault Leros, resulting in the capture of thousands of Allied prisoners of war. Fortunately, at 7 a.m. on October 4, when the *Mary B.* and the other craft entered Vathy Harbor at Samos, Taylor saw the British and Greek flags flying, signifying that the port remained in Allied hands.

While at Samos, Allied authorities informed Taylor that the Germans had captured Kos and heavily bombed Leros. With the potential for German invasion weighing on his mind, Taylor quickly delivered the cargo, including the much-needed emergency food and medical supplies, to the archbishop of Samos, who was also an agent for MI-6, Britain's foreign intelligence service.* The bishop informed Taylor that many of the people, including guerrillas, desperately needed items that could only be secretly procured on the Turkish black market, including insulin. Taylor agreed to undertake the mission. From Samos, Taylor and his small flotilla set sail for Turkey.

---

*Because of their unique backgrounds, which included archaeology and anthropology, the OSS operatives often displayed an unparalleled cultural awareness, which they needed to operate with the local population effectively. These pioneering OSS recruits were the precursors to the Human Terrain Teams that were active in the modern wars in Afghanistan and Iraq. Cultural awareness is a key skill set that America's special operators strive to master.

8

"HAGGLING, BRIBING, FINES, DELAYS, INSPECTIONS, BULLSHIT"

DESPERATE TO GET TO THE ISLAND of Leros where his battalion was fighting, Colonel May, a British doctor temporarily detached from his duty on Leros, approached the leader of the Greek guerrillas on Samos. Although he pleaded his case valiantly, the command major gave him little hope. Everyone knew the Germans were attacking Leros, and most believed the island would soon fall—if it hadn't already. The guerrilla leader knew of only one man who might be willing to risk his life to make that journey: "If that crazy Yank doesn't come back, I'm sure I won't be able to get anyone else to take you," the command major told May.

The "crazy Yank" was Taylor, of course, and he was already on his way back to Samos. The streetwise lieutenant and the shrewd "Duck" had savvily handled the negotiations—for which no spy training could possibly have prepared them—to procure the insulin and other supplies for the archbishop from the Turkish black market. However, getting out of Turkey proved its own ordeal. Taylor and his companions endured "three hours of haggling, bribing, fines, delays, inspections, bullshit, and just plain uncooperativeness" before obtaining authorization to leave the port. Fortunately for them, the journey back to Samos on the *Mary B.* was largely uneventful.

However, their next mission proved even more dangerous than the first. On Samos the *Mary B.* picked up Colonel May and two other doctors who were determined to travel to the island of Leros to rejoin their British units and support the defense of the island. The only problem was that the BBC had reported that Leros had already fallen to the Germans. Taylor "checked with the signals office, and they said it was still in British hands." So the intrepid American began plotting a daring nighttime mission to drop the doctors off at daybreak—hopefully before the serious fighting resumed. May confided in Taylor that "he had thought his last chance [of getting to Leros] was gone."

Before departure, Taylor once again radioed Leros, and although there was some contact, they were not able to communicate clearly. Taylor recalled, "The operator assured me the signal I heard was his operator in Leros and not a German operating his set. That was all the confirmation I could get" that the island had not yet fallen.

The "Crazy Yank" was willing to risk his life to transport the doctors, but the Greek caïque crew demurred. Taylor remembered, "We prepared to shove off, but it seems the Greek crew had heard the BBC report about Leros too and weren't eager to go into Naziland. I told them we were going and if they didn't want to come that they could stay and I would take the boat. They decided to go." Of course, Taylor had some misgivings of his own. Of Colonel May he wrote, "It seemed all wrong to return such a good man and excellent Doctor to be captured so soon. That was the way he wanted it however, as it was his battalion and he wanted to be with them at the end. He reminded me it was an Irish Battalion and not to sell them short."

As the *Mary B.* got underway in the strait between Samos and Turkey they came under fire in the darkness from the Turkish side. So they sailed closer to Samos, but then took rifle fire from that island as well. They arrived at Leros at 5:30 a.m. on October 7, 1943, just as the sky was beginning to lighten. Taylor recalled,

"Departing, we were picked up by a searchlight and followed out of the bay until overtaken by a British [motor launch] and an Italian MAS (Torpedo Armed Motor Boat). The British checked us for a few seconds (we were flying the American flag) satisfied themselves and left, but the [Italian boat] insisted on stopping us with all guns trained. Not to be outdone, [one of the OSS agents on the *Mary B.*] picked up his Tommy gun and with barrel pointed at the skipper of the MAS, continued the discussion, which was not only useless and annoying but wasted valuable minutes when we should have been clearing the island." At this point in the war, the Italians, whose government had recently left the Axis and sided with the Allies, were unsure who was friend or foe.* Eventually the Italian crew let the OSS boat pass, and the flotilla departed Leros, making "more knots than *Mary B.* could comfortably handle with motor and sail."

Taylor's group left the island just in time. By 7:00 a.m. they could hear the first wave of Nazi war planes arriving on Leros. "Bomb burst and ack-ack were heard a few minutes later. Several groups followed, and detonations could be heard after we reached the Turkish coast."

* * *

WINSTON CHURCHILL CONTINUED to push for operations in the Aegean with an eye on a postwar world; however, the Allies lacked sufficient resources to conduct operations in the area. As a result, the British operations failed. Ultimately the Germans boldly counterattacked with a combined airborne and amphibious

---

*The Italians, who had broken from the Axis not long after the Allies landed at Salerno, Italy, on September 9, 1943, surrendered to the Allies. To prevent Italy's collapse, the Germans quickly occupied Rome and other portions of the country with their forces. For several weeks the Italians were unsure of their alliances. Later the Italian change of allegiance would provide a unique opportunity for MU's underwater operations.

assault. They crushed the British garrison on Leros, which had a critical airfield, and seized the island of Kos. Soon they also encircled Samos and cut it off. In an unheralded operation, OSS caïques successfully evacuated hundreds of Greek and British personnel from the island.

* * *

TAYLOR'S EXPERIENCE ON the missions to Samos and Leros highlighted the glaring need for high-speed motorboats. The caïques were mechanically unreliable and extremely costly to operate. The OSS took a number of stopgap measures to compensate for the boats' problems, including swapping out the marine engines for tank and aircraft engines that the service somehow obtained. For months Taylor hounded OSS and Allied headquarters in the area to provide his fledgling Maritime Unit with fast motorboats.

Despite the lack of high-speed craft, Taylor accomplished a great deal in the few months he was in Egypt. Additional MU personnel hadn't left the United States by October 8, so Taylor had to rely entirely on himself. Of his accomplishments in the region the chief of the Maritime Unit in Washington noted, "Lieutenant Taylor has been successful in establishing water transportation out of Alexandria to various island contacts, and his service is being enthusiastically received by all parties in the Middle East. Lieutenant Taylor is the caliber of a man who can do a big job in his field; in spite of all handicaps he has proven his worth to Maritime."

Always forward thinking and pioneering, Taylor realized the fast craft he was requesting suited a range of missions, including those of the underwater variety that Taylor had spent so much time planning for in the States. He would later write, "Provisionally tried underwater swimming apparatus now includes underwater breathing apparatus and mask; luminous and waterproof watches, depth gauges, and compasses; protective underwater suit; auxiliary swimming devices; and limpets and charges. With this equipment and proper training, operatives could make a simple and almost perfectly secure underwater approach to a maritime target and effect a subsequent getaway. An underwater operative, for example, could place a limpet against the hull of an enemy munitions ship in a crowded harbor with good chances of destruction."

Taylor also saw the opportunity to open up a new dimension of warfare, one that would become a hallmark of the U.S. Navy SEALs: parachute insertion. Taylor was one of the first OSS officers to document this groundbreaking method of delivering underwater commandos to the target, stating, "Underwater operatives and equipment might be landed by parachute to attack targets in inland waterways, such as hydro-electric dams on a lake or important locks in canals. Such an approach offers a unique technique in the penetration of enemy defenses." Several months later Taylor's innovative ideas were incorporated into the Maritime Unit training manual, which included an exercise to destroy a canal by parachuting underwater swimmers into the target, where they would don rebreathers and plant limpet mines along the enemy-held waterway.

* * *

AFTER THE ASSAULT ON Salerno in September 1943, the Allies trained a significant focus on Italy. Determined to remain in the midst of the fighting, Jack Taylor requested and received a transfer to Italy to set up Maritime Unit operations in the port city of Bari on the Adriatic Sea to implement the plans he hatched with Hayden and Tofte to complete the supply service to the Yugoslav partisans. Led by Josip Broz Tito, the partisans numbered about 180,000 men. Joining forces with the Loyalist troops led by Draza Mihailovic, Yugoslavia's insurgent troops embarked on a series of military operations that tied up roughly fifteen German divisions. The Allies wanted to keep those German troops in Yugoslavia rather than fighting in Italy or on the Eastern Front. In this context, supplying Tito's forces became a key priority for the Allies and the OSS.

Taylor's request for transfer was helped along by a letter from the British governor general of the island of Samos, which thanked the OSS and expressed "his appreciation for the services rendered and for the medical supplies." According to official MU history, "It was experience of this type that caused Lieutenant Taylor to be appointed OSS Operations Officer at Bari when the decision was made in December, 1943, to establish a base there to service Yugoslav partisans."

As Taylor was leaving for his new post in Italy, additional Maritime Unit men from Washington arrived at the Greek Desk in Cairo to augment Taylor's command of one. Along with the men, word came that the long-awaited high-speed boat would also arrive, on loan from the U.S. Army. Taylor's parting words to his replacements were "sign for it in my name before they change their mind."

* * *

TAYLOR WOULDN'T BE heading to Italy alone: Hayden, Tofte, and Smith would accompany him, although it looked at first as though Hayden would be taking part in a very different mission. Initially Hayden received orders for a proposed mission in the Greek isles. Handing the former leading man "a formidable sheaf of documents, Colonel Guenther advised, 'I suggest, lieutenant, that you study these intelligence reports. Familiarize yourself with the situation in Greece. But I warn you, you will find it a most complex situation.'"

Weeks passed, and no one in command followed up with Hayden, who was under the impression he was taking "a group of escapees from Greece fitting out a cargo ketch, and running her up through the Greek Islands." Guenther, after returning from Washington, finally informed him that "The British have that mission sewn up."

"I see," responded Hayden.

"Well, [Hayden], a report has just come in that there is a man named Tito up in Yugoslavia. They say he's a Communist, but apparently he's in control of quite a large guerrilla organization, so why don't you hop up to Bari, Italy . . . and see whether you can be of some service."

With a "fistful of orders," Hayden joined Taylor, Smith, and Tofte, and they departed for Bari.

9

TREASURE ISLAND

BACK IN THE UNITED STATES, under Woolley's direction, the original handful of combat swimmers multiplied, morphing into Operational Swimmer Groups I, II, and L, comprised of thirty to forty men per unit.* Woolley's vision of creating combat swimmers on par with the Italians was becoming a reality. With Christian Lambertsen finally graduated from medical school, the newly minted naval captain joined the OSS on a full-time basis. He would play a key role in the swimmer groups' ongoing development as well as the continuing development of the LARU.

Recruiting men to utilize the rebreather equipment proved a challenge. Instead of looking for former Navy divers, who often used hardhat-like diving equipment and worked on everything from submerged wrecks to ship repairs below the waterline, the OSS wanted expert swimmers. The MU didn't want average swimmers who needed instruction; they sought out the best in the world—Olympic-caliber swimmers and national champions. The OSS knew these men were in excellent physical condition and were experienced in the use of swim fins and face masks. A large number of these world-class swimmers were, in

---

*Eventually a fourth group made up of many men from the L-Unit would be formed into Operational Swimmer Group III.

fact, Southern California "beach rats." Undoubtedly spurred on by Taylor's early experience testing the rebreather in the waters of Santa Monica with Wadley and Peterson, OSS combed the beaches as well as the Coast Guard and Navy ranks, looking to recruit lifeguards and expert swimmers. One Southern California beach rat, James Eubanks, later reflected,

> I was a lifeguard in L.A. County. If you've seen *Baywatch* on TV, it was *Baywatch* minus the babes. We had a boat named *Baywatch*, but we didn't have girls in the lifeguard towers. Prior to the war, I was a diver who won quite a few rough-water swim meets. The Coast Guard put out a call for expert swimmers to help with operating landing craft since we knew surf conditions. Two of us volunteered. They gave us a Second Class Boatsman rating. After boot camp, they placed me as a swimming instructor and I couldn't get off the base camp. After several months of boring duty (with the Coast Guard), we received notice that the OSS wanted volunteer swimmers for hazardous work with a ten percent chance of coming back. It sounded like a good way to get off the base, and a way into the war, so I volunteered.

After Raider training at Camp Pendleton, which included small-boat handling and beach assaults, additional training commenced at Catalina Island on the West Coast on the leased grounds of a former Boy Scout camp. MU dubbed the facility "Area WA."

OSS Maritime Unit underwater training then migrated to the sun-swept beaches of the Bahamas, specifically Treasure Island, a spit of land only two and a half miles long and three hundred feet wide. Only an elderly black caretaker and his family occupied the limestone-formed island. The remote location offered security from the prying eyes of the Bahamians and the unlikely prospect of German spies.

In sharp contrast to the chilly, polluted Potomac River in which earlier swimmer training took place, the pristine, crystal waters of the Caribbean offered excellent visibility. The men were hit with a massive amount of vivid sensory detail, including gorgeous reefs and a variety of colorful, exotic fish. They frequently encountered a four-foot barracuda "who was jokingly named Horace." One operative recalled, "He seemed to take great delight in rushing at a swimmer and then stopped about three feet away to work his jaws. As soon as the swimmer made a flick at him with a spear, he would dash off with a swish of his tail."

Though Horace never posed a problem, the sharks did. As one OSS swimmer colossally understated, the sharks caused "a certain amount of consternation" as they approached many of the swimmers. In a display of true OSS ingenuity, the operatives invented a solution for the unwelcome interlopers: shark repellent. One version included copper acetate powder that was capsulated in a cloth sack. When a menacing shark approached, the swimmer released the powder, creating a dark cloud in the water similar to the inky fluid a squid emits.

The men continued their diving near Treasure Island, where they found an old shipwreck that proved "ideal for planting limpet mines and other underwater demolitions." At Nassau, Operational Swimmer Group II was split into two groups of twenty men each. The final training exercise was a mission to penetrate American harbor defenses at Guantanamo Bay, Cuba. This exercise, code-named "Operation Cincinnati," would serve both to gauge the effectiveness of the Swimmer Group and to test the Navy's vulnerability to these types of attacks.

Each of the swimmers was outfitted with fins and mask, waterproof wristwatch and compass, an M-3 grease gun in watertight covers, and a waterproof flashlight. They carried with them the explosives in special containers, and some also had sidearms. John Booth, a blue-eyed northerner and national champion swimmer

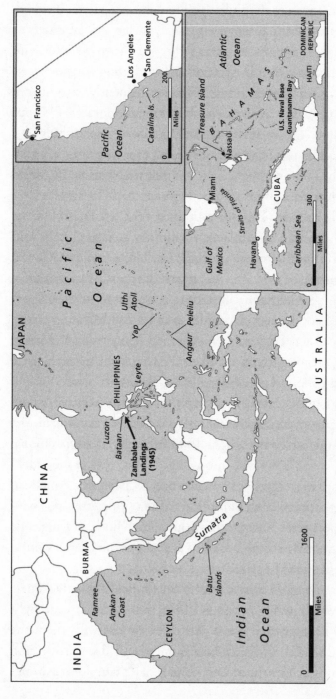

CATALINA ISLAND-TREASURE ISLAND-PACIFIC AREA OF OPERATIONS

who commanded the attacking "Red Group,"* recalled the mission:

> The first few days were spent in dispatching swimmers with cable and bolt cutters against standard A/T and A/S nets to determine whether or not it was possible or plausible to have swimmers cut the cables in the net. It was possible to do this and if better and newer cutters had been available, it would have been easier. Next, the swimmers were sent out with Composition "C" [explosive] and primacord and ½ lb. of "C" was placed under each buoy (15) and all charges were put on a main line. The net sank immediately and only two charges failed because of faulty primacord. This was an A/T net. It was possible for swimmers to swim over or climb over all types of nets and booms and under A/T nets or through the overlap. A/S nets presented no obstacle to swimmers. The mesh is 1' x 2' at the smallest and is possible to swim through. Lifting A/T nets by means of a block and tackle was tried. It is possible to lift the net within 8' or 10' of the surface, but it takes about eight or ten men and two blocks. The breach thus made is about 8' wide at the top and 20'–30' at the bottom.
>
> Seven-man LCRs, flying mattresses, and 2-man kayaks were taken across the anti-motor boat boom without too much trouble. There were two problems testing the net and boom and harbor defenses. The first time two 7-man LCRs and fourteen men left a submarine 100 yards off the A/S net, negotiated all of the harbor defenses, attacked target and returned to submarine without being detected. The second time six men and one LCR left from a point 1000 yards off net, negotiated net and harbor defenses, paddled for seven hours

---

*John Booth passed away in 2012. He was a lifelong friend of the author and would frequently stay at his residence on his many trips from Rhode Island to Florida. I will never forget what Booth, ever the optimist, told me after my divorce: "I was divorced around the same age you are [thirty-five]. You are in your prime and at the height of your power!"

around harbor, coming as close as 75 yards to some ships, bivouacked for one day on shore, attacked ships and installations in harbor, and returned to rendezvous without being detected.

President Roosevelt also noted the success of the mission and noted in his report, "In these tests, the lengthy training showed commendable results, because the swimmers were able to circumvent the net defenses in each instance. An additional point of value was proof that the Navy sound detection gear did not reveal the presence of underwater swimmers."

This mission, although it seemed fairly insignificant at the time, was actually tremendously groundbreaking, laying the foundations for America's future combat swimming programs, including the U.S. Navy SEALs. Lieutenant Commander Michael Bennett, U.S. Coast Guard, would later note, "The exercise was the first of its kind in an actual maritime environment and took place almost 40 years before the Navy commissioned a US Navy officer from SEAL Team Six to set up Red Cell teams in 1984 to ascertain the Navy's vulnerability to terrorist attacks."

* * *

AFTER EXTENSIVE TRAINING on the West Coast and in the Bahamas, the three swimmer groups were finally ready for overseas deployment. Lieutenant Arthur Choate, a former Wall Street millionaire, headed Group I, the first to deploy into combat.

Headquarters initially allocated Choate's group to the Aegean. Plans were underway to send them to the island of Karavostosi to concentrate attacks on German shipping on the island of Rhodes. They hoped the combat swimmers could also work with the British, specifically a commando group known as Force #133, and focus on German targets along the Thracian coast. However, Donovan personally interceded and canceled the planned deployment of Choate's group, sending them to Hawaii instead, where they would enter the Pacific war.

Lieutenant Frederick James Wadley, whom Taylor had met back in the winter of 1942 in Santa Monica while testing Browne's Aqualung, commanded L Group. Wadley's group included former Navy diver John P. Spence as well as one of the OSS's first frogmen, Norman Wicker. The group was sent to England, where they would train and prepare for missions related to the invasion of Normandy.

Operational Swimmer Group II, led by Dr. Lambertsen himself as well as senior combat swimmer John Booth, headed to the Far East to operate out of Ceylon, running missions into Burma and Malaysia.

10

THE *YANKEE*, OPERATION AUDREY, AND THE BOOT

Hayden, Taylor, and Smith looked over the long, local fishing boat covered in layers of grime as she wearily rocked in Italy's Bari Harbor. The repurposed, aging craft with a sloping deck and broad bow was outfitted with a radio antenna resembling a crucifix that incongruously stood more than ten feet above the pilot's cupola. Fifty-two feet long, fourteen feet wide, with a German two-cylinder eighty-horsepower engine, the *Yankee* was a far cry from the sleek, high-speed boat Taylor envisioned to be the ideal vessel for engaging in covert, treacherous missions across the enemy-infested waters of the Adriatic Sea. Even with a .50 bolted to her foredeck, she didn't look like a boat built for war. However, such prosaic features would make it easier for the craft to fit in with the local vessels and avoid suspicion. In spite of her unimpressive appearance, Hayden took a liking to the boat and promptly christened her the *Yankee*, after another vessel he had sailed.

Taylor and Hayden, both experienced men of the sea, would captain the *Yankee* on numerous operations, aided by a crew of

eleven: pilot Voyeslav Ivosevitch, one Marine sergeant, eight partisan seaman-gunners, and a cook named Tony. Taylor and Hayden
would also use the craft to run supplies to Yugoslavia for Tito's
partisans. The *Yankee* would also play a big role in Smith's life. He
didn't know it yet, but for Lloyd Smith the *Yankee* represented his
ticket out of the most dangerous mission of his life.

As in Cairo, Jack Taylor was the first MU representative to set
foot in Bari, Italy, a new theater of OSS operations. Since their
landings in Salerno in September, the Allies had been slowly clawing their way up the spine of the Italian boot: the Fifth Army and
Americans on the western side with the British Eighth Army on the
east coast facing the Adriatic. The OSS established a base in Bari.
Recently liberated by the Allies, the port lay on the heel of the Italian boot with a key entry on the Adriatic. Because of Italy's recent
switch to the Allied side, "everything was in turmoil . . . to find
lodgings was difficult; to visit the officials and make arrangements
necessary to procure labor, fuel, transport, berthing for ships, and
so forth seemed at first impossible," recalled one OSS agent.

Despite the challenges, Taylor, Hayden, and Tofte got to work
almost immediately. Their first task was to build a fleet for a clandestine supply operation dubbed "Operation Audrey." The *Yankee*
was but one craft, and they would need dozens to carry out their
plans.

* * *

WHEN ITALY SURRENDERED to Allied forces on September 3,
1943, the Italian army still occupied much of Yugoslavia.* Tito's
partisan forces who sided with the Allies quickly disarmed many
of the Italian troops, taking their weapons and artillery for themselves. After the Italian surrender, mountains of equipment, including shoes, uniforms, rations, and weapons stored in warehouses in

---

*The official announcement came on September 8, 1943.

Sicily, fell into Allied hands. Tofte, Taylor, and Hayden immediately recognized that this gear would well serve and support the guerrilla forces fighting the Germans in Yugoslavia. Tofte, Area A's former hand-to-hand combat instructor and now a major in the OSS, was charged with managing supply runs in the Adriatic to distribute the seized largesse to the Yugoslav partisans.

The gargantuan task included a laundry list of activities: establishing the supply line, finding and mapping minefields in the Adriatic, assembling a fleet and crews for forty vessels, arranging for maintenance and fuel of the ships, acquiring weapons and other supplies for Tito's forces, finding food and housing for all the personnel required for the supply operation, establishing security and armed guards, organizing recordkeeping for the supply mission, and attending to innumerable other small details. Obtaining the necessary supplies for maintenance activities proved especially difficult. The OSS requested materials from the British and other U.S. military sources of supply; if that failed, they turned to the black market. One report noted, "It has simply been a beg, borrow and steal policy to keep these vessels running."

Despite the challenges, the new base was quickly up and running. The OSS recruited partisan laborers, who did much of the work, toiling "virtually without a rest." "[In] the next few days, coal, repairs, and ship stores for the battered little partisan boats arrived." According to official records, "Within three weeks, the OSS officers made a complete reconnaissance, gathered considerable intelligence, established bases and trans-shipping facilities, and procured a fleet of small ships. In another six weeks, they had set up a supply service more than able to handle all that the Allies were at the moment prepared to send or Tito to receive." This small group of men, placed in the right area with the superb ability to innovate and improvise, would have a distinctive impact on the war in the Adriatic.

By the end of the year, the OSS had twenty-five boats in the port of Bari, with as many as twenty making runs at any one time,

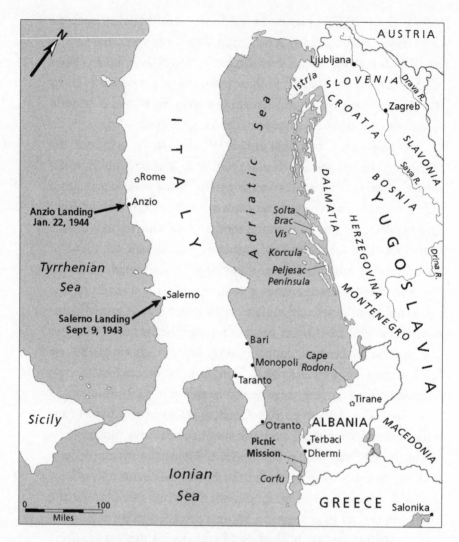

ITALY AND YUGOSLAVIA AREA OF OPERATIONS

all carrying crucial supplies ultimately bound for Yugoslavia. Under Major Tofte's direction the decrepit fleet of "battered, leaking fishing schooners" made more than sixty voyages through enemy waters without losing their cargoes even once. Operation Audrey would later be called "quite remarkable since the unseaworthy fleet sailed in seas which the Royal Navy would not risk."

Hayden and Taylor piloted many of the craft in the OSS fleet on a countless number of covert missions across the Adriatic. Taylor, MU's only operative in the Mediterranean Theater, would work closely with the Special Operations branch of OSS. Eventually he was named OSS's operations officer in the Mediterranean. As operations officer, he was "responsible for the activities of SO, MU, Schools and Training, Operational Supply, and Field Photographic (before its transfer to Intelligence). His responsibilities included planning and coordinating SO and MU operations, and establishing and maintaining adequate training sections for all types of instruction except communications." With Taylor's appointment, the lines between the Maritime Unit and Special Operations continued to grow blurry—and they would remain that way for some time, largely because there simply weren't enough bodies for all the duties.

Unfortunately, because most of the craft depended on wind power, the vessels averaged only seven knots, or around eight miles per hour. With the partisan main supply base on Vis about eighty miles away from Bari, it was a hazardous, approximately ten-hour journey through hostile waters. Hayden described the perils of making a daily run: "By plunging through the Allied minefield late of an afternoon a schooner always had a fighting chance of reaching Vis at dawn—barely in time to be backed into a precipitous cove where she could be hastily camouflaged with pine boughs festooned in her rigging, unloaded the following night, the camouflage repeated, and then driven toward Italy as soon as the weather served." The fighters on Vis would then pack the supplies into small fishing boats, which would take on the dangerous task of getting the materiel to the mainland.

Most of the boats used to deliver cargo from Bari to the partisans were similar to the caïque craft used in Greece—in fact, many of the boats actually came from British contacts in Greece. Though useful, the slow, aging craft weren't suitable for all OSS missions. Taylor thought that relying solely on the British to supply boats for various OSS missions was unwise and "repeatedly asked the Maritime Unit in Washington to supply him with fast surface craft." OSS headquarters agreed, but it took considerable time for the bureaucrats to locate suitable vessels.

The first to arrive were two eighty-five-foot Army Rescue craft, and with the boats came additional MU men. After long delays, the two boats finally made it to Naples, Italy. There one of the boats, P-568, needed additional repairs and was delayed in dry dock. Lieutenant Ward Ellen, Taylor's fellow instructor from Area D, successfully sailed the other vessel, P-584, all the way from Cairo to Bari, where it joined the fleet used for ferrying cargo to Yugoslavia. Ellen would later help establish and oversee a maintenance base in Monopoli, Italy, just up the coast from Bari. This base would soon become unexpectedly important to Allied operations in the region.

11

"THE LITTLE PEARL HARBOR"

OSS officers and partisans alike ran for cover as the roar of more than one hundred German bombers filled the overcast skies above Bari. Water splashed as boat crews hastily jumped into the sea, knowing that their ships would be prime targets of the attack. "A mob of Italian stevedores ran madly" away from the boats at the dock, trying to avoid being hit. An air siren wailed, and soon the sound of exploding bombs thundered as the Luftwaffe crews dropped their payloads in the crowded harbor. Gun crews from three of the ships at port "pumped tracers over each other's heads with no effect whatever." Screams joined the din as the explosives fell on the twenty-five Allied ships in the area. Seventeen sunk almost immediately, while seven others burned. Shrapnel soared through the air, tearing into people and objects indiscriminately, and one of the nearby buildings caught fire. The attack was over in minutes, but the horrors were just beginning.

Unbeknownst to the civilians and military in the port, one of the ships carried liquid death in its belly. The American freighter *John Harvey* was secretly carrying mustard agent, in violation of international agreements. The devastating impact of mustard gas in World War I had convinced the world's powers to ban its use.

However, President Franklin Roosevelt had covertly ordered the shipment of one hundred tons of mustard agent in hundred-pound bombs to Italy.

When the German bombs fell on the *John Harvey*, the ship's hold immediately exploded with devastating violence, killing all those who knew of the existence of the banned chemical ordinance. Deadly mustard liquid and gas flew high into the air and then slowly settled back down into the harbor, coating everything and everyone in the vicinity. When the injured began to arrive at Bari's hospitals, doctors and nurses treated them for conventional burns, not realizing they had been exposed to mustard. They failed to remove the chemical-soaked clothing, so the chemicals continued to penetrate and burn the patients' skin. Soon victims began complaining that their eyes burned. Then their skin began to blister. Shocked, the physicians searched for the cause. Eventually one of the American doctors interviewed some longshoremen, and one mentioned the possibility that he might have unloaded mustard. The military began treating its patients for exposure to the chemical, but they failed to share their knowledge with the civilian hospital. More than a thousand civilians perished in what became known as "The Little Pearl Harbor."

For Hayden and everyone else except Taylor, the air raid was an unexpected baptism by fire. Still Hayden noted that the attack was over so quickly that "there was hardly time to be scared." He attempted to take his cues on how to respond from the Yugoslav partisans, who were used to these types of raids. He recalled, "We were trapped on the end of a dock, and eighty partisans from Yugoslavia went right on with what they were doing in spite of the commotion, loading ammunition, blankets, and high-octane gas into a pair of wooden schooners. The leader of the Yugoslavs, a man named Stipanovitch, fired at the low-flying German planes with a machine pistol. 'Bloody fucking buggers!' he yelled over and over again in a deep voice that boomed through a broad mustache."

Hayden started to run for cover behind a nearby latrine. He thought better of it and recovered enough dignity to light a cigarette. The watching partisans noticed. "Hamil-tone!" hollered Stipanovitch, using Hayden's recently changed name. "Give to me please one nice cigarette if you will."

The movie star handed over a cigarette and noticed Stipanovitch's hands remained perfectly steady as he lit it. "Some fucking welcome for you, eh Hamiltone?" the Yugoslav continued in his booming voice. Then he turned to a young, one-legged boy standing nearby and threw his pistol at him. "Here boy!" he growled, "Cool this bugger off." Hayden was tremendously impressed by the partisans, "whose spirit made anything he'd seen before sophomoric." He would have the chance to interact with them again frequently over the coming months.

Taylor and Ellen arrived on the grisly scene shortly after the attack. They assisted with the massive cleanup, and later, with the relocation of the base to Monopoli. Somehow the *Yankee* survived the carnage unscathed and would be put to use on an important mission.

12

THE ULTIMATE RESCUE

Twenty-six American nurses and medics sat tensely in the back of the C-53D Skytrooper plane, which was a variant of the famous C-47 transport.* They were en route from Sicily to Bari, carrying out their duties to evacuate the critically wounded from the front lines. Injured soldiers had been piling up in Bari, and they needed to be moved to more secure locations. Since their arrival in the Mediterranean region a few months earlier, the men and women of the 807th had saved many lives, transporting hundreds of wounded soldiers from combat hotspots to safer venues for medical treatment.

Peering out the rectangular windows of the bird, the anxious pilots and passengers nervously watched the sinister-looking clouds in the distance and the massive tornado-like waterspouts racing across the Adriatic directly toward the plane. The pilot frantically radioed the tower at Bari for instructions and an updated weather

---

*Eisenhower considered the C-47 to be one of the key tools that helped the Allies win World War II.

report. However, in a shocking oversight, he lacked the proper codes to identify his incoming flight as "friendly," placing its passengers in serious danger of being shot down by area defenders who could mistake his approach for that of an incoming enemy aircraft.

The pilot turned the big bird northwest, away from the impending danger, toward the heel of Italy's boot. Once there he could safely follow the coastline to Bari. Soon heavy fog engulfed the plane, precluding visibility. The crew managed to finally establish radio contact with Bari, and the tower agreed to turn on the homing beacon for ten minutes. But the crew's relief was as short-lived as their luck. Much to their dismay, the C-53 suddenly lost all contact with Bari, as the plane's radio communication and magnetic compass simultaneously failed.

Flying blind, the pilots attempted to find a place for an emergency landing. Through a break in the fog, they observed an airfield and moved in to take a closer look. Their hope of a safe landing turned to terror when they made out the black swastikas adorning the wings and tails of enemy fighter planes lining the airstrip. A sharp crack of anti-aircraft fire sounded over the dull drone of the engines. The pilot and copilot desperately hauled back on the wheel, pushing the C-53 upward and into the cloud cover. Now flying at over eight thousand feet, the crew and passengers felt a sudden drop in temperature, as biting, frigid air entered the cabin. The plane seemed doomed, as its wings began to ice because the ground crew had neglected to reinstall the rubber de-icing boots normally fitted on each wing.

Suddenly, a German *Focke-Wulf* 190 bore down on them, aiming to destroy the defenseless cargo transport. Knowing he couldn't possibly outrun the German fighter, the pilot's only chance to save the plane and its passengers was to duck back into the dense clouds and attempt to elude the enemy's guns. But hiding the C-53 in the cover of the clouds only exacerbated the icing problem. For fifteen tense minutes, fear gripped the pilots and passengers alike, as the ailing transporter lumbered from one cloud formation into another, engaged in a deadly cat-and-mouse game with the nimble German fighter plane.

But now the crew faced yet another peril: the plane was nearly out of fuel. In a last ditch attempt to find a safe area to put down, the captain lowered his altitude. As the pilots' visibility improved, they saw sharp craggy mountain peaks directly ahead of the C-53. Desperate, they scanned the unfamiliar landscape feverishly searching for a place—any place—to land. The pilots headed the plane in the direction of a patch of flat ground next to a small lake that offered the best chance for a successful emergency landing. The plane descended, and the pilots lowered the landing gear and, with a combination of skill and sheer luck, deposited the plane onto the tiny field. Both men applied the brakes as the lake loomed in front of them. The dry, open pasture soon gave way to mud, and the wheels sank into the soupy mess, abruptly halting the momentum of the big bird. The nose tipped forward, and the plane's tail jerked upward, violently throwing the crew and passengers forward. The C-53 hopped up briefly, shuddered, then collapsed like a dead beast into the thick of the marsh.

Miraculously, everyone on board survived. However, the pilots had inadvertently landed the medics and nurses of the 807th smack in the midst of an Albanian civil war. German forces occupied the nation and were actively engaged in an antipartisan operation designed to clear the countryside of opposition to the Third Reich. They found themselves surrounded by hostile forces intent on eliminating them.

It would fall to Jack Taylor, Sterling Hayden, and Lloyd Smith to get them out.

* * *

WHEN THE OSS HEARD about the downed aircraft, they quickly began plotting a rescue operation. "It was learned that several of the nurses were in poor physical condition as a result of hardships they had endured while traversing difficult mountainous country behind the German lines in Albania," Allied reports noted.

With rescue by air seeming impossible, the Maritime Unit became the natural choice to conduct the rescue operations. Hayden explained, "When the brass in this outfit heard about that they became all fired up—one man in particular who had just arrived from the States." This major called the OSS agents into his office and told them they were going to rescue the nurses. Although the officer had no combat experience—he had recently been the credit manager for a restaurant chain—he had planned out the mission in intricate detail, "like we were holding up a bank." Hayden, Taylor, and the others agreed to the mission, but only if they could have a larger role in the planning.

That task fell primarily on Taylor's shoulders. As MU's representative in Italy, Taylor had started to wear many hats, including that of operations officer. Although a gifted planner, Taylor despised sitting behind a desk and yearned for adventure. The mission into Albania would give him a chance to do both. And the mission would pose plenty of danger—an earlier British attempt to make contact with the nurses had already failed.

As in Egypt, a lack of high-speed boats plagued the Italian MU section. To evacuate the nurses from Albania, Taylor had a few craft at his disposal—the *Yankee*, the *Maryk*, and a British MBT boat. Initially crewed by partisan personnel, the vessels would eventually be manned by MU staff as they filtered into the theater. Hayden and Taylor, who were the most experienced seamen of the lot, would skipper the boat for the rescue mission.

But before they could get the nurses out of Albania, someone first had to get into the country and find them. For this task Taylor chose Lloyd Smith, the Special Operations operative who accompanied Hayden on the trip from Cairo to Italy. He would infiltrate the country and make contact with the survivors of the crash.

Rough seas delayed the mission twice. In early December, Taylor, Smith, and Hayden set out in the underpowered craft. Smith was armed only with Taylor's .357 Magnum, which he won in a poker game en route to Italy. Moving through the German-infested waters of the Adriatic, they dropped Smith off at the small Albanian port of Seaview. At the same time, Taylor and his crew delivered some badly needed supplies to the Albanian partisans fighting the Germans. While Smith searched for the medical team, Taylor and Hayden planned to conduct numerous dangerous additional supply runs over the coming months.

Meanwhile Smith linked up with fellow Secret Intelligence (SI) agents who had been working in the country along with elements of the British Special Operations Executive (SOE), including future actor and star of *The Guns of Navarone* Sir Anthony Quayle. With zero knowledge of the culture or language, Smith (with an assist from the British) somehow had to locate the nurses, who were in hiding nearly a hundred miles away. He would need to traverse treacherous mountains and survive the cauldron of an active civil war raging among the various resistance groups within the country.

Like most insurgencies, the Albanian resistance was divided into several major groups each with their own agenda: the Nationalists (also known as Ballists), the Royalists (Zogists attempting to restore King Zog I who had fled the country in 1939 after the Italians invaded), and the Communists. Elements of the Albanian establishment openly collaborated with Germany. Communist partisans, allied to the Soviet Union, refused to cooperate with the other factions and often fought against the other resistance groups. Smith would have to navigate through this cultural and ethnic jungle, and of course, he would need to avoid the Germans.

At first, guides provided by the SI men helped guide him through the hostile territory. Smith constantly found himself negotiating for his life with the violent groups. He wasn't afraid to pull out some big names to accomplish the mission. At one point he encountered a large group of heavily armed Ballists (whose ever-so-welcoming-to-foreigners motto was "Albania for the Albanians, Death to the Traitors"). He recalled, "I arrived at the small town of Dukati and was met by fifty armed Ballists, who tried to persuade me not to enter partisan territory." Smith implored the armed fighters to let him through, saying that he was on a mercy mission, stating, "We have people in your country that are by themselves; they are not soldiers but medical personnel. Right now, our President knows that they are in your country. I am sure that he trusts you people. He expects your help."

The mission did indeed have a high profile, and President Roosevelt was briefed on it. Smith's name dropping worked, and the Ballists provided him with three guides. They trekked deeper into partisan territory that was occupied by Germans who were actively trying to crush the insurgency. Once there, he had several close calls, including numerous occasions when he and/or his guards were almost taken prisoner. But Smith and his small group of guides always seemed to be one step ahead of the Germans. Smith recalled one such incident: "It was still raining and since my clothes were wet, I decided to stay in Dhermi that day. I received word that over a hundred Germans were making a house-to-house search of a nearby village for Partisans and weapons. Suspecting that Dhermi would be next on their list, I moved to a house at the extreme western end of the town and made ready for a fast getaway. Before they arrived, I moved to a cave and spent the remainder of the night sleeping there with a shepherd and his flock. This is standard operating procedure with the Germans. They move into a village, kill a few Partisans, and after a few days move out again."

Smith's mission was like finding a needle in a moving haystack. He and his guides were moving through hostile territory and so were the nurses—both groups trying to avoid roving patrols. To find them, Smith split up his small group of guides, and they fanned out in three different directions. By working with the SOE missions on the ground, bribing local strongmen, and relying on a lot of persistence and luck, Smith eventually found the medics and nurses on January 6, 1944. Now the sizably larger group had to somehow make its way back through hostile territory and link up with Taylor.

Once again traversing the enemy-infested waters of the Adriatic, the *Yankee*, piloted by Hayden and Taylor, made it to the rendezvous off the coast of Albania. According to plan, a small boat made its way to the *Yankee*. Hayden, clad in a large, dark overcoat, stared down at the nurses and Lloyd Smith. With his bellowing voice, it is likely that it was Hayden who hollered, "Crawl up. Hold the rope tight!" The nurses clambered aboard safely. Taylor, Hayden, and the crew greeted the exhausted Americans who had spent nearly two months behind enemy lines in Albania, giving them ample quantities of rum and candy along with blankets and pillows. Twenty-three Americans were finally safe in the hands of two of the best seamen in the Adriatic, but the count was three short.

* * *

DESPITE THE AIR RAID and base relocation, the OSS supply operation continued from Bari. Sterling Hayden received orders to undertake another highly dangerous mission in the Adriatic. The Allies had heard that Germans were attacking and invading several islands off the Dalmatian coast. Hayden was to travel by boat to the islands of Korcula, Vis, Hvar, and Brac to make contact with Tito's officers and "to find out on the spot whether the islands in question had actually been occupied by German landing forces."

Heedless of the predicted bad weather in the area, Hayden set out for Yugoslavia on Christmas Eve. But the night's storms proved impossible to overcome. His ship stranded not far from the Italian coast and soon sank. Undeterred, "Captain [Hayden] managed to get ashore and returned to Bari, from where he proceeded on board another ship on the morning of the 25th."

The weather wasn't much better on Christmas day, but this time Hayden managed to make it to the island of Korcula. Under cover of darkness, he came ashore and made contact with Tito's operatives in the area, who confirmed that the Germans were, in fact, attacking the islands. When morning broke, Hayden set out in a Jeep, accompanied by a Yugoslav officer and two partisans, to ascertain the situation for himself. Suddenly, Germans waiting in ambush began firing at the vehicle. They shot and killed the driver sitting next to Hayden. "However, Captain [Hayden] and the remaining Partisans managed to shoot their way out of the ambush and escaped with the Jeep."

Korcula was overrun. With no hope of stopping the German onslaught, Hayden and what was left of the partisan garrison escaped by boat on the night of December 26. "After a hazardous sea voyage through waters patrolled by enemy E-boats and landing craft, [Hayden] arrived on the Island of Hvar on the morning of 27 December." It too was under attack. With German dive-bomber Stuka JU-87s roaring overhead, Hayden calmly sat in the open for six hours, collecting as much intelligence as possible from the partisans on the island. Hayden later explained, "No Allied aircraft [come] near this part of the world, so the Krauts patrol up and down in little training planes called 'Storches' with wheels hanging down. And when the pilot sees you he leans over the side and drops little bombs by hand."

Confident he had obtained as much information as possible about the enemy movements on the Dalmatian coast, Hayden set out on yet another perilous sea voyage on the night of December 30. Lashed by the winds of a severe winter storm on the Adriatic, the small, local boat successfully dodged the enemy patrol boats that infested the area. At the last minute, however, the craft's mechanical systems gave out, and the boat sank. "On the way back south the water pump let go," recalled Hayden. "We paddled and drifted into the mainland, said goodbye to the boat, and took off on foot toward where some friends were rumored to be."

Undaunted, the shipwrecked Hayden somehow procured another boat and made it back to Bari with the precious intel. On the basis of that information, "immediate steps were taken to bring aid and relief to the threatened islands. Furthermore, Allied naval operations were initiated without delay and obtained extremely favorable results against German naval craft. Also, Allied air operations were at once undertaken against German occupation forces in Dalmatia, causing the German military operation to come to a temporary standstill."

After this successful mission, the assignment of establishing a base to continue supplying the partisans on Vis fell to Hayden and Ward Ellen. They set up in the port city of Monopoli, about thirty miles south of the OSS operation at Bari. Their MU fleet consisted of fourteen schooners (sailing vessels with multiple sails and masts), six ketches (sailboats with two masts), and two brigantines (another type of small sailboat that was a favorite with pirates).

However, the business of supplying Tito's partisans didn't always sit well with the Allies, particularly the British. The political implications of aiding an openly Communist organization troubled them. That hesitation came to the fore when a British general visited the port at Monopoli. Hayden recalled that "the British arrived all decked out with red bands on their sleeves and caps and there were drivers holding car doors open. It was quite a show." One of the partisans, a friend of Hayden's named Stipanovitch, came crawling up "from the bowels of a schooner all smeared with dirt" at about the same time. Unimpressed by the general's splendor, Stipanovitch marched right up to the Brit and saluted. "General," he began, "I must ask you the one question. On the Dalmatian coast we have gunboats made from fishing launches with antitank guns made fast on deck. They go almost as fast as eight knots, some of them. Here in Italia are five once upon a time Royal Yugoslav motor torpedo boats with armor plates and hinges and they go the forty knots. Now why, I ask it of you, why does your command not turn them loose to us partisan peoples? Why?"

Somewhat sheepishly, the general kicked at a stone and replied, "My dear chap, there are such things as politics to be considered, you know."

This answer touched a nerve with the Yugoslav, who exploded in response. "And I say fook your politics," he yelled before storming off.

13

BACK TO ALBANIA

LLOYD SMITH ENJOYED A STRONG SENSE of satisfaction as he leaned over the sink at the OSS base camp in Bari with a shiny flat razor in hand, finishing a long overdue shave. He had just completed the mission of his life. The OSS chief, General Donovan, had reviewed his mission report, and it was now on its way to the president of the United States. It was an accomplishment that would make any operative proud.

Suddenly Smith felt a presence in the room. Turning around, he saw Wild Bill Donovan striding toward him. Stunned, Smith dropped the razor into the basin as Donovan grasped his hand in a warm handshake, congratulating him on a mission well done.

Donovan often spoke with agents in the field and, whenever possible, would personally thank the men and women of the OSS and see them off on their missions. He respected their courage and sacrifice because he himself loved action. Donovan led by example and would never ask one of his agents to do something he wouldn't do. Never lacking in bravery, he participated in many of the war's crucial amphibious landings, including the invasion of Italy at Salerno and later, D-Day. After thanking Smith for leading the successful rescue mission in Albania, he asked the former wrestler for more details about some of the events. After carefully listening, Donovan looked Smith straight in the eye and said, "We're sending you back in."

Three nurses from the group of twenty-six somehow had become separated from the rest of the party. Donovan was sending Smith back to bring them out. And once again he would rely on the expert sailing skills of his friends and fellow OSS operatives Jack Taylor and Sterling Hayden to navigate the *Yankee* through the German-infested waters of the Adriatic, transport him into Albania, and be there to carry him and the three remaining American nurses safely home.

* * *

FEBRUARY 24, 1944, "SEA ELEPHANT," A CLANDESTINE BASE IN CENTRAL ALBANIA

In a repeat of the first infiltration, Taylor and Hayden successfully re-inserted Smith back into the country. After successfully reaching the covert base "Sea Elephant," he worked closely again with the Albanian Ballists as well as SOE and the OSS operatives in Albania to locate where the nurses were hiding, though he could not make contact right away. In fact, meeting up with the nurses wasn't going to be easy. Since his last mission, the Germans had moved into the area by force. The Allies knew it was only a matter of time before the Germans located "Sea Elephant," and it wasn't safe for Smith to leave. Because he couldn't go himself to fetch the three women, he was forced to rely on the cousin of one of his key Albanian supporters to carry a message. "This cousin was provided with money to secure credentials and to purchase civilian clothes for the nurses to make the trip from Berat by automobile should they decide to get out of uniform," noted Smith. "In my letter to the nurses, I told them the decision as to whether or not they wished to change to civilian clothes and make the trip by car or have me come up and bring them down by foot was entirely theirs." One of the partisans, who believed it would be too risky for Smith to get the women by himself, was incredulous that Smith was leaving the decision about how to travel up to the women. He said that in Albania, "We always tell our women what to do."

Several tense days followed, and the Germans grew ever closer to the location of the secret base. Local shepherds stood on watch nearby, ready to inform the Ballists and Smith as soon as enemy soldiers approached. Four Germans moved into the area, forcing Smith and his comrade, Sergeant Nick R. Cooky, an OSS agent and Marine who was leading an SI mission in Albania prior to Smith's arrival, to flee into the snow-covered mountains, but the trip was far from easy. He reported, "We waited in a gulley at the snowline and then started towards the top. After traveling for four hours in knee-deep snow and walking against a wind that was knocking us off our feet every few yards, we decided to come back down the mountain a few hundred yards and find shelter. At this time we came into a hard rain. That night we bundled together under a rock ledge with our two blankets. The next morning I had the feeling that I had not slept at all, however, [Sergeant Cooky] insisted that I was both snoring and shivering, not just shivering."

Smith and Cooky proceeded over the mountains to Dukati, avoiding German patrols along the way. The Nazi soldiers somehow overlooked the base at the coast, but the Allied agents in the area decided to remain in Dukati, believing it to be more secure. Weeks passed, but there was still no word from the nurses or the cousin who had gone to retrieve them. Smith's Albanian contact reassured him, "If my cousin does not return within ten days, you can shoot me. I'll bet my life on him."

It wasn't necessary. Nine days later, on March 19, Smith "was awakened at 0700 hours by a very excited English corporal," who announced, "They have arrived!" Smith noticed the British agent's "suspenders were dangling down the sides of his trousers, and his gun belt was doing the work his suspenders should have been doing. Seeing him in such a state of excitement and figuring that he was warning [him] of the approaching Germans, [Smith] reached for [his] gun belt and panic pack," ready to fight or flee.

But his Albanian friend, who understood the true meaning of the corporal's words, spoke up, stopping Smith in his tracks. "See, God-dammit, Major, I told you my cousin would bring them."

The nurses had opted to disguise themselves in civilian clothing and make the trip with the cousin by car. They arrived "in the best possible physical condition and spoke very highly of the care they had received." That night Smith and the nurses began their long and treacherous trek back to the coast.

They arrived back at the prearranged location where they were to meet an Italian MAS boat led by Ward Ellen on the night of March 21. However, according to reports, "The coast was considered 'hot,' and the waters were believed to be mined. When the MAS boat arrived off the pinpoint from O'Taranto, the Italian captain refused to go as close to shore as planned. The Italian dinghymen refused to take the canvas boat to a German-held shore." At this point Ward Ellen stepped forward to take the smaller craft to the shore. Inspired by his example, several Italians volunteered to crew the canvas dinghy. It took them three trips to unload all the supplies on shore and evacuate the three nurses, plus one American operative and one British officer. The Italians' fears of a German attack never materialized, and all made it safely back to Bari.

Lloyd Smith, like Jack Taylor, never rested long. He would soon command the Brenner Assignment, a daring plan to gather intelligence and sabotage the Brenner Pass, the main German supply artery from the Third Reich into Italy.*

* * *

LIKE TAYLOR, HAYDEN continued crossing the Adriatic with no let up between missions. He traveled several times to the islands off the Dalmatian coast to gather intelligence and deliver aid to the partisans there. Hayden described one group of fighters there as "about

---

*The author tells the story of this incredible mission in his fifth book, *The Brenner Assignment.*

thirty of the toughest bastards on earth. None of them had a bath in years. All of them had been in the thick of the fighting and marching all up and down Bosnia and Croatia. They would only take one cigarette at a time, which they passed around in circles."

While Hayden was with the group, a scout brought word that a German gunboat was laying up in an inlet a short distance away to ride out the weather. After hearing the message, "No one said a word. [The partisans] just loaded up two sorry-looking horses with machine guns and ammo and we all took off."

They soon located the 120-foot craft "in a cove so small she was tied up aft to some trees." Although "nobody gave any orders," the experienced fighters knew what to do. "We fanned out on a bluff full of dwarf pines directly over the vessel," recalled Hayden. "A kid no more than twelve stayed with the horses and kept stuffing dead grass in their mouths."

One of the German officers chose that unlucky moment to make an appearance on deck. "This fat bastard comes out on the bridge in his slippers and yawns and stretches," said Hayden. "And the fellow in charge of our group fired at him—and missed. Hell broke loose, of course." Within minutes the skirmish was over. One of the Germans held a towel out of a porthole as a sign of surrender. Not one of the Allies was injured, but several of the enemy had taken grievous wounds. "It made me sick to see the crew—mostly just fuzzy-faced kids—some with their faces half shot off and one holding his eye in his hand, which he kept trying to put back." A French surgeon with Hayden's group immediately set to work patching up the injuries and even "shared his cigarette with two Germans." But the operating conditions were far from ideal. "In place of anesthetic, they took the butt of a pistol and gave the patients a crack on the temple, which laid them out for a time."

On another mission Hayden sailed the *Yankee* to Albania to pick up a group of thirty Italians who were hiding in a cave. For more than a year the group had been on the run, trying desperately to return home. "I had agreed to carry the Italians back to Otranto, but I reckoned without my pilot, Ivosevitch," recalled Hayden. "He took a Thompson gun ashore with the rubber boat, and then I heard the firing. He came back on board alone."

"We go!" shouted Ivosevitch.

Hayden, knowing that Italian soldiers had previously raped the man's wife to death, had nothing to say in response.

* * *

NOT FAR INTO THE NEW YEAR, the Yugoslav supply operation underwent a major change. Tofte, Taylor, and Hayden "were suddenly relieved of their duties," to be replaced by U.S. Army personnel. "This sudden change left the new officers in complete ignorance as to how [the mission] operated and the reasons why." Eventually, British forces began taking over the operation from the clueless Army personnel. "Soon the American officers were simply figure heads." Lieutenant Ellen recommended, "Since the British Army has shown so much interest in the Shipping Operation, this officer suggests that it be turned over to them."

Despite the change of command, the mission was a resounding success. A small number of the right men in the right place made a difference. Altogether the operation shipped around 6,500 tons of supplies to the partisans, including "18,932 rifles, 20 field pieces, 33 mortars, 659 machine guns, 72 anti-tank rifles, 165,775 hand grenades, 3,567½ bales of overcoats and woolen clothing, 1,325 bales of GI shoes." They also transported more than two thousand troops from Bari to Yugoslavia as well as evacuating more than eight hundred wounded soldiers. According to the OSS, "These figures indicate that OSS made possible the activation of a force of 30,000 or more guerrillas. So effective was this aid, that the Germans diverted [several units] from their winter offensive solely to attack the supply line itself. Thus, the impact on the enemy of this operation may conservatively be considered equivalent to that of three American divisions." It had kept German forces busy in the Balkans so they couldn't attack Allies elsewhere. In addition, it provided the Allied forces with valuable intelligence.

Yet this tremendous undertaking cost the OSS amazingly little—just $35,000. And of that, $29,000 was a loan that the partisans promised to repay. By comparison, according to the OSS, "the cost of putting only one American division in the field [at the time was] $57,000,000, or about the total yearly expenditure for the whole of OSS."

14

NO PICNIC

As the operation to supply Tito ended, activities behind the lines seemed to increase over the course of several months. Jack Taylor never let up and conducted eight separate missions into enemy-occupied Albania, repeatedly transporting intelligence agents and necessary supplies to the war-torn region. He also captained two sorties to the Greek island of Corfu, delivering and picking up agents as well as "supplying ten tons of food to starving islanders." Taylor planned and participated in actions, and in addition to being chief of the Maritime Unit, he continued to serve as the operations officer and principal planner for SO and MU missions out of Bari. Although the British had intelligence agents in place in the country and OSS had an SI presence, Taylor recognized the need for additional eyes on the ground. His objective was to have an American covert base of operation. The OSS had been "using British pinpoints, and he wanted to establish greater independence." Once again taking matters into his own hands, Taylor outlined a plan for establishing a base in Cape Rodoni, Albania, and convinced his superior officers to approve the mission, code-named "Picnic I." However, bad weather caused repeated delays, and Taylor's commanding officer "strongly recommended that the project be postponed because the dark moon was practically over." He was concerned that Taylor might end up stranded in the country for more than a month until it would again be dark enough to approach the enemy shores at night. Despite his misgivings, OSS HQ allowed Taylor to conduct the operation "because he had confidence in Taylor's ability and judgment" and because the mission had already been approved.

At 8:30 p.m. on the evening of March 31, 1944, Operation Picnic I got underway. Taylor along with two other men under his command boarded an Italian MAS boat and left for the Albanian coast. Around 1:30 in the morning they arrived at their destination and began the laborious and perilous process of unloading the passengers and gear. For more than two hours the ship, anchored about five hundred to seven hundred meters off shore, remained undetected by roving German patrol boats as two small rubber boats ferried the men and equipment to shore. Taylor and the others planned to conduct reconnaissance on land for a couple of days and then be exfiltrated by boat. But as his commanding officer had feared, the retrieval operation did not go as planned.

To their horror, Taylor and the two other operatives soon realized that they had landed in an area crawling with Germans: "We discovered that we landed between two machine gun nests about three hundred yards apart." On April 2, the night of the scheduled pickup, he radioed back to the OSS base in Italy: "Since the sector is full of Germans, boat must come even if moon is shining. No shore signals should be flashed by the boat. Two boats must first come to the beach."

But the dangerous situation on the shore soon became much worse. A short time later Taylor sent a follow-up message: "Every hour men's lives are becoming more perilous. Surf is all right. The boat should come but no signal given. We shall signal from 0100 to 0300 hours GMT." Headquarters responded, "Please stand by from 0100 to 0300 hours GMT as the boat is coming tonight. Boat will not signal."

Once again, however, bad weather intervened. The boat radioed Taylor with a second, more urgent message: "Because of bad weather could not possibly send sortie tonight. Please maintain contact if possible. Will make another attempt during the night of April 3." The boat continued its efforts to reach the MU officer and sent one message assuring him they were "doing everything possible." Surrounded by the enemy, Taylor could not respond.

Plans moved ahead for another attempt to extract Taylor and his fellow agents on April 4. Once again the Italian Navy, most likely the San Marco Group, provided transportation, but when they arrived at the cape where they had dropped off Taylor and the others they found artillery emplacements capable of hitting the ship. The Italians cut their engines about six hundred yards offshore and settled in to wait for the signal from Taylor.

When the signal came forty-five minutes later, it wasn't the Morse code flash of the letter "T," which they had been expecting. Instead, the Germans fired a "pyrotechnic signal flare" that lit up the night sky. The captain started the engine just as small-arms fire broke out from the shoreline. German bullets whizzed "over their heads on the port side." Concerned about being intercepted by enemy boats, the Italian captain abandoned the mission and raced back to his home port, leaving Taylor and the others behind. Taylor recalled, "The vessel returning for the pickup was fired on, and we spent sixteen days getting back to the interior: four days without food and two days without water."

It would be three long months of ongoing hardships and continuous efforts to avoid capture before Taylor returned to Italy again. Trapped in an area infested with Germans, he and his comrades spent their time as productively as possible, gathering and communicating actionable intelligence. An after-action report recorded,

> At all times surrounded by enemy forces and on three occasions forced to flee from enemy searching parties when his whereabouts had been discovered, Lieutenant Taylor, nevertheless, maintained his party intact and through frequent clandestine radio contact with

his communications base at Bari, Italy, transmitted intelligence as
to enemy troop movements, supply dumps, coastal fortifications,
anti-aircraft installations and other military intelligence of value to
the Allied forces. All of this intelligence was collected either personally by Lieutenant Taylor or at his specific direction by the men under
his command. Lieutenant Taylor himself operated the clandestine radio transmitter.

Taylor made the most of a botched mission. Stranded, he
pushed inland, "dodging Germans and unfriendly Albanians."
Taylor carefully navigated his small party through this political
minefield, and on his own initiative contacted Abaz Kupi (the Zogist movement leader, loyal to the king). Kupi gave Taylor documents outlining their geopolitical positions during and after the
war. Contact with Abaz Kupi put Taylor into the highest levels of
World War II geopolitics; SOE and the British government largely
supported the Communists, the group that was ultimately victo-
rious and would run the government after the war. Taylor and his
party, which now included six downed airmen from the U.S. 15th
Air Force, traversed their way across the beautiful yet treacherous
snow-capped Albanian Alps, through Montenegro, and eventually
to Yugoslavia, where an Allied OSS mission arranged for them to
fly to Italy.

The documents Taylor carried from Kupi went to the highest
levels, and Donovan personally wrote to Secretary of State Cordell
Hull, "The enclosed communications from the Albanian Legitimist
Committee (Zogist Movement) were brought out of Albania by
Lieutenant J.H. Taylor. They are unknown to the British Government." According to Taylor, the British prohibited communication with the Zogists because it potentially could threaten their
relationship with the Communists. Donovan pressed Hull: "If it
is necessary to call them [the documents] to the attention of the
British, it is requested that this agency be consulted in advance."

The letters included a manifesto on the history of Albania and what the movement hoped to achieve after the war and from Britain and the United States:

- Full political and economic independence for Albania according to the Atlantic Charter

- Restoration of the monarchy under Zog I and the preservation of our democratic constitution

- Restoration of a just political order in the Balkans and participation of Albania as a sovereign state in the family of the Balkan states

- To have a legal government in London nominated and presided by our King who continues to enjoy Royal power until a new national assembly freely elected does not take away from these powers

The documents beseeched Britain and the United States to understand their position: "In the name of the Legitist Movement which comprises the best element of the fighting forces implores the United States to take [this] into consideration."

Taylor and the airmen returned to Italy in July 1944. The letters never had the intended effect of persuading the United States or Britain to support the Zogist cause. By November 1944 the last Germans evacuated Albania, at which time the Communists took power and ruled Albania with an iron fist until 1992, when it became one of the last Balkan Communist countries to fall.

15

THE KELLY PLAN

The twenty-seven-year-old OSS lieutenant scrawled his slanting signature across his proposal and then leaned back in his desk chair. Richard M. Kelly had just put his name on a daring proposition: integrating former enemy forces into the OSS Maritime Unit. The document he had just signed would come to be known as the "Kelly Plan," and it would play a significant role in the development of America's combat swimmer program.

Before joining the OSS, Kelly had worked as an adman on Madison Avenue in New York, and if there was one thing he knew, it was how to sell an idea. Kelly had also served two and a half years with the New York National Guard and a little over two years on active duty with the U.S. Naval Reserve. Due to his experience on the water, the OSS Maritime Unit drafted him into its ranks.

In 1944, Kelly devised an audacious, unorthodox plan, and he doggedly pursued it. Following Italy's capitulation to the Allies, roughly half the *Decima MAS* unit surrendered, whereas the other half fought for the Germans. The experienced operators of *Decima MAS* and its attached San Marco battalion remained idle in Allied custody. What if these former enemy units could be folded into the MU? The OSS would profit from their underwater and special operations expertise and the groundbreaking technology *Decima MAS* had painstakingly developed over many years. In his proposal, Kelly summarized the merits of the idea as follows:

> Realizing: (a) The superb training and outstanding achievements of these Italian swimmers, (b) The ideal operating conditions in the Mediterranean, (c) Their intimate knowledge of likely targets, (d) The great difficulties and delay involved in the transportation and supply of even a small number of American swimmers in this and other theaters; It is recommended that [the OSS] be advised at once to explore to the fullest the immediate utilization of this available Italian personnel.

Making an argument in favor of haste and capitalizing on agency rivalries, Kelly added, "MU-OSS is the only organization specifically authorized to utilize such personnel. Further delay will undoubtedly permit these swimmers to be taken over by other branches of OSS or the British." He also noted that *Decima MAS* could be valuable for training American swimmers in Italy. He closed out his appeal with Madison Avenue confidence and spin, predicting that adoption of the Kelly Plan "would in a relatively short time result in successful action against the enemy. This project seems to offer the Maritime Unit not only the *quickest* but the *most important* contribution to the war effort of any under discussion for any theater."

* * *

IN ORDER TO SET UP ITS own combat swimmer program, the OSS carefully studied the operations conducted by similar units in other countries, particularly those of Italy's *Decima MAS*. The Italians first experimented with maritime "sneak attacks" during World War I, but the idea didn't really take off in that country until the advent of World War II.* At the time, OSS sources credited *Decima MAS* with "the sinking or serious damaging of approximately 140,000 tons of shipping" during the war. It also suggested, "This form of warfare seems peculiarly suited to the Italian temperament. Their success must also be attributed to the high morale and careful training of the units involved, and the ideal operating conditions to be found in the Mediterranean, such as mild water temperature, etc."

The founder and leader of *Decima MAS* was Prince Junio Valerio Scipione Borghese, who became known as "The Black Prince." Born near Rome to an aristocratic family, the prince was educated in London before attending the Royal Italian Navy Academy in Livorno. He began his naval career in 1929 and by 1933 was already commanding his own sub. Prior to World War II he saw action in the Second Italo-Abyssinian War and the Spanish Civil War. A hard-line Fascist, he remained committed to his ideology during and after the war, eventually becoming an anti-Communist leader in Italian politics.

To train its Gamma men, the Italian 10th Flotilla MAS established a combat diving/sabotage school in Valdagno, located in northern Italy. According to OSS reports, about half of the students who attended the training there were German. The facility included "a large swimming pool, at the deep end of which was the complete hull of [a] ship fitted with stabilizing ridges." At the school "the men were thoroughly trained in all possible phases of swimming and marine sabotage; swimming with fins and camouflage nets for several hours at a time; diving both rapidly and

---

*Until this time many countries considered this type of covert operation to be bad form. In fact, during the Battle of the Nile in 1798, when a British boatswain suggested planting explosives on an enemy ship, he was charged with "suggesting methods not compatible with the traditions of His Majesty's Navy" and discharged from duty.

slowly, always avoiding splashing the water; learning to know the various parts of a ship in the dark; practice in the use of the respiratory mask for the mouth; passing through various barricades; and swimming underwater with full equipment for about an hour." The *Decima MAS* operators intensely trained for a year. They learned how to exit and enter a sub and simulate the approach into a harbor full of Allied ships. They operated the pigs (*maiali*) and practiced cutting/passing through antitorpedo nets to penetrate a harbor and plant charges.

To aid in their maritime sabotage, the Italians developed a wide array of specialized equipment, including manned torpedoes, explosive motorboats, miniature submarines for crews of two to six men, diving suits, and underwater explosives. One particularly insidious explosive included a small propeller. The Gamma men would attach the device to the bottom of the ship, and once the craft reached a particular speed, the propeller would spin and detonate the device. "Thus, by proper regulation, the explosion would take place on the high seas, indicating that it had been caused by a mine or torpedo, rather than by sabotage," noted an MU technical study on the Italian equipment.

The Italians also pioneered the equipment individual divers used, drawing on the fins and face masks that had become popular with Italian spear fishermen prior to the war. A typical Gamma man was outfitted as follows:

1. A close-fitting rubber suit, completely covering the body, fitting snugly at the neck, wrists and hips

2. A woolen suit worn under the rubber one

3. A large jacket of impermeable cloth for carrying equipment, with several rings for attaching explosives, contrivances and tools

4. A net, to camouflage the face while swimming

5. Fins to attach to the feet as an aid to swimming

Although *Decima MAS* began operations in 1940, they didn't experience true success until 1941, when they crippled or sank Allied ships in several stunning operations, including the famed attack on Alexandria Harbor. In 1942, they began preparations for another legendary operation. Over the course of six months they converted a formerly scuttled, five thousand-ton Italian tanker known as the *Olterra* into a covert mission base. While the oiler sat in the harbor under the pretext of making repairs, *Decima MAS* made structural alterations to enable "Italian divers and the human torpedoes used in attacks against Allied shipping in Gibraltar Bay to be launched from her port bow. . . . These alterations were carried out under the cover of painting and minor repairs to the ship. When they were finished, the trapdoor leading to the torpedo chamber was almost invisible while closed."*

Over the next several months, *Decima MAS* launched a series of elaborate attacks from the *Olterra*, destroying numerous Allied vessels, including the America Liberty ship the *Pat Harrison*. By the time of the armistice in September of 1943, the unit had damaged or sunk more than thirty enemy ships. Although many of their planned operations did not succeed and despite the capture of several Gamma men, *Decima MAS* became one of the most feared and revered Axis naval threats to the Allies.

This was the very same unit Kelly proposed integrating into the OSS.

---

*Ian Fleming, a World War II British intelligence officer and later author of the James Bond series, immortalized the secret trapdoor of the *Olterra* and the exploits of *Decima MAS* in the film *Thunderball*.

* * *

IN FEBRUARY 1944, an arrangement was concluded between the OSS and Prince Aimone, Duke of Aosta, to "make available the techniques and services of San Marco Battalion," an "elite" unit attached to *Decima MAS*. One operative described the duke as "about fifty years of age, very tall, most distinguished, and sincere in his desire to help the Allies." The men of the San Marco looked up to him and followed his lead. Some even believed he could be king if Italy returned to a monarchy.

The job of vetting the Italian operatives who wished to work with the Allies fell to twenty-seven-year-old James Jesus Angleton, code-named "Artifice," a superbly talented, rising star in the OSS. In many ways Angleton was perfect for the job. He had lived in Italy for many years during his childhood, and prior to the Rome assignment he distinguished himself as an agent in X-2, the counterespionage branch of the OSS, earning the trust and respect of his superiors, both British and American. Angleton's appointment as counterintelligence chief of Rome was met with enthusiasm and relief, as operations in the area were becoming "considerably more dangerous" than ever before. One of the San Marco recruits was, in fact, a German agent. A cable to the X-2 office in London from the administrative head of OSS counterespionage in Italy read "Air much clearer" upon Angleton's arrival in Rome.

Born in Boise, Idaho, Angleton moved with his family in 1933 to Milan, Italy, where his father assumed leadership of National Cash Register's Italian subsidiary and served as president of the American Chamber of Commerce for Italy. Before entering the war, Yale-educated Angleton had been a passionate poet and carried on a correspondence with luminaries like Ezra Pound, T. S. Eliot, and e. e. cummings. His temperament and exploits on campus indicated Angleton possessed a predilection for secrecy and covert activities. Classmates described him as a "fanatic in the making" and as "a mysterious Satan" who lived a sly life of "mysterious guile."

In 1943, Angleton joined the U.S. Army at the age of twenty-five before being recruited into the X-2 or counterintelligence branch of the OSS. During World War II, he was considered one of the preeminent "experts" on the unit; this, coupled with his deep knowledge of Italy and fluency in the language, made him ideal for interacting with the *Decima MAS* operatives and the men of the San Marco Battalion.

Most within the OSS viewed Angleton as the right man to revamp the operation in Rome. Security and compartmentalization were lax, and his predecessor at X-2 had recommended the OSS cease operations with the San Marco men. Though betrayals were a possibility, like Kelly, Angleton felt the short- and long-term benefits of working with the group outweighed the security risks. He emphatically urged the OSS to keep the San Marco unit active, arguing that it would allow him to strengthen X-2's relationship with the Italian Secret Intelligence Service (ISIS) of the Italian Royal Navy, which had been key in eliminating the German intelligence network and saboteurs north of Florence. Angleton had intelligence indicating the Germans were intending to plant "sleeper" or "stay behind" Italian agents in key centers in Italy upon evacuation of the areas to report on Allied troop movements and provide other actionable intelligence. Many believed Borghese, the former leader of *Decima MAS*, was likely overseeing some of these activities.

Angleton was convinced the San Marco commandos now working for the OSS would prove to be invaluable assets. He also believed that ISIS could be a powerful partner in eradicating the covert Axis network and participate in a myriad of other joint intelligence operations. Angleton's and the OSS's renewed confidence in ISIS was a tremendous boost to their relationship. This prompted an offer from the Royal Navy Intelligence Service to allow the OSS to "take over the Gamma frogmen school in Taranto, Italy," which boasted specialized equipment and expert instructors, so the "OSS could prepare its own naval sabotage group for operation in the Pacific." The OSS cataloged and inventoried the techniques and equipment of *Decima MAS*, though they were never deployed in the Pacific.

OSS records report, "It was the San Marco Battalion which eventually enabled MU to perform its most valuable work." The portion of the battalion that had come over to the Allied side was divided into two groups: surface swimmers and underwater swimmers. Those who had been trained in the use of human torpedoes and other underwater devices were based at Taranto under the supervision of the British. However, their usefulness was limited because "lack of German targets prevented this division from engaging in sabotage activities." As operations officer, Jack Taylor played a key role in the negotiations with the group and had a hand in setting up their training and organization under the OSS. Ward Ellen was initially tasked with commanding the surface swimmers.

Under Taylor and Ellen, men from the group immediately started contributing to the Allied war effort in Italy as the OSS peeled off select San Marco men for missions. During the Allied invasion at Anzio, a bloody amphibious landing resulting in a months-long battle that raged on the western side of Italy near Rome, one former sergeant in the San Marco Battalion infiltrated behind German lines, and as he returned through friendly fire with a "rough but accurate plan of German fortifications," was seriously wounded by an American soldier who thought he was an enemy combatant. He refused medical treatment until he made his full report to the OSS officer. In and out of consciousness and revived with injections of plasma, the Italian operator made his report and received an American decoration for his valiant efforts.

In May, Richard Kelly was ordered to "take charge of MU activities in Italy, also to contact members of the Italian San Marco Battalion, who had been assigned to OSS." His fellow Navy officer Ward Ellen would continue to assist Kelly in training the Italians and integrating them into MU.

MU oversaw the second group of "surface swimmers," which was based in Naples. It included "six Italian officers and 44 enlisted men, all surface swimmers." Although not trained in underwater combat, "they were, however, qualified to undertake infiltrations by sea for the purpose of attacking supply dumps, beach installations, etc." For several weeks Kelly and Ellen trained this second group of Italians in demolitions and in the use of MU equipment. However, friction developed between the two men, as Ellen considered himself independent of Kelly's command.

The Italians brought with them the latest in covert maritime tech, including swimming gear, two-man "mattresses" called *tartugas* (turtles) powered by silent electric motors, their own rubber swimsuits, high-speed boats, and "other assault, reconnaissance and demolitions equipment." However, the Germans retained much of their equipment in addition to the loyalty and services of nearly half the unit's members. One OSS operative reported, "The duke and his men saved three one-man human torpedoes, similar to the British chariot. They hid them by sinking them in a river. . . . They are there still. The duke said he would be more than pleased to raise them and turn them over to us to use as models for similar craft, that our own men could operate."

A study of the captured equipment became of paramount interest to the Allies. Donovan ordered an inventory of the equipment and personnel that the duke had offered for Allied use.

One of the earliest studies concerned Italy's MTM explosive craft. Essentially it was a motorized speedboat that contained five hundred pounds of TNT in the bow. "The main charge detonated either hydrostatically or on contact. The operator of the craft could set the method of detonation. . . . If the boat hits head on . . . the operator aims the boat, locks the speed and the steering gear, arms the firing mechanism, and then releases the raft attached to his body and drops off the stern," the OSS recorded. Hopefully he would survive what was nearly a suicide mission.

* * *

Plans were also underway for the OSS to bring over an entire Operational Swimmer Group, the one led by recently promoted Lieutenant Commander Arthur Choate. However, General Donovan himself rescinded the order "because of commitments which General Donovan had made in the central Pacific area and because of his own orders in this matter." MU and Italy continued to press for an entire swimmer group, and they eventually received a couple of swimmers, Norman Wicker, whom Taylor had trained in Annapolis, and John J. Stanaway.

As additional MU officers and enlisted men continued streaming in, the entire Maritime Unit organization in Italy began to take on a more military structure. In May 1944, OSS-METO was designated the 2677th Regiment OSS (provisional). The actual regiment itself remained provisional and was not activated until July 1944. Taylor, who abhorred paperwork, relied on newly arrived MU officers to handle bureaucratic matters while he continued to go on missions. But the days of an operations officer going into the field were becoming numbered, and soon MU put in place procedures and rules to minimize the danger of officers being captured. At the same time, "Lieutenant Kelly immediately began laying the groundwork for a series of combination sabotage and intelligence missions behind the German lines, on the northern Adriatic coast of Italy," relying on the expertise of the San Marco Battalion's special operators.

16

OSSINING

As quietly as possible, the six-man demolition team of Italian San Marco commandos, now under the command of Lieutenant Richard Kelly, climbed off the *MAS* boats and onto rubber boats. The shadowy flotilla managed to avoid a German minefield in the vicinity and slip past enemy boats patrolling the area. Beaching the boats, the team made their way to the mission's intended target, a German rail track on which trains filled with supplies and enemy troops traveled as they hastily retreated north.

This was the third attempt to put the demolition party ashore. "Considerable [enemy] personnel" and searchlights on the beach had foiled two earlier attempts. Hiding in wait, the team heard nearby "enemy MPs blowing whistles and shouting at traffic" as the German military police ushered men, tanks, and trucks of the retreating army moving to another belt of fortifications known as the Gothic Line.

Finally, one heavily guarded supply train stopped on the track. Under the noses of the Germans, the special operators of the San Marco Battalion stealthily approached the target and set pressure charges to go off as the train rolled over the rails. To ensure the

track was vaporized, the demolition party placed timed pencil detonators set to explode in the morning in the event the pressure
detonators failed.

The six commandos and their leader returned to the beach,
launched the rubber boats, and returned to the *MAS* transports
to await the blast. Tensely, Kelly and his Italian special operators
waited in silence for the German ammunition train they believed
would soon arrive.

Finally, they heard the whistles of an approaching train, soon
followed by deafening explosions as the bombs ripped through the
steel and wood, destroying the train and a section of track. Simultaneously, the Italian *MAS* boats opened fire on two trucks in the
vicinity, destroying them as well. Air reconnaissance revealed all
German traffic was held up for more than thirty-six hours, and
Kelly brought back actionable intelligence to the British Eighth
Army Headquarters.

Reports indicated that the "intelligence information, which
Lieutenant Kelly brought back from this first mission was considered extremely valuable by British Eighth Army Headquarters, and
other operations of a similar type were given high priority."

This was Kelly's first mission with the San Marco Battalion, and
it was dubbed "Operation Ossining I." Only a small portion of
the San Marco Battalion was now working with the OSS—about
fifty of the original members. Unlike the frogmen of *Decima MAS*,
these men were "not adept at underwater swimming and the use of
one-man torpedoes, etc. Instead, they specialize[d] in sea landings
of the commando type, going in to plant demotions and blow up
bridges."

The Italian special operators were noteworthy for their confidence, often bordering on arrogance. One of the operatives at
the Italian base noted, "They are cocky young men, sure of themselves, most of them with no political convictions, but playing this
game for the adventure, for the privilege of U.S. support, and U.S.
rations, like cigarettes and food. They can be surly, and damned

independent. It has been no easy job for Kelly to win the confidence of these men and their leader, but I believe he has succeeded, and while they seem a little vain because of what they have accomplished for the Allies, I think they deserve our admiration and gratitude."

At the end of July, Kelly moved his group's base of operations about a hundred miles north, near the city of Ancona on the Adriatic Sea. He would soon be joined by two more MU officers: Lieutenant John Chrislow of the U.S. Navy Reserve and Lieutenant George Hearn of the U.S. Marine Corps.

Hearn had joined the Marines right out of college and had served for eight months before being recruited into the OSS. He enjoyed being part of the action and thrived on assignments behind enemy lines.

In his training, Chrislow had received particularly high marks and was singled out for his leadership potential. His teachers wrote, "Handling other trainees, performance of field duties, physical stamina, initiative, intelligence, demolitions, pistol and field craft are all very satisfactory. Attention to duty in operation and code speed are all excellent. Map reading-excellent. Rifle and close combat satisfactory." They also noted he was in "good physical condition" and thoroughly capable to be an instructor: "Quiet, sincere, cooperative, and a good mind. A good field man."

With the help of these new officers, Kelly devised plans for a new mission dubbed "Ossining 3." Acting on intelligence supplied by Allied intelligence sources, MU hoped "to destroy two road bridges over a small stream, approximately five kilometers south of Pesaro." The bridges formed a key part of a German supply route, and their destruction would make it difficult to move tanks, artillery, and troops.

On the night of the raid, two Italian *MAS* boats transported Chrislow, who led the mission, and eleven other men from the OSS/ San Marco group to the vicinity of the bridges. The twelve operatives then boarded two seven-man rubber boats and one of the electric surfboards for the final leg of the journey. Avoiding detection by "four Nazi armored cars, two tanks, several heavy vehicles and three German soldiers on foot," the MU operators managed to plant six hundred pounds of plastic explosives on the pair of bridges, which were about ten kilometers behind enemy lines. The explosion wiped out the bridges "blocking all traffic for several days," and all of the Americans and Italians safely made it back to their base.

Joining the new MU officers, Ward Ellen continued to command an Army rescue boat, P-583. The boat participated in numerous infiltrations and exfiltrations and helped save countless lives of downed airmen. On one mission, Ellen crossed the Adriatic with cargo for Tito's partisans. High storms and heavy seas forced the boat to stay at port at the partisan island of Vis, which put him in the right place to take part in another vital mission. According to mission reports, "A seven hundred plane sortie [of Allied bombers] to Vienna produced seven Liberator crash landings on Vis. Four landings were on the rocks, and three were in the sea. There were 71 parachute jumps [crews bailing out]." Lieutenant Ellen rescued "some thirty downed airmen." He then returned the downed crews to Bari.*

Reports later noted, "Although the Maritime Unit was severely handicapped due to the lateness of its arrival in the Italian and North African Theater, its work, even in a few months, was considered highly commendable by the Allied High Command. Without casualties or loss of equipment to date, it has contributed greatly to the campaign in Italy."

★ ★ ★

---

*Not all the group's operations were successful. On a mission known as "Ossining 4," the boats failed to find the insertion location. And on "Ossining 5" Germans bombed the MU craft from the air while ground troops fired from shore. Still, the mission was at least partially successful because "all personnel escaped without injury," and they succeeded in at least temporarily tying up German troops and diverting them away from the front lines.

IN THE EARLY MORNING HOURS of August 23–24, 1944, the long shadowy silhouette of the Castel Di Mezzo lighthouse loomed in the distance as one of the San Marco operatives guided his raft along the coast looking for a landfall for the Packard Mission. Twenty minutes later the recon squad of San Marco commandos returned to the *MAS* boat, informing the mission commander, Lieutenant Mini Enzo, that he saw a boat sailing north but found an "excellent point to land." Enzo, a grizzled vet with years of combat experience and countless missions under his belt, ordered his team to switch positions with the recon squad. Enzo and a couple of his operatives clambered aboard the silent craft and made their way to the pinpoint.

Reaching shore, Enzo hastily disembarked, constantly on the watch for German patrols or roving Axis boats. Moving silently to avoid patrols or German observation posts on the bluffs above and in the lighthouse, the Packard team crept one hundred yards inland, where they buried equipment they couldn't carry, including a rubber boat.

Enzo decided to hide the team until the morning before entering high-risk inhabited areas. "The region was very unfavorable for us due to the complete lack of any natural hiding-place," he noted. The team had to traverse Highway 16, the German-controlled supply line that cut across Packard's area of operation. Enzo explained, "[Crossing the highway] was most dangerous . . . capture would have meant death in case the Nazis or fascists stopped us."

Fortunately, the team found a helpful farmer working the fields. After feeding the local a story about who they were, the Packard team received food and a crucial safe house away from roving German patrols. From their new base camp the team contacted the Garibaldi and Pesaro partisan units.

Enzo's mission involved gathering information on the formidable Gothic Line, a belt of German pillboxes, minefields, and artillery emplacements that stretched across the neck of Italy. The Germans remained masters of defensive warfare, and since the

Allies had landed in 1943 they had been decimated by one German fortification after another.

The intrepid San Marco operatives gathered tactical information on the entire line. Most importantly they secured a crown jewel of strategic and tactical intelligence: an Italian engineer who worked on the line along with his blueprints marking all the gun positions, minefields, and entrenchments. Knowing the information "was of the greatest importance and urgency," Enzo decided to escort the engineer back to Allied lines, leaving half the mission behind to gather additional intel.

Uncovering the buried rubber boat, Enzo and the engineer paddled back to Allied lines, where Polish MPs picked them up. The engineer and plans went back to the British Eighth Army intel section. As planned, two *MAS* boats picked up the rest of the Packard Mission on August 28.

When the Eighth Army attacked, they used the priceless information to save Allied lives as they broke through the Gothic Line. The British noted that the partisans contacted through the Packard Mission "were of tremendous help to the Eighth Army in their breakthrough."

By all accounts, the Kelly Plan was succeeding.

17

SWIMMER COMMANDOS

SILENTLY THE FOUR SWIMMERS GLIDED through the darkness, intent on reaching the submarine pens they knew were close at hand. They lay on two OSS-developed teardrop-shaped rubber rafts, known as "Water Lilies" or "Flying Mattresses," to keep a low profile and avoid German radar—as well as any curious locals who might be nearby. Silent electric motors powered by twelve-volt batteries took them within striking distance of the pens. Then the four men slid into the water, making as little noise as humanly possible.

Their assignment was to "reduce the striking power" of the German U-boats docked in Lorient-Kéroman, France, by taking them out four days before the planned Allied invasion of Normandy. Gordon Soltau, an MU swimmer who would become an all-pro receiver and kicker for the San Francisco 49ers after the war, was assigned to plant explosives on the locks, the underwater gates that guarded the sub pens. The others planted limpet mines on the subs inside. Then they began swimming for their rendezvous point on shore, leaving as silently as they arrived.

Fifteen minutes later, the explosives detonated. The subs sank into their cradles in the pen; the gates were completely destroyed. Mission accomplished. Now Soltau and the others had only to make their way to their safe house, where they could meet up with friendly forces on D-Day.

But this was just a dress rehearsal. Soltau and the three others from L-Unit, who sailed to England after training exclusively on Treasure Island, were practicing in the chilly waters of the Thames near Oxford, preparing for the actual invasion. The local eyes they were trying to avoid were British villagers and students. "Right before D-Day, we got word that Operation Betty was scrubbed," recalled Soltau. Getting ready for a mission only to have it canceled would soon be a familiar experience for the group of seventeen MU agents assigned to England.

While Taylor and Kelly conducted operations in the Adriatic, Operational Swimmer Groups I and II conducted operations in other parts of the world. Soltau and sixteen other men of L-Unit went to London. One OSS report notes, "The most conspicuous role played by the Maritime Unit in the European Theater was the work of its individual officers in planning and conducting ferrying operations across the English Channel to France." Frequently they worked closely with the British to conduct reconnaissance and plan for missions to insert OSS agents along the French coast: "MU officers acted as official observers in charge of transferring landing parties from ship to shore." In addition to delivering agents to enemy territory, the ferry service also exfiltrated local resistance fighters from German-occupied areas to London: "Their purpose was to bring back natives of these countries who had thus far escaped Nazi suspicion, give them a brief period of training in London, and then ship them back to their respective home areas to perform definite missions."

Heading up the L-Unit was Lieutenant Fred Wadley, the national champion swimmer whom Taylor first met in Santa Monica testing "Browne's lung" and with whom he later trained at Area D. Former Navy diver John P. Spence joined Wadley along with Lieutenant F. Michael Carroll, and Captain James J. Kamp, an Australian who established and ran a training camp at Helford in southwest England. Although they intended to establish a swimmer unit in the area, the cold temperatures made it impractical, as the L-Unit History records:

It was obvious before long that swimming operations were impractical in this Theater. The temperature of the water at Helford stayed in the vicinity of fifty degrees. The weather was so cold that on many days it was impossible to do any swimming at all, or at best a very limited amount. Even when attired in rubber suits, the longest time they could stay in the water under favorable conditions without getting chilled was about 45 minutes. Furthermore, the practical range at which they could proceed entirely underwater and locate targets was found to average between 150 and 200 yards. Frequently, it was much less than this.

But the water temperature wasn't the only obstacle facing the MU in England. Much of their equipment proved unusable. The motors on the surfboards hadn't been waterproofed and would break down after less than four miles of travel. In addition, their waterproof suits sprung leaks. The LARU also developed problems from being exposed to cold water, only some of which they were able to correct. On one tragic occasion, one of their swimmers, James E. Clark of the U.S. Navy Reserve, accidentally drowned "when he became panicky due to failure of his Lambertsen unit." The swimmers' health also suffered from the climate: "Dampness and cool air common to the British Isles caused head ailments such as colds and frequently rendered the swimmer liable to ear difficulties in rapid variations of depth."

Nevertheless, Wadley and his crew planned several daring missions, including a one-way suicide mission using an old freighter to block traffic in Denmark's Kiel Canal. Several of the men went as observers into France to deliver supplies and men to the resistance, but the frigid temperature of the water iced all combat swimming operations. Faced with this reality, the OSS reluctantly accepted that there likely would be no underwater combat missions launched from England. The British had already shut down their swimming operations, and the Americans followed suit.

In July 1944, L headed back to the States, likely bringing with them a special piece of equipment that the MU and the SEALS that followed them would adapt. Similar to the "pigs" *Decima MAS* used, the "Sleeping Beauty," or Motorized Submersible Canoe, was a craft the UK's SOE developed for underwater use. The twelve-foot-long submersible weighed six hundred pounds and carried a twenty-four-volt electric motor that could propel it at speeds up to 3.5 knots. Today's SEALs use a modernized version of the same device, which they call a SEAL Delivery Vehicle, or SDV.

* * *

AUGUST 11, 1944, THE WATERS OFF THE SOUTHEAST TIP OF PELELIU, SOUTHWEST PACIFIC

A handful of men inflated their rubber boats on the surfaced deck of the U.S. submarine *Burrfish*. Their faces blackened with paint, the detached OSS swimmers of Navy Underwater Demolition Team 10 (UDT 10) quietly paddled their craft under the cover of darkness toward the shore. Time after time they changed course to evade the numerous Japanese patrols before eventually making their way to the beach. Exiting the boats, the OSS swimmers crept along the shoreline, taking measurements and observing the conditions. It was one of the more pioneering recon operations of the Pacific War.

Now finished with their work, one of the men chanced a little noise. He tapped a prearranged signal with his KA-BAR knife onto one of the large chunks of coral in the bay. No one heard the soft sounds except the sonar operator of the USS *Burrfish*, and the team of swimmers slipped back into the water to rendezvous with their submarine. This endeavor, the first mission that involved American combat swimmers launched from a submarine was a success: the men determined that the beach on Peleliu was suitable for landing craft. Weeks later, based on the information obtained by the combat swimmers, the Allies successfully conducted a massive invasion of the island.

* * *

THE MU ALSO DEPLOYED combat swimmers in the Pacific Theater. Initially, neither Admiral Chester Nimitz nor General Douglas MacArthur was interested in utilizing agents from a rival branch of government. However, at the urging of General Donovan, a number of OSS combat swimmers did see action after they became part of UDT 10.

The Navy was compelled to strengthen the UDT program in the aftermath of the bloody battle at Tarawa, a small chain of islands in the central Pacific. The Americans sent in landing craft to storm the beaches, but unbeknownst to them, reefs blocked the way, preventing the boats from reaching their intended destination. The men inside the crafts became sitting ducks for the entrenched Japanese forces on the shore, resulting in hundreds of Marine and Navy casualties.

Determined to learn from the catastrophe at Tarawa, the Navy bolstered its training schools. The curriculum trained recruits in the art of underwater demolition, hydrographic surveys, and reconnaissance. In the summer of 1944, Major General Donovan and Admiral Nimitz of the U.S. Navy met, and Donovan offered Nimitz the use of the MU. In order to strengthen the UDT, the Navy brought in twenty-seven OSS operatives from Operational Swimmer Group I. OSS Lieutenant Commander Arthur Choate, a multimillionaire and Wall Street investor, was placed in charge of the team, and four other OSS officers provided additional leadership. The OSS Swimmer Group I arrived in Hawaii in June before heading out on a convoy destined for the Solomon Islands.

The MU training program was far superior in many ways to that of the Underwater Demolition Teams. MU combat swimmers were highly trained and superbly skilled in raiding techniques, infiltration and exfiltration, intelligence gathering, underwater operations, and land and sea sabotage. They used rebreathers, while the UDT used only face masks and snorkels. Furthermore, the MU's familiarity with weapons was superior. Some had been to parachute school, and all were trained in hand-to-hand combat. As one historian observed, "the [OSS swimmers] were much more like the Navy SEALs would be than the UDT men were by then." Another area in which the OSS swimmers were more advanced than their Navy counterparts was in the use of swim fins. Although the Navy had fins, most of the UDT teams were swimming either barefoot or in athletic shoes. After the OSS taught the Navy UDT swimmers how to use fins effectively for both swimming and moving across the coral reefs, the commander of the Hawaii training school placed a massive order for more fins for all of the UDT team members. However, before their first mission, the Navy stripped Choate's men of most of their high-tech equipment and forced them to conduct swimmer missions with just face masks and fins.* The LARUs were put into storage in Honolulu, and the loss helped to set the UDTs' use of rebreathers back by many years.

* * *

AUGUST 18, 1944, NEAR THE ISLAND OF YAP, SOUTHWEST PACIFIC

In the dead of night, the submarine *Burrfish* surfaced near the small, verdant island now transformed into a highly fortified Japanese stronghold. A handful of men, their faces blackened with grease,

---

*It's probable that the Navy took away the equipment after Choate, citing equipment failures and a lack of training, refused to go on a reconnaissance mission that the Navy had ordered UDT 10 to undertake. OSS's MU chief in Washington disagreed with Choate's assessment and said that the men were trained for exactly that type of recon mission. The incident went all the way up the chain of command to Donovan and almost led to Choate's removal.

exited the vessel and inflated their rubber boat. In pitch darkness they paddled their craft toward the shore as quietly as possible, amidst strong gusts of wind. Time after time they were forced to change course to evade numerous enemy patrols. Armed only with grenades and razor-sharp KA-BAR knives, five swimmer commandos—John Ball, Robert Black, Emmet Carpenter, Howard Roeder, and John MacMahon—set out to survey the beach and determine whether it was suitable for a landing. Earlier, the men, detached from UDT 10 and comprised mostly of OSS swimmer commandos, had launched the first successful swimmer-born recon mission from the *Burrfish*, but this night off Yap would prove fateful.

About a quarter mile from shore the men encountered a reef, where they stopped paddling and dropped anchor. Ball stayed with the boat while the other four slid silently beneath the high, white-capped breakers, equipped only with face masks and flippers. Making their way as discreetly as possible through the rough ocean water and powerful undertow, they struggled to swim toward the enemy-infested beach, taking measurements and observing the conditions along the way. Carpenter soon returned to the boat "in distress and too tired to swim further." He and Ball waited patiently in the craft for their comrades to return.

The time designated for returning to the sub came and went. Five minutes passed. Then ten. Fifteen. Twenty. At thirty minutes past the deadline Ball and Carpenter risked detection and paddled the boat to within one hundred yards of the beach. For fifteen more minutes they frantically searched in vain for their missing comrades. Eventually "they abandoned all caution and flashed their flashlight all around in hope of picking up the other three men. They had no success."

Ball and Carpenter reluctantly returned to the sub without the other swimmers. It wasn't until later that they discovered what had happened to Roeder, MacMahon, and Black. After surveying the beach, the commandos attempted to swim back out to the reef and rendezvous with the boat. But the wind and breakers made the swimming difficult, and the men failed to locate Ball and Carpenter. They had no choice but to return to the island. Dripping wet and wearing only their swim trunks and camouflage paint, they avoided detection for an entire day and returned to the water that night, hoping for a boat to pick them up.

On the *Burrfish* the surviving swimmers pleaded with the captain for another chance to pick up their comrades. They rightly believed that if the three were still alive they would return to the reef again that night. However, the surf conditions had grown even worse, and the captain didn't want to lose any more of the commando swimmers. He gave the men up for lost and headed for the sub's next mission.

Roeder, MacMahon, and Black again returned to hide on the island, but they were found and captured on the evening of August 20. Their captors brutally tortured and interrogated them and transmitted their findings in a report that the Americans intercepted. The swimmers were never heard from again.

* * *

THE CLOUD OF THEIR DISAPPEARANCE hung over UDT 10 as the rest of the team on board the destroyer *Rathburne* prepared to support the invasion of Peleliu and Angaur. The OSS operatives traded in their LARUs and other high-tech underwater spy gear for KA-BAR knives, swim trunks, and plastic pads with wax pencils. Although trained as special operators, their key duties were underwater demolitions and hydrographic survey. The assignment didn't sit well with some of the swimmers, who had been trained for more complex work, but they carried out their mission as ordered.

On September 14, 1944, the swimmers left the *Rathburne* on a mission to survey a landing on enemy-occupied Blue Beach on Angaur, part of the Palau Island group. Angaur and the nearby island of Peleliu were assaulted at heavy cost to secure the flank of U.S. forces for the upcoming attack on the Japanese-held

Philippines. UDT 10 team member Robert Kenworthy recalled, "I jumped up like on a diving board, curled my body, and dove into the water. This was in broad daylight; we were at least 300 yards from the beach, all the while avoiding getting shot." But the water offered little safety. "As we were approaching the beach, we were expecting them to open fire, but they were waiting for us to get closer," said Kenworthy.

After all their months of training, the swimmers felt "perfectly at home in the water," but that didn't mean the swim to Blue Beach was comfortable. Kenworthy noted, "The water was mighty cold but crystal clear. But we were used to it. Fifty-four-degree water after several hours becomes very untenable. Your testicles climb up inside. It's later when they come down that it is not very nice."

As they closed in on the beach, the swimmers suddenly encountered the intense fire they had been dreading. "Just remembering it makes the hair stand up on my arms," recounted Kenworthy. "We were about 75 to 125 yards away from it when all hell broke loose. I turned my head and from the right end of the beach I saw three Jap soldiers push palm fronds aside and open fire. We were caught right between the two machine guns. Then came several [unreadable] Wildcats (our own planes) firing, accidentally strafing us. Bullets were hitting the water all around us."

Breaking radio silence, the UDT commanding officer yelled at the admiral, "Get your goddamn cowboys out of there!"

The planes broke off the attack before the friendly fire caused any casualties. Despite the barrage of bullets, the swimmers managed to complete their measurements of the beach and safely return to the destroyer. After determining that demolition would be required for the landing craft to approach, the combat swimmers returned to the water, this time towing explosives. Without their LARUs, the men had to resort to other techniques to set the charges. "I held my breath over two minutes so we could go down and stay down and set the charge," recalled Kenworthy.

"Boom!"

The explosives detonated, shooting shards of coral high into the air. "It was sickening because thousands of fish were also killed by the explosion. I still remember their white little bellies," added Kenworthy.

The reef was clear, providing passage into the beach, but the job wasn't done yet. Hovering five or six feet below the surface, the swimmers carefully guided the landing craft through the holes in the coral blown by Kenworthy and his men, allowing the young men who would take part in the assault access to the enemy-infested beach. Kenworthy remembered, "This was a powerful thing as you looked at the clenched faces of these 18- and 20-year-olds and in another fifteen or twenty minutes they were dead. It's a visual thing you carry with you all your life." Despite the UDT casualties, the Allies successfully assaulted and seized Angaur.

★ ★ ★

UDT 10'S NEXT MISSION was to lead the invasion of the Philippines. On October 19, 1944, six American battleships began their bombardment of the island of Leyte, the first stop in the liberation of the Philippines. About an hour after the big guns started firing, the swimmers of UDT 10 scrambled down cargo nets into the waiting boats that would take them closer to shore. Their job was to level the beach to enable landing craft to bring American troops to shore. The order called for them to conduct their mission in broad daylight, armed only with combat knives and the explosives they needed to blast a path through the rocks and reef.

The boats carrying the swimmers stopped about four hundred yards off shore—well within the range of the Japanese guns and mortars on the beach. The swimmers methodically dropped over the sides and got to work. OSS operative and former Marine Les Bodine recalled, "As we swam forward the water around us was being peppered with machine-gun, rifle, and mortar fire. Water was splashing up around me from the rounds. I noticed that the Japanese had fish traps in the water in front of the beach. They turned out to be markers that allowed them to direct their mortar and cannon fire."

One of those mortar rounds landed nearly on top of Bodine, and he lost consciousness almost immediately. (Years later he learned that the concussion blast had pushed his body down to the ocean floor—about ten feet underwater.) "When you get hit by an explosion like that," he said, "water goes into every orifice: The ears, nose, rectum, and tears things up a little bit. I was spitting up blood and blacked out." One of Bodine's team members inflated the life preserver connected to his swim trunks and towed him back to the boats, where the doctor dosed him with whiskey. "It burned," remembered Bodine. "My eardrums and stomach have scar tissue, but the next day we went back in."

* * *

OPERATIONAL SWIMMER GROUP II, ARAKAN COAST, BURMA, EARLY 1945

As his small craft bobbed on the ocean waves, John Booth squinted ahead, searching the horizon in vain for any sign of the *chaung,* or tidal river, that was the mission target. His hands, like those of his companions, were rough and raw from nine hours of paddling his two-man kayak. The night was dark, limiting visibility and making it all but impossible to see the tiny waterway. "We had a compass bearing to a line of blackness," recalled Booth.

Finding the passage at last, they headed upstream, scouting for Japanese activity. Not too far ahead, they observed an enemy patrol boat approach their position. "We were along the banks in our kayaks," remembered Booth. "They missed us as they went by." The swimmers completed their reconnaissance and turned around. After nine more brutal hours of paddling, they returned safely to base.

Upon reading the mission report, one of the British officers assigned to work with the MU asked, "Why didn't you put a grenade in that Japanese boat?"

Annoyed, Booth immediately shot back, "What does clandestine mean?"

Later he noted, "We weren't there for a shoot 'em up; we were there to get information. These were second generation British officers who were trying to make a name for themselves, earn medals, and they died by the bushel."

*　*　*

LATER DURING THE SUMMER of 1944, a separate group of OSS swimmers, led by Chris Lambertsen and Lieutenant John Booth, known as Operational Swimmer Group II (OSG II), headed for the Pacific, independent of the group that became part of UDT 10. The swimmer commandos first went to Burma. Due to a lack of Japanese shipping targets, their primary task would be to conduct reconnaissance along the Arakan Coast, but they also assisted with transporting agents, particularly when operatives were to be dropped off on a beach that needed to be scouted ahead of time. The swimmer commandos were combining intelligence gathering with special operations much like their later-day SEAL counterparts. To assist with their mission they brought with them a variety of gear, including LARUs, a submarine, fast patrol boats, and two-man kayaks, as well as the "Sleeping Beauty" submersible. Booth, assigned to pilot the underwater craft, didn't feel it was up to the task of navigating the treacherous Pacific waters. "It ran pretty good, but it wasn't good enough to risk my life with it," he explained. "The batteries leaked acid, and the currents were too strong in Burma." He continued, "These days, most high school projects are more advanced. However, the mission and the tactics we were developing helped pioneer underwater demolition."

The Burmese mission also helped modern military forces, like the SEALs and the Green Berets, understand the need for local language experts. When the MU team returned to the Burmese coast for additional intelligence gathering, they encountered a group of natives in a canoe. Unfortunately none of the Americans spoke

Burmese fluently. Booth put his pistol to the head of one of the men in the craft. "Where are the Japanese?" he recited in Burmese. It was one of the few questions he knew. But when the scared villager responded, Booth "was lost." He later remarked, "It was kind of ridiculous. A lot of stuff we did, the Special Forces refined." Today Special Operations forces typically have at least two men on a team who speak the native tongue.

* * *

OVER THE NEXT YEAR, the MU conducted a number of other missions in the region, including several that involved OSS operative Walter Mess. A former lawyer from northern Virginia, Mess headed off to war at the age of twenty-eight, and the OSS soon recruited him. (Later he would become a prominent real estate mogul involved in the development of the Watergate complex in Washington, D.C., and live to the ripe old age of ninety-eight.) He transported Booth and the men of OSG II on many occasions. Of his time in the Pacific, Mess recalled, "Shooting wasn't our mission. Our mission was taxi driver. Our mission was not to fight, but we were prepared to do it." Many of the transportation assignments required the MU operatives to memorize elaborate course changes and follow a path based on dead reckoning. "Many of the missions were fifty to seventy miles behind the lines, moving up shallow *chaungs*," explained Mess. "Try picturing running a patrol boat up Washington, D.C.'s Rock Creek Park River without attracting attention." Somehow the teams managed it, moving "silently at night right through Japanese gun emplacements and encampments." Mess added, "I still remember going by the Japanese camps at night seeing the soldiers and their fires."

MU operatives were routinely assigned to protect SO agents who were returning from completed missions. Mess recalled, "If we were under fire, we would use a bicycle tire to snatch the men. They would stick their arms up, and we'd hook them with the bicycle tire and swing them into the boat, using the bicycle tire as a hook."

Although many of the MU missions on the western coast of Burma involved transporting agents and swimmers into and out of the country, they did get to employ their swimming skills on a few occasions. In January 1945, the Allies began the invasion of Ramree. In preparation for the assault the OSS set up a new base of operations in the coastal town of Kyaukpyu. Believing the area around the main jetty was mined, the OSS sent John Booth and three other swimmers on a reconnaissance mission. Using their LARUs and other underwater gear, the four men determined that there were no active mines in the area. However, they did discover "several wires and old wreckage," which they removed. As a result, they were able to bring boats safely into the area.

The swimmers also took part in several operations to determine whether various beaches were suitable for use in invasions. On January 25–26, a team of ten, including Booth, Eubank, and Lambertsen, conducted a reconnaissance of Sagu Island off the Burmese coast. PT boats took the men into the vicinity of the area, then they switched to kayaks before swimming the final leg of the journey. Again their underwater equipment proved invaluable as they were able to find a suitable beach, which the British forces used for their landing.

During the course of their operations, Lambertsen continued to enhance the capabilities of the LARU. As the rebreather evolved, the men conducted even more difficult missions and remained underwater for longer periods of time. As a scientist and a medical doctor, Lambertsen was also reporting the impact of underwater activity on the human body. His extensive scientific research and the ongoing development of his device helped set the stage for future underwater activities by the SEALs and would be invaluable to the military and underwater diving in general.

On the same day as the Sagu Island mission, another MU officer assisted in a similar underwater reconnaissance effort on Ramree

Island. He and another OSS operative also gathered intelligence on both Ramree and neighboring Cheduba Island that proved valuable to the Allies. Two admirals with the Royal Navy thanked the men personally for their services and "expressed a desire to use the facilities of the [OSS] again."

The MU continued to work very closely with the British throughout this time. On another occasion Booth and four other swimmers using their rebreathers surveyed a British minesweeper that had sunk after running aground. They were able to provide a detailed report to the Royal Navy commander, who "expressed his appreciation and satisfaction."

In February, MU swimmers, including Booth, took on a vital reconnaissance mission. Utilizing their kayaks, they penetrated deep up two of the coastal rivers to determine their feasibility as an invasion route. They successfully "obtained hydrographic and coastal intelligence of value to Allied forces, and later used in planning of invasion of Burma mainland at this point." They also encountered Japanese patrols. They not only avoided detection, they "also learned of [the Japanese] tactic of maintaining sentry platforms on banks of chaungs." The mission required the swimmers to spend long stretches of time in their kayaks, at one time paddling for sixteen hours straight.

* * *

AFTER THE BRITISH LAUNCHED two spectacular raids on Japanese shipping in Singapore Harbor in 1943 and 1944, sinking several enemy vessels, OSS put out requests for additional swimmers to target Japanese shipping. The MU chief in Southeast Asia noted, "This area abounds in reconnaissance and similar raids, which can best be carried out by swimmers and that enthusiasm exists in Allied High Command relative to the possibilities." Accordingly, the OSS sent another swimmer group to the region in October 1944: Operational Swimmer Group III (OSG III). The combat swimmers arrived first in Ceylon. The group included many former members from L-Group in London, such as Gordon Soltau.

OSG III conducted missions in Burma and in Sumatra. One operation, dubbed "Sugarloaf 2," sent operatives to an island off the west coast of Sumatra to conduct reconnaissance of a site for a possible Allied airfield. The swimmers worked closely with OSS's SI group, utilizing British submarines to put agents ashore, often in rubber boats, on islands swarming with Japanese troops.

Many of the British subs used to transport the MU men on missions were nothing more than rotting tubs that should have been headed for the scrap yard instead of embarking on covert missions. For instance, the *Severn* lost her port engine, followed by the radar, refrigerators, and air conditioning, while en route to the mission pinpoint. The MU operatives aboard the vessel had to endure spoiled food and temperatures averaging 120 degrees Fahrenheit. In a scene that could have been ripped from the film *Das Boot*, they also endured "a siege of depth charging by the enemy."

The MU also conducted "prize crew" operations, a euphemism for "snatching" local natives and their boats to glean intelligence on Japanese troop strength in the native's home area. The OSS illegally pressed some Sumatrans into service as agents working for the OSS, and sent them through a "rugged training course" in Ceylon.

One series of operations that involved an eclectic group of natives pressed into service by the OSS was known as the Caprice Missions. Launched from a British submarine, the small group of local agents infiltrated a tiny Japanese-held island off the east coast of Sumatra by rubber boat. They went by code names. For example, "Johnny" was a former member of the Dutch Army, and "Redja" was a native Sumatran who had lived in New York for a time and "jumped ship from the luxury liner *Marnix* in New York City." "Biden" was a fisherman before the war, and "Tdar" was a "paddy [rice] farmer." However, shortly after going ashore, the Japanese captured them. OSG III immediately put plans in motion to get them out.

* * *

MANY OF THE MU operatives thrived on the dangerous missions. Walter Mess summed up the feelings of many operatives when he explained, "You are not alive, unless you are living on the edge. And living on the edge like these swimmers and the rest of those men, you are alive. I mean you are *alive*." He added, "I think that was the most fun I had in my life."

Hollywood dentist Jack Taylor, then a lieutenant commander, was a lifelong adventurer, expert swimmer, sailor, pilot and—arguably—the first SEAL. Taylor did it all—Sea, Air, and Land operations—swimming above and below the water and parachuting behind enemy lines into Austria.

One of the only Americans to survive Mauthausen Concentration Camp, Jack Taylor spent months at the work camp, during which he was under the constant threat of execution. The Germans routinely worked their prisoners to death, and hundreds died every day from starvation alone.

Commander H.G.A. Woolley, a British Navy veteran of World War I and a Hollywood screenwriter, advised the OSS on amphibious special operations throughout World War II. A true visionary and "out-of-the-box" thinker, Woolley's leadership served as the mainspring behind the Maritime Unit (MU) and America's first underwater combat swimmer program. *(National Archives, courtesy of B. Danis)*

All photos from National Archives unless otherwise noted.

Doctor Christian Lambertsen (later known as "Dr. Scuba") personally models the rebreather he developed. Lambertsen pioneered rebreather and SCUBA technology and is credited by many with coining the iconic acronym. When he invented the Lambertsen rebreathing device, he was a medical student at the University of Pennsylvania.

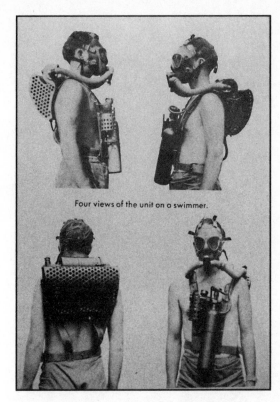

Four views of the unit on a swimmer.

The Lambertsen Amphibious Respiratory Unit (LARU) was a revolutionary closed-circuit breathing device that allowed divers to swim more than a mile underwater without coming up for air. Unique for the time, it eliminated the telltale bubbles that could give away the presence of an underwater combat swimmer.

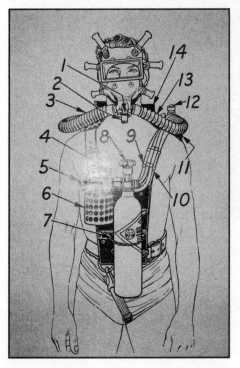

The components of the LARU. The earliest versions of the rebreather were constructed from an old World War I gas mask and a common bicycle pump. The innovative device evolved over time, and America's combat swimmers used components of the pioneering device well into the 1980s.

A leading man in Hollywood films both before and after the war, Sterling Hayden, also known as John Hamilton, was a Marine who served in the OSS alongside Jack Taylor, conducting missions in the Adriatic. His film credits include Gen. Jack D. Ripper in *Dr. Strangelove* and Captain McCluskey in *The Godfather*. *(Columbia Pictures)*

An expert sailor and unsung hero of the war, Lieutenant Ward Ellen, USNR, helped shape the Maritime Unit. He captained OSS boats on numerous missions until a shipboard explosion left him severely wounded.

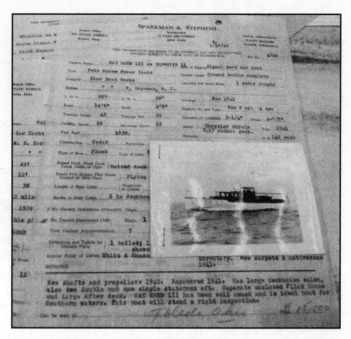

A curious photo of one of the vessels considered for use in training missions by the OSS. Lacking sufficient funds but not ideas or initiative, the Maritime Unit deployed two rotting cabin cruisers that played the role of submarines in training exercises in the Potomac near the covert facility known as "Area D."

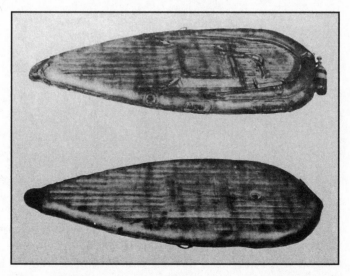

The OSS and Dr. Lambertsen not only developed a precursor to SCUBA (the LARU), they also created a variety of other diving and special operations gear for combat swimming, including a novel inflatable two-man surfboard with a silent, battery-operated motor that stealthily propelled teams to their targets.

The two-man surfboard carries swimmers equipped with a rebreather during a training exercise in Helford, England. The OSS worked closely with the British in planning highly dangerous missions in German-occupied France.

A two-man rubberized kayak invented by the OSS. The handling of these small craft required highly specialized training, which was provided by the OSS Maritime Unit. Operatives used these lightweight craft on intelligence-gathering missions in the Pacific.

The "Sleeping Beauty" or Motorized Submersible Canoe was a craft developed by the UK's SOE for underwater use. The 12-foot-long submersible weighed 600 pounds and carried a 24-volt electric motor that could propel it at speeds up to 3.5 knots. Today's SEALs use a modernized version of the same device, which they call a SEAL Delivery Vehicle or SDV.

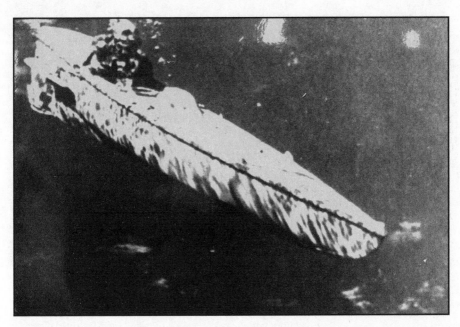

The Sleeping Beauty in action. Testing by the Maritime Unit proved that the vehicle could be successfully launched from a submerged submarine, allowing combat swimmers to approach targets without ever surfacing.

Combat swimmers in special wetsuits developed by the Maritime Unit. The term "frogman" allegedly originated when someone spotted swimmer John P. Spence in the green suit and yelled, "Hey Frogman!"

OSS combat swimmers trained for a variety of missions, including underwater sabotage by planting limpet mines on the hulls of enemy ships. True visionaries, the Maritime Unit saw the possibilities of parachuting teams to an underwater target, much like today's SEALs, putting them decades ahead of their time.

Maritime Unit combat swimmer. The OSS recruited world-class swimmers—many of them Olympic competitors or national champions—for its Maritime Unit.

A "chariot," or human torpedo, developed by the innovative Italians of *Decima MAS*. The 24-foot, 1.6-ton torpedoes, also known as *maiali* (pigs), sank several British warships in Alexandria Harbor in December 1941, setting off an underwater arms race among the world's major powers. Unlike the Italian program, which had frogmen riding on the surface of the water and diving under for a short time to set charges, the OSS developed a novel, breakthrough approach that utilized combat swimmers who would stay underwater for an extended period of time and cover distances over a mile using a rebreather designed by Dr. Christian Lambertsen.

Additional views of the chariot. The Italians used these vehicles to sink two Allied battleships in Alexandria Harbor, immediately altering the balance of power in the Mediterranean.

Members of the San Marco Battalion, elite Italian commandoes who initially fought for the Axis, but later provided expert assistance to the MU. They frequently transported covert agents into hostile territory.

Special operators of the San Marco Battalion working with the OSS. Although they had once been enemies, the two groups put their differences aside to accomplish missions that represented the Maritime Unit's "most valuable work."

A MAS boat, a high-speed torpedo boat used by members of the San Marco Battalion under the command of the Maritime Unit in Italy. The highly maneuverable boats were ideal for covert operations in the Aegean.

A caïque. The MU utilized the small, wooden-hulled vessels extensively for covert operations in the Mediterranean. Weighing 10 to 40 tons, the boats had auxiliary sails, but most were powered by gasoline engines and carried crews of two to six.

The Maritime Unit's caïque fleet would eventually swell to thirty-six boats, which were captained and operated by their local owners. "Some of these men showed great loyalty and daring in their operations under OSS; others (occasionally the same ones) were masters of smuggling, thievery, and goldbricking."

This photo captures a typical covert OSS operation across the Adriatic. These missions were often perilous because Axis craft occupied the waters and German planes patrolled from the skies above.

Hans Tofte, "the world's second best killer." As a trainer for the OSS, he helped turn Ph.D.s into men and women who could win a bar fight. He later served in the CIA.

A photo showing German U-boat pens along the French coast. The Maritime Unit planned a daring combat swimmer operation to disable the pens prior to D-Day.

Various SS officers who ran the Mauthausen Concentration Camp, where Jack Taylor was a prisoner. They committed numerous atrocities, which came to light during the Nuremberg Trials.

A Mauthausen inmate who met his death (one of many) on the electrified barbed wire that surrounded the camp. Mauthausen was the epicenter for a string of labor camps in Austria that could house tens of thousands prisoners at a time. Experts estimate several hundred thousand men, women, and children died in the camps.

The crematorium at Mauthausen Concentration Camp, where the SS burned the dead bodies of tens of thousands of inmates. Jack Taylor and other inmates were forced at gunpoint by vicious German guards to build the ovens, brick by brick.

A member of the Maritime Unit receiving Airborne training. Many of the unit's members were parachute-qualified, unlike the Navy's Underwater Demolition Teams (UDTs). Maritime Unit operatives, much like modern SEALs, combined special operations with intelligence gathering.

A Maritime Unit submarine-launched operation in the southeast Pacific. Maritime Unit swimmers also conducted critical reconnaissance and demolitions that enabled the Navy to land on key islands in the later stages of World War II.

AIR

18

THE DUPONT MISSION

BY THE SUMMER OF 1944, the Allies had Italy contained and continued the long bloody advance up the mountainous spine of the country. The OSS's focus shifted farther north to the Third Reich itself. The fledgling intelligence agency had successfully utilized many Italian recruits in their campaign to take that country, and now they hoped to do the same in Austria.

The Allies tapped Oxford-educated OSS Major John B. McCulloch, stationed at the base in Bari, to head up the search for Austrians who could be persuaded to support the Allied cause. Wealthy and affable, McCulloch spoke three foreign languages, including German, which served him well in his role as a recruiter. He was particularly good at disguising interrogation as small talk, ferreting out valuable intelligence, and helping to identify prisoners interested in changing sides.

When McCulloch and those who worked with him identified potential recruits, they sent the "Deserter-Volunteers," or DVs, to a pair of villas in Bari. There the would-be operatives received American GI uniforms and began training, for their new careers as spies. One incident drove home the perilous nature of their new occupations. During training, the parachute belonging to one of the Austrians got tangled up as he was jumping from the plane. He perished, pummeled to death when the wind battered him against the fuselage of the plane.

It was from this group of DVs that McCulloch would select the men for the Dupont Mission, a daring parachute drop into the heart of German-held Austria. It would be OSS's deepest parachute penetration into the Third Reich. The operatives would collect intelligence on the Austrian city of Wiener Neustadt. Located about twenty-five miles south of Vienna, the city was a major transportation hub and key stop on the German supply lines as well as the home of an airplane factory. In addition, the Allies had heard rumors that the Reich was constructing a belt of defensive fortifications known as the Southwest Wall in the region.

Obsessed with being in the heart of the action, Taylor once again left his operations officer's position and volunteered to lead the Dupont Mission into Austria. After spending weeks behind the lines in Albania, surviving an experience that would kill most men, Taylor convinced McCulloch he should lead the mission. It wasn't an easy sell: despite being one of the OSS's most experienced operators, he spoke almost no German. Therefore, it was essential that he have comrades who were not only fluent in the language but also well acquainted with the region and its culture.

The first DV selected to accompany Taylor went by the all-too-Anglified name of Underwood. A sandy-haired, blue-eyed Austrian, he had been drafted into the Reich's Army in the winter of 1942. Coming from an intensely anti-Nazi family, he had one goal: to desert at the first possible opportunity. In January of 1944 he finally saw his chance. Newly assigned to the infantry, he arrived at the Italian front and asked for permission to scout the American lines. With permission granted, he left camp and summarily tossed his weapon into the underbrush. After an hour and a half walk, he arrived at a group of green tents that he knew housed U.S. soldiers. Cautiously, he walked up to one and drew back the flap. The four sleeping GIs inside barely stirred. He crept over to one of the men and gave his blanket a tug. "I am an Austrian," Underwood announced in English. "I want to help you."

The OSS first assigned Underwood to its propaganda section, Morale and Operations (MO). Under their direction he wrote German leaflets full of misinformation. Occasionally he would slip into a German uniform and infiltrate enemy lines. There he would attempt (often successfully) to convince the men that their German officers had ordered them to surrender. But McCulloch snatched up Underwood for the Dupont Mission, offering him the chance to do more serious damage to the Germans.

Underwood felt something bordering on hero-worship for Taylor, who would lead the mission. The taciturn American with a drive to be part of the action seemed an inspirational figure to the younger Austrian, the only deserter-volunteer selected for the mission who spoke English. But Underwood had less fondness for the other two men McCulloch selected for the mission: another Austrian, code-named "Perkins," and a former member of the *Luftwaffe*, code-named "Grant." With only a grammar school education that ended when he was fourteen, Perkins, a stonemason, was of a lower social class than Underwood, a distinction that was intensely important in the European society of the time. Underwood's father had been a personal friend of the Austrian chancellor, and he felt that working with both of the other Austrians, Perkins in particular, was beneath him. However, the uncouth Perkins did have some attributes that made him well-suited for Dupont. The dark-haired, stocky twenty-three-year-old had been a paratrooper, a skill that would be valuable on the mission, and he came from the village of Saint Margarethen, which was very close to the drop zone and provided him with invaluable contacts.

The final member of the team, Grant, was from Prague and had Czech ancestry. Grant said he had been a medical student before being conscripted into the German air force, but he later demonstrated a willingness to stretch the truth that led some, including Underwood, to question his story. Underwood disliked the blond-haired, gray-eyed man, but Grant seemed to get along well with most other people. The former officer claimed to have been married and that his father had been the director of a glass factory. He loved to talk, but he also gained a reputation for severe mood swings. His predilection for womanizing would cause trouble for the team later on.

The team didn't get along well. Due to the language barriers, they couldn't even communicate well. But despite their tensions, they would be forced to cooperate, as they would be virtually alone, deep in the heart of enemy-held territory. For the rest of the summer Taylor and his team prepared for their mission.

Taylor went on a training blitz, learning many of the same sorts of skills that would be necessary for the future SEALs. His first stop: parachute training at the Royal Air Force (RAF) facility located at the Rabat David Airport in Haifa, Palestine. The RAF put Taylor through the paces—fourteen days of intense training divided into three parts: physical conditioning, synthetic training (tumbling, exits from a grounded plane, including being dragged across the ground in a parachute harness), and, finally, actual parachute jumps. Taylor would make eight practice jumps to become airborne qualified by the Brits. Unlike American paratroopers, who exited the side door of transport planes, Taylor dropped through a hole in the belly of a British bomber, an exercise that foreshadowed Dupont's actual parachute drop into Austria only a few weeks away.

Next Taylor went though Lysander training. Renowned for its ability to land in a fifty-yard field, the Westland Lysander single-engine aircraft was ideal for covert operations. It dropped and picked up Allied agents throughout occupied Europe. Taylor learned how to fly the plane and quickly get in and out of the aircraft. Shortly after Lysander training, he went through Container School, where he learned to pack and parachute-drop the type of containers that would bring Dupont's gear and equipment into Austria.

The final leg of Taylor's training regime in Haifa included a "refresher course" known as ME-102. Here Taylor practiced with silenced pistols, blew up bridges, and sharpened his skills at sowing mayhem behind German lines. Based on the intense training and his past experience, Jack Taylor felt ready.

19

"I WAS PROMISED THIS MISSION, AND I WANT IT"

The sudden flash of the red jump light inside the fuselage caught Jack Taylor's attention. It was 10:15 p.m., and in fifteen minutes he would be parachuting into the middle of Nazi-held Austria with no support other than his three companions. For the past several hours the drone of the "Liberator" bomber had made conversation nearly impossible, and Taylor became absorbed in studying the maps of the area where he would be gathering intelligence. One of the Polish crewmen pulled away the piece of plywood covering the jump hole, and the four-man team of the Dupont Mission got their first glimpse of the terrain below. For the most part they could see nothing but fog, water, and the seemingly impenetrable black of the moonless night.

The pilot descended sharply to four hundred feet, the minimum height required to make a safe jump. Over the intercom came the call for action stations. The jumpers rose to their feet. Their commander, Major John McCulloch, who was aboard the flight despite the fact that it violated regulations, shook each of their hands in turn and wished them good luck. This practice, intended to inspire and support the operatives, emulated Donovan's hands-on leadership, but today these actions might be considered reckless: if a senior officer with detailed knowledge were to fall into enemy hands, it could compromise American operations.

Suddenly the light in the back of the plane switched from red to green, signaling their arrival over the drop zone. Taylor positioned himself over the edge of the hole and fell into the darkness.

* * *

TAYLOR WOULD HAVE PREFERRED to make the jump another night. Friday the thirteenth seemed an inauspicious day to launch one of the most dangerous intelligence-gathering operations of the war. But the mission had already been postponed in September because of weather, and the positions of enemy searchlights and flak guns made it necessary to fly in on a night with no moon. Rather than wait another month, Taylor's superiors ordered them to proceed.

At the American intelligence base in Bari, operatives and military personnel had been placing bets on whether the men of the Dupont Mission would survive. Odds were ten to one they would not.

Dupont called for one American and three Austrian operatives to parachute deep into the heart of Austria. The drop zone was "a flat cultivated strip about two miles long by one-half mile wide on the northeast fringe of the city near Neusiedler See (40 km south of Vienna near the Hungarian border). The area was sparsely settled and bordered on marshy land with tall reeds which would serve as excellent cover." After landing in the marshes on the edge of the lake the men would make their way to the city, where Taylor and his team were to gather intelligence about Nazi operations in the area, gauge the local level of support or resistance to the Germans, and radio back their findings.

Because Dupont placed Taylor and his men so far behind enemy lines, it was considered extremely dangerous, even foolhardy.

157

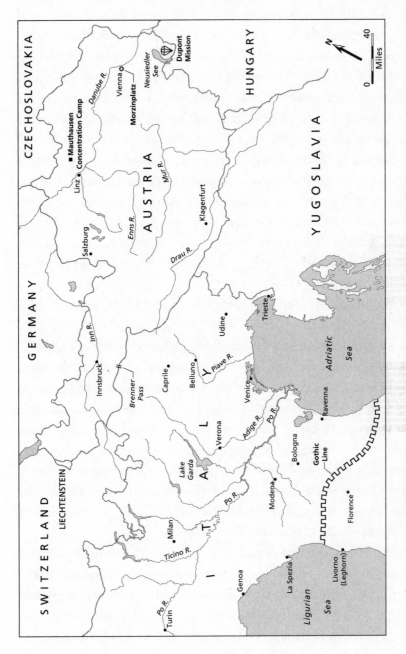

NORTHERN ITALY AND AUSTRIA AREA OF OPERATIONS

Some questioned Taylor's inclusion on the mission, noting that he spoke almost no German, and the mission included nothing in the way of maritime operations other than parachuting near a lake. Taylor, however, didn't believe the language barrier would be a problem, and he thought it was important to include an American officer to inspire the local Nazi resistance, so he fought to stay on the team. His stalwart determination and willpower won the day. Taylor simply stated, "I was promised this mission, and I want it."

The other three team members had all been born in the area around Vienna. Although adamantly opposed to the Nazis, all were forced to serve the Third Reich. After capture by the Allies they readily switched sides. In his report Taylor noted all three men "were in their early twenties, single, in excellent physical and mental condition and eager to participate. There was no question of their integrity."

Perkins came from the town of Saint Margarethen, about fifty kilometers south of Vienna, and the team hoped they could set up a base in his parents' home. Grant, a former butcher's apprentice and something of a ladies' man, assured them that the team could also find safe harbor in the homes owned by the family of the butcher's daughter, with whom he was very well acquainted. (In the coming days, Grant's womanizing would have a profound effect on the mission.) The operative also believed the butcher, named Buchleitner, "could be depended upon to help in an emergency." The third Austrian, Underwood, came from Vienna, an area that was too dangerous for the team to enter, but he also had local knowledge that could prove helpful.

Due to the dangerous nature of the mission, the flight plan and drop procedures would be "entirely abnormal." Taylor explained, "Of necessity, it had to be a 'blind' drop, i.e. without [a] ground reception committee or pattern lights, and with absolutely no circling. Three containers, two containing duplicate radio equipment, were to be dropped in salvo followed immediately by the four bodies." However, shortly after takeoff Taylor was stunned to learn that the Polish pilot was expecting to do a "normal drop" with lots of circling. Taylor explained the mission plan to the pilot, stressing that there should be absolutely no circling so as to minimize their detection by the enemy.

* * *

WITH THE WIND IN HIS FACE, Taylor fell through the cold night air and struggled with the risers attached to his parachute canopy. "I pulled down on my risers to check a bad oscillation," remembered Taylor. With the lines finally untangled, he looked down to see the ground rushing toward him. "I . . . saw to my horror that I would land on the roof of a house not more than twenty feet below. As I was slipping in that direction, I released the risers in order to drop straight down and barely missed the eaves, landing instead a few feet away from the house in the front yard." Mistakenly believing the building to be a radio station, Taylor fled the yard.

The call of a marsh bird sounded in the distance. Knowing it to be the team's prearranged signal, Taylor followed the call and met up with the other agents. They quickly buried their parachutes and jump suits and began searching for the containers with their supplies and the all-important radio that would be their lifeline to the outside world. Though the Polish pilot spoke excellent English, he failed to heed Taylor's instructions. "To our amazement and chagrin, our plane returned and flew directly overhead in line with our previous run," Taylor remembered. But they quickly turned their attention back to the ground and within thirty minutes found the first of the dropped containers, the one holding supplies but no radio. They stowed it behind some reeds when, suddenly, the drone of an airplane engine broke the silence of the night. The team found themselves in grave peril. Taylor recalled, "To our utter horror, ou[r] plane returned again, passing low directly overhead. This was practically signing our death certificates as the German radar was so very accurate that circling over any area by a lone plane at night was bound to create suspicion and lead to an investigation."

Searchlights and antiaircraft fire arced across the inky black sky as the Germans attempted to shoot down the plane. Finally the bomber left the drop zone and headed back toward Italy.

Angry over the pilot's inability to follow his orders, a distracted Taylor suffered another mishap. "I stepped in a hole in the marsh wrenching my knee badly, which made walking on uneven ground very painful, but we continued searching throughout the night and in desperation even into the dawn. From a hillock, we ventured to look out over the lake and marsh but could find no trace of the other two containers."

The loss of the other containers had cascading consequences that threatened the success of the mission and placed the agents' lives in jeopardy. Without a radio they could not report back their findings or be resupplied or extracted from Austria. The Dupont team was trapped behind enemy lines with little hope of accomplishing their mission. They continued to search through the night before finally giving in to exhaustion. For several days the four men remained in the area, desperately hoping the plane would return again and finally drop the containers with the radios. They remained hidden from enemy eyes, but not from the wildlife. Taylor awoke, startled, to find "a medium-sized marsh snake lying alongside my sleeping bag."

On the third day, the team abandoned all hope that the plane would return to drop a radio. The men set out on the day-long journey to the town where Buchleitner the butcher lived. However, after only a few minutes Underwood became severely ill. He struggled along for a mile before admitting he could not continue. Determined to gather the intelligence and fulfill their mission, the rest of the team left him behind with food and water. They "continued past Nougledel where thousands of foreign (slave) workers were being herded for work on the Southeast Wall, a line of defense utilizing, in this area, the natural water barriers of Neusiedler See and the Leithe Geb."

At 2:30 in the morning on October 17, Taylor, Perkins, and Grant arrived at the Buchleitner home. Although they fiercely opposed the Nazis, the butcher's family had some trepidation about allowing the OSS operatives to stay in their home. They fed the men and showed them to some beds. But only an hour later they woke the team, requesting that they leave. German troops were arriving in the village, and the family feared what would happen if they were found harboring spies. Taylor recalled, "As it was nearly dawn and we had no place to go, we begged to stay and were allowed to hide in the hayloft."

So began a lengthy and perilous saga of trying to find a safe house. According to Taylor, "Buchleitner and family were devout anti-Nazis, as were eighty percent of the people in this vicinity, but in spite of a token of a few gold pieces and several hundred marks, he wished us to be on our way. This was the first demonstration of fear growing into terror, which we were to see several times later." The group traveled from village to village by night, desperately seeking a place where they could set up a permanent base. Along the way they bluffed their way through *kontrols* (checkpoints) by pretending to be soldiers and saluting "*Heil Hitler.*" The old villagers manning the stations allowed them to "slip by, although it was ticklish." They begged several contacts for a place to stay, "but all were unwilling to keep us permanently although they were entirely friendly and willing to be hospitable for one night," said Taylor. Many of those they met expressed support. In particular, one "middle-aged woman wept and almost became hysterical when I was introduced to her as an American officer," noted Taylor. "She was unusually intelligent and vehemently denounced the Nazis. She begged me to send for American or British paratroops, stating that 90% of all Austrians would assist. This plea was repeated many times later by others."

As they traveled from place to place the team gathered intelligence, despite the loss of their radio. They discovered an ammunition factory that employed forty thousand workers, as well as many other targets, such as "a locomotive factory in [W]iener Heustadt, turning out one a day, a powder factory in Winzendorf employing 2000, a *Wehrmacht* lager in Vienna containing all materiel of war, an artillery school, flak school, numerous airfields and woods where the German fighters were hidden when the American bombers came over, government food storage houses in Vienna, etc." They also amassed data on the Southeast Wall, a belt of fortifications protecting southern Austria. The team took down "the exact location of the fortified hills, anti-tank ditches, barbed wire and mine fields, pillboxes, artillery sites, etc. At this time (1 Nov.) there were 50,000 foreign workers and several hundred Hitler Youth preparing this defense line under the direction of *Todt* and R.A.D. It was expected to be finished by the middle of January [1945]."

In addition, Taylor and the others witnessed the conditions in which the Reich was warehousing slave laborers and implementing the "Final Solution," the Holocaust. One former theater "housed several hundred foreign (slave) workers, mostly Ukrainians, but including Poles, Czechs, French, Italians, Etc., approximately 25% were women. They had practically nothing to eat and were the worst specimens of humanity I had ever seen," recalled Taylor. On another occasion "two trains of 28 cars each with approximately 6,000 Hungarian Jews passed through on their way to lagers in Austria. They had had no food or water for three days and when [a Red Cross nurse] took them a pail of drinking water, the guards (SS or SA) objected and told her that Jews didn't deserve to be treated as human beings."

However, they found that some prisoners received much better treatment. At one point they made contact with British POWs who were working on a railroad line. A small stream ran behind the home where they were staying, and it "was being widened into an anti-tank ditch by many hundreds of foreign workers and their Nazi overseers. We observed and photographed them at close range through a crack in the roof made by sliding a tile up. Early one morning I thought I heard swearing in English and, on sliding the tile up, we saw about eleven British POWs working on the railroad with no guard except the railroad inspector." The OSS men waited for their chance to make contact, and a few days later they caught the Brits' attention when the overseer left for a moment. "They were so surprised that it was difficult for them to conceal their excitement," remembered Taylor. "We told them we were U.S. Air Corps men who had bailed out and were on our way to Yugoslavia. They offered a map and good advice. They said they were not treated badly, extra food was issued for railroad work, their Red Cross packages were coming through regularly, and from what we saw they didn't strain themselves working." In his report Taylor noted,

Political information showed that approximately 2% to 5% of the farmers and villagers were devout Nazis, 10% to 15% were on the fence and 80% anti-Nazi, with 50% rabid anti-Nazi. In Vienna, estimates were difficult because of extreme Gestapo control, but it is safe to say that not more than 20% were strong Nazis and certainly 50% were rabid anti-Nazi. Later American bombing of non-military targets, particularly pure residential districts and the beautiful art gallery and opera house, reduced the Anglo Americanophiles to nil. It was very bad psychology and positively stiffened morale. The feeling among the Austrians, particularly the Viennese, was that the Allies were making no differentiation between the Austrians and the Germans, which did more to squelch budding resistance movements than the Gestapo. In the later months, coupled with the Russian atrocity stories, it actually united Austrians and Germans as never before and made possible a real *Volksturm* (people's army).

Although the Dupont team had collected troves of valuable information, without a radio, they had no way to transmit it to the Allies. Eventually they regrouped at the butcher's house, where they met up with Underwood and his mother, who assisted them with trying to make connections to the Vienna underground and get their intelligence out of the country. They set up a temporary base of operations in the hayloft of a friend and developed a daring plan to get out of the country. Perkins and Grant "would go to the front in Italy via Udine and attempt to infiltrate through the American lines." Meanwhile Taylor and Underwood would attempt to make their way to Yugoslavia, contact the partisans there, and somehow find a way back to the base at Bari. Through their contacts they made arrangements to travel from Vienna on a freight train carrying machinery for a ball-bearing factory. "Underwood would go as a civilian employee, and [Taylor] would be encased in a box as machinery." Grant and Perkins set out from the farm for the Italian front.

Before long, one of the men made a critical mistake that would place the entire team in jeopardy. Living up to his reputation as a womanizer, Grant had seduced one of the locals and used his mission funds to purchase a diamond ring for his girlfriend. Suspicious of this outlay of cash, the Gestapo swooped in and picked up the two men. Under interrogation, they confessed their actions and gave up the location of their two fellow operatives.

Unsuspecting, Taylor and Underwood remained at the farm that had been their most recent hideout, making the final preparations for their own dash to the border. As the two agents were steeling themselves for one last freezing cold night in the hayloft, they heard visitors approach the main house. They turned off their light, expecting no trouble, as the family with whom they were staying frequently entertained guests. There was nothing friendly about the visitors that night. Taylor recalled, "Suddenly, the door was thrown open and eight plainclothesmen rushed in." He grappled with the Germans for a few seconds, but eventually they forced him into a corner, where they beat him over the head with a blackjack until he was groggy. Four men jumped on him and twisted his left arm "backwards until the elbow joint was torn loose, much as you would the joint of a chicken leg." Taylor realized further struggle would be futile. "Blackjack taps on my head continued while my wrists were chained together behind my back, painfully tight, and locked with a padlock."

Taylor looked over at Underwood, who had suffered much the same treatment. His friend was "bleeding profusely from several cuts on his head." The plainclothes Gestapo agents hauled the two men to their feet and dragged them out into the night.

LAND

20

VIENNA CAPTIVITY

THE GERMANS HAULED AWAY TAYLOR and Underwood for "questioning," a process that involved as much intimidation and torture as actual interrogation. Taylor noted, "We were led to the Burgermeister's office in Schutzen, and with our arms still chained behind us we were slapped and kicked while being questioned. Although in opposite corners of a large room with our backs turned to each other, we could each hear what was happening to the other."

The officer pointed to Taylor's collar and asked what the insignia there meant. "*Hauptmann* (Captain)," responded the operative.

"*Falsch* (false)!" announced the German slapping him across the face.

The same interchange repeated several times, and each time Taylor kept his answer the same. He later learned "they were trying to make me admit that I was a civilian in uniform."

Taylor and Underwood weren't the only ones brought in. He also saw the family that had sheltered them hauled off by the authorities, all of them weeping except the housewife. The Germans executed the head of the family, while the others remained in German custody.

The Germans took away Taylor's uniform and offered him civilian clothes, which he refused, believing they would take photographs of him in the clothing and use it as evidence that he had broken the rules of the Geneva Convention. After more interrogation they transported Taylor to Gestapo headquarters in Vienna. In better days the building near the center of the city had served as the Hotel Metropole. The Gestapo had converted it into a prison. "In underwear only . . . and with clumsy wooden shoes, I was taken to Morzinplatz IV Gestapo [Headquarters] in Vienna and placed in cell No. 5 on the mezzanine at 0500 on the first of December," recalled Taylor, "even my shoe strings being removed so that I could not hang myself. I was not allowed to lie down nor to sleep nor was any food or water allowed." More grilling and intimidation followed. "At this time, I never expected to live another day and consequently slept very little," noted Taylor. He was held in an eight-by-seven-foot cell with no view of the outside, and the lights were left on continuously. He finally received meager food and water and realized he fared better than some other prisoners, who were "chained backwards to the bars in the cell with their toes barely touching the floor, [while] others were permitted no 'food' for several days while others had their wrists chained together at night."

On a typical day, the prisoners were awakened at 5:00 a.m. "After washing and making one's 'bed,' [they] waited until [8:00 a.m.] for breakfast, which consisted of hot water (very diluted unsweetened ersatz coffee) and a thin slice of black bread. One must then sit on a stool but not sleep and must jump to attention whenever the '*Kontrole*' made the rounds, usually about four times daily. Lunch consisted of a very weak erpsin (beet) soup (no meat-broth, bone, or other vegetable), about four tablespoons of vegetable stew such as erpsin, carrots, or potatoes, and one thin slice of bread. For supper, one had the same stew and a similar slice of bread. For Saturday supper, a small cube of cheese was substituted for the stew and for Sunday a small slice of wurst the size of a silver dollar was substituted. One was permitted to go to the toilet only at three specified times daily when there were two guards on duty, and no prisoner ever saw any of the others."

Periodic questioning continued over the course of several days. Disturbingly, the Germans "showed a remarkable knowledge of

OSS including names and had a diagramatic relationship of OSS Theater Hq to Washington. They were particularly interested in northern Italy and told me several things about the organization which I didn't know, such as the establishment of a detachment at Cannes," he added. Making matters worse, Taylor caught a glimpse of Perkins and Grant, who were also in custody, which meant that no one from the team had made it back to the Allied lines with their intelligence.

After some time passed, they placed Taylor in a cell with Hungarian General Tabornok Wattay Anton, Hungary's former war minister. In addition, he met several other prisoners, including a Bavarian count. Frequent Allied air raids resulted in the prisoners being taken to shelters in the lower levels of the prison, but no opportunity for escape presented itself.

Taylor's injured arm continued to be very painful. "In spite of the fact that my arm was green and blue and terribly swollen, no doctor nor X-ray ever came although promised innumerable times," he said. "It was five weeks before I could use it to button my pants or tie my tie. I finally became resigned to my death and with the aid of Wattay, who was very religious, I prayed twice a day for myself and my comrades."

Soon the holiday season approached. The Bavarian count Taylor had befriended "was released the day before Christmas and left a small wreath with candles for us. On Christmas Eve we lit it and tried to be happy, but Wattay was so worried and nervous about his family in Budapest during the siege that he couldn't control himself. In trying to comfort him, I broke down myself, which was the only time during all my captivity," recalled the OSS officer.

In mid-January, Wattay was taken away, and Taylor received a new roommate, one who brought with him a very welcome radio. Although Allied stations were blocked on local frequencies, Taylor jerry-rigged the set to get shortwave bands. Soon they were happily listening to news from the BBC and America. In fact, the very first time they got it to work they heard "Vice President Wallace giving the oath of office to Truman and a moment later the President was heard being sworn in by a chief justice. It was a real thrill." Many of the prison guards were former members of the Vienna police who opposed the Nazis, and one stopped by the cell door on several occasions in order to listen to the news from the Allies. This guard told Taylor that "only three out of the twenty police guards were Nazis, and their treatment bore out his claim. They were regular Vienna police, most having 20 to 30 years' service and not SS or *Wehrmacht*," Taylor noted. "With the exception of the above mentioned three, they were all kind and sympathetic with us; however, very strict Gestapo control was exercised over them."

Through his cellmate, Taylor also learned about the "top-floor" prisoners. The Germans had captured nine agents (five women and four men) sent into Austria by the Russians and British. The Germans forced them to remain in contact with their handlers and "to save their lives, they operated their radios in daily contact with Moscow, also ciphering and deciphering all messages. A radio room on the top floor was in charge of a Gestapo operator who supervised and monitored each transmission." In addition to feeding false information to the Russians, the *Wehrmacht* attempted to lure other agents into traps where they could also be captured.

Eventually the harsh conditions began to take a toll on Taylor. He spent two months in "absolute solitary confinement, only seeing and speaking to other people during the air raids." He also grew ill. "I had severe dysent[e]ry and much loss of blood the last two weeks of January, and although medical attention or medicine was promised daily, neither were ever forthcoming," Taylor later wrote. "By the middle of February, I had lost much weight and had long ago stopped exercising because it made me too hungry. About this time I succumbed to pneumonia with very high fever." Again Taylor made repeated requests for medical attention, but the only help he received came from fellow prisoners. With the help of one of the Viennese guards, a prisoner passed him a package of sulphanilamide, which Taylor believed helped save his life. A female

prisoner named Louisa Scuchek, who was one of the top-floor radio operators, "was allowed to come into my room at intervals and
change the cold towels on my head," Taylor remembered. "She
was a wonderful nurse and made me feel much better. We became
very good friends."

At one point, Scuchek confided to Taylor that she believed the
Germans would execute her and the other Russian operatives at
the last minute before Russia invaded Austria. But she was not
afraid. "I have no fear, I am a Communist," she explained.

Later, due to damage to the prison, Taylor and radio operator
prisoners were moved to a villa formerly owned by the head of an
Austrian-American rubber company. The villa sat on a park, and
the prisoners were herded through the picturesque area during the
daily air raids. "It was the first time I'd seen the sun in five months,
and the 'special' prisoner food was far superior to anything previous, although meager." Taylor was even taken out to saw firewood
and prune trees in the park when he was well enough to work.

But his stay in the relatively posh surroundings didn't last. After
only a week in the villa, a guard awakened Taylor in the night and
told him to get ready to leave. *This is the end*, Taylor thought to
himself.

21

DECIMA MAS STRIKES BACK

THE NIGHT OF NOVEMBER 18–19, 1944, LIVORNO, ITALY

The sound of a cough that emanated from somewhere in the darkness suddenly broke the silence of the calm, starless night, immediately attracting the attention of Able Seaman P. R. Thompson. It was just after one in the morning, and Thompson was throwing out an anti-limpeteer charge in the harbor at Livorno,* Italy, where dozens of Allied ships were moored. Steel nets and other obstructions had failed to stop enemy frogmen, so the Allies had resorted to the use of miniature depth charges that created shock waves powerful enough to shred human tissue, muscle, and bones. Thompson and the other three men on duty at the lighthouse at Diga Di Marzocco took turns trudging out along the stone breakwater and dropping the explosives every five to twenty-five minutes, at random intervals, to make underwater swimming perilous for the enemy.

Thompson's head turned in the direction of the cough, and he noticed a dark shape beneath the surface of the water. He threw his charge. The shadow moved. The seaman charged back to the lighthouse and quickly informed the other two guards that he thought

---

*Sometimes referred to by English speakers as Leghorn.

there were limpeteers in the bay. Rushing back along the rocky breakwater with their loaded rifles, the three men opened fire on the amorphous shape now clinging to the rocks. Almost immediately a trio of Italian frogmen climbed up onto the breakwater.

"Put your hands up!" ordered the Americans.

The Italians obeyed, but they began walking along the rocks.

"Halt!" the men shouted.

Two complied, but one frogman clad in a dark green rubber suit continued walking. Thompson and the others fired a warning shot near his feet, and he came to a sudden stop. The Americans searched the three men for weapons, found only their knives, and hauled them back to their post for interrogation.

The frogmen were clad in multiple layers for protection against the elements. Closest to their skin they had a set of woolen clothes for warmth. Next came a rubber suit and rubber shoes. On top of that were dark blue coveralls. On their heads "all three wore dark green felt skull caps of the Balaclava helmet type, with dark green camouflage netting attached." They had blackened their faces with paint, and each wore a set of flippers and an underwater breathing apparatus. They also had weighted belts with two hanging clamps, and they carried fifty thousand lire each.

After inventorying their belongings and noting their rank badges, U.S. Navy personnel began interrogating the three men. Initially "all three prisoners made clumsy attempts to mislead and deceive." But a quick look at their dog tags revealed their names: Sub-lieutenant Bruno Oswaldo Malacarne, Petty Officer Marcello Bertoncin, and Sailor Edmondo Sorgetti. All three were members of the part of the *Decima MAS* who, along with their leader, Borghese, had joined the German cause rather than the Allies when Italy switched sides in the war. The Black Prince and his Gamma men were back in action.

For six days, the Navy interrogators questioned the trio. Thanks to intelligence provided by the *Decima MAS* men now working with the OSS, the interrogators had files on all three, which helped coerce the truth out of the frogmen. By talking to each of the men separately, the Navy was eventually able to piece together a story that "in the opinion of interrogators, approximates the truth."

The OSS learned that planning for the *Decima MAS* mission had begun in October when an Italian reconnaissance plane took photographs of the port at Livorno. On November 8, their German handlers gave the Gamma operatives a final briefing and they left the city of Valdagno the next morning by truck. On November 10, they reported for duty at the German Navy base in Varignano, a village on Italy's northeastern coast. They intended to set out on the mission immediately, but bad weather delayed them until November 18. That evening they set out in a small, high-speed motorboat, eventually stopping about two or three kilometers northwest of the entrance to the port at Livorno.

Around 10:30 p.m., the three men slipped into the frigid water, each "towing two bilge keel bombs of a new type" as well as civilian clothing, identity cards, money, and other effects that would enable them to survive and establish a base in Italy. They planned to attach the limpets to at least two Allied ships. Sometime during the long swim one of the frogmen tore his rubber suit, and he "was suffering from muscular convulsions" due to hypothermia by the time they approached the breakwater. They paused there for a rest, when Thompson spotted them. As soon as the Americans began firing on the frogmen, they dropped their limpet mines and other gear and surrendered.

The interrogation also revealed a future planned human torpedo attack on shipping at Livorno. In response to this intelligence, the Allies set up "artificial moonlight," created with "a series of searchlight beams in a cone."

* * *

COMPANY D'S NEWLY MINTED executive officer, Ted Morde, was present at the interrogations of the Italian frogmen.

In an agency filled with colorful characters, Lieutenant Ted Morde stood out as one of the most vibrant. Before joining the

MU, he had been a radio announcer and journalist, but the most notorious episode in his past, by far, was his work as an archaeological explorer. In 1940, Morde led an expedition to Honduras in search of "The Lost City of the Monkey God." Five months later he returned to the United States, claiming to have found the site. He brought back thousands of artifacts in support of his claim and also published a record of his adventure in *The American Weekly*. The headline proclaimed, "Explorer Theodore Morde finds in Honduras jungles a vanished civilization's prehistoric metropolis where sacrifices were made to the gigantic idol of an ape—and describes the weird 'Dance of the Dead Monkeys' still practiced by natives in whom runs the olden blood." Morde wrote, "I am convinced that we have found the site of the legendary Lost City of the Monkey God, the ancient capital of the vanished Chorotegans—of a civilization older perhaps than those of the Mayas and Aztecs—tales of which have lured explorers for years deep into the jungles of Honduras." He went on to explain local customs and legends in graphic detail before concluding, "That we can hardly wait for the weeks to pass before we can reenter the City of the Monkey God and begin to uncover the wealth—archaeological and perhaps other kinds as well—goes without saying."

However, Morde never made a return expedition, nor did he ever tell anyone else where to find the lost city. When the war broke out, he joined the OSS and was detailed to the Cairo headquarters. Morde eventually worked on a high-profile mission in Turkey where he met the German ambassador to Turkey, Franz Von Papen. During World War I, the United States had expelled Von Papen for allegedly sabotaging rail lines. Back in Germany he rose in politics to become chancellor.

In 1944, Morde became executive officer of the Maritime Unit in Italy and began serving as its eyes and ears on the ground, reporting on the activities of the *Decima MAS* units for Commander Woolley and Marine Major Alfred Lichtman, who was then serving as Area Operations Officer for the MU. Morde had a very favorable opinion of Richard Kelly's unit, which had been renamed "MU of Company D." In a letter to Major Lichtman, Morde wrote, "Frankly I am pretty proud of OSS in this theater. It is my opinion that some day long after the war, when permission is given to present the facts about OSS accomplishments to the public, or for the judgement [*sic*] of historians, there will be utter amazement that OSS has been able to accomplish so many magnificent deeds for the good of the cause. We have over here a group of men who live, eat and breathe this war."

* * *

DESPITE THE THWARTED ATTACK on Livorno and the capture of key *Decima MAS* operatives, enemy underwater sabotage in the harbor continued. On several occasions the German-controlled Italian swimmers of *Decima MAS* attempted limpet attacks against MU and other Allied craft in the area. Another Company D officer wrote, "Mines go off almost every day, and shooting takes place at reconnaissance planes . . . air raids are expected anytime, and limpeteers swim in, as they have twice in the last three weeks, to blow up the harbor." The Allies would need to be on high alert to prevent future underwater sabotage missions.

In addition to defending against attacks from the Axis frogmen, MU of Company D continued to launch missions into northern Italy. On October 10, 1944, they received a shipment of "ten Lambertsen Diving Units Model #10, complete with extra type B oxygen cylinder to each unit" and some extra soda lime absorbent material to aid in these efforts. The MU continued to entertain the thought of converting the San Marco commandos into underwater swimmers like their brethren Gamma men in *Decima MAS*; but the war came to an end before it could happen.

* * *

THROUGHOUT THE FALL AND WINTER of 1944, the MU conducted numerous clandestine missions, such as the Lupo ("Wolf") Mission. On December 16, 1944, in the dead of night, Ward Ellen transported three Italian OSS-trained agents to a point just north of the Po River. The three operatives then paddled a small rubber boat to the desolate beach. Once ashore, a "boatman" who was supposed to guide them to a pinpoint and reception committee of partisans "disappeared." After hiding all day, the men got back in their boat and rowed, unguided, to locate the rendezvous location. Keeping about three hundred yards from the shore, they fruitlessly searched until exhaustion set in. They beached the craft, and "forgetting to be careful," they succumbed to sleep in the unprotected sandy dunes near the Po.

A German patrol surprised the three men at dawn. Attempting to protect their gear, they shot their way out, fleeing into a nearby swamp. "All day on December 18th we wandered about in the swamp, followed by the Germans, who gave us no peace. The water reached our chests."

Evading the Germans, the "Wolves" stumbled upon a local with a boat who took them to dry land and shelter. But the man, a collaborator, returned with a patrol of Fascist Italians. Near the door of the house, Lupo's team leader drew his pistol and fired several shots. Simultaneously, bullets tore through his chest and spine.

With their team leader dead, and suffering grievous gunshot wounds of their own, the other two men of the Lupo team hid behind a table with their pistols drawn, waiting for the Fascists to enter the house. The men anxiously waited, planning to play dead, aided in their deception by the streams of blood flowing profusely from their wounds. No one came. After losing several men in the firefight with the OSS operatives, the Fascists had fled. Eventually, the two remaining OSS agents crawled out of a window and escaped to a nearby hut and later into a thicket. "[One agent] lost a great deal of blood. Having no bandages to stop the bleeding, and thus able to go no further we decided to spend the night there."

The men hid in the thicket "entirely surrounded by Germans, who kept beating the bushes to find us." Somehow evading the dragnet, the wounded men continued on the run until December 20, when they were stopped by a patrol from the Italian Republican Guard, who demanded their papers. When they were unable to produce the proper papers, the Fascists stripped the agents and uncovered their wounds. The Republican Guard turned the two men over to the Gestapo for torture. "The methods used by German SS troops to wring confessions from Patriots were like those used in the Middle Ages; they used hot irons, steel rods and chains, and made us drink salt water. Their most modern device was passing a wire charged with an electric current over our genital organs." Despite the SS's cruelty, the brave men of the Lupo mission survived the war.

Kelly and Ellen conducted countless missions like Lupo. Many of them were joint operations between the MU and one of the most successful OSS units of the war, the Eighth Army Detachment.

22

THE EIGHTH ARMY DETACHMENT

THE BRIGHT LIGHT OF A FULL MOON shone through the fuselage windows of the cramped Italian bomber as it made its way deeper into occupied Italy. On board a team of Italian spies geared up and prepared to drop into the darkness. With them was twenty-five-year-old American OSS Captain Alphonse P. Thiele, the leader of an extraordinary team of Italian agents committed to the Allied cause. Like many of his fellow OSS officers, he liked to accompany his men as they prepared to venture behind the lines, conducting many of the infiltrations himself:

> Captain Thiele personally made twenty-five landings and infiltrations behind enemy lines, five of which were by PT boat through heavily mined and German-patrolled, Adriatic waters, as well as numerous flights for air-supply and agent-drops into enemy territory. On these numerous operations he was constantly in danger of discovery by enemy patrols and on many occasions narrowly missed capture. Several times during amphibious operations Captain Thiele and his crew were fired upon by German patrol craft and in one instance struck a floating mine; the speed however, of his PT boat prevented any serious damage.

Thiele was born in Constantinople shortly after the close of World War I, the son of a German army officer who married an

Italian. The family immigrated to America in the early 1920s, and he became a naturalized citizen. Prior to the war Thiele led an ordinary existence, working as a welder and mechanic and later owning his own gas station at 113 Wales Avenue in Jersey City, New Jersey. At the end of 1940, Thiele packed up the business and enlisted in the U.S. Army, eventually becoming an officer in the 458th Parachute Field Artillery Battalion (later attached to the 13th Airborne Division). Not long after his parachute qualification and during his brief time as an instructor, the OSS recruited him. His fluency in Italian and German made him ideal for deployment to the Mediterranean. The five-foot-six, brown-eyed man with a medium build had a "flair for handling [Italian] agent personnel." For most of the war he "led his own team, agents, and airplanes."

Walkiria Terradura, a beautiful Italian partisan, assisted Thiele throughout the war. The two fell in love and would later marry. She helped Thiele develop key contacts and relationships within the Italian resistance that were critical to the success of the Eighth Army Detachment's activities in the Adriatic. Although the Italian men first had doubts about a woman's ability to conduct guerrilla operations, Terradura proved her worth, taking part in several operations to blow up bridges. In fact, her name inspired fear in the Fascists, who referred to her area of operations as "Walkiria Territory" and carefully avoided it. Less easily frightened than their Italian counterparts, the Germans issued no less than eight different warrants for Terradura's arrest, but she managed to stay one step ahead of them. Of this time in her life she wrote, "I lived through hours of unbearable anxiety, a nightmare that would stay with me for years to come."

Originally formed from the British X Corps, which fought with U.S. General Mark Clark's Fifth Army shortly after the Salerno landing in Italy in December 1943, the Eighth Army Detachment was assigned to aid the British Eighth Army. It was one of the smallest yet most able detachments in the entire OSS. It originally consisted of one officer (Thiele) and four enlisted men. The men in the unit all spoke Italian fluently. They included Frank Monteleone, a burly, down-to-earth Italian American from Staten Island, New York. Considered by OSS leadership to be "unusually frank and engaging," Monteleone was a "motivated and highly reliable" agent. He began his military service as a radio operator with the U.S. Navy but later volunteered for the OSS. He put his language and radio skills to use on many missions within the Italian Theater, including a special mission with OSS superspy Moe Berg, who was assigned to track down Axis high-tech and atomic secrets. Berg's most famous mission involved the potential assassination of German physicist Werner Heisenberg, the man in charge of the Reich's quest for a nuclear bomb.*

The British Eighth Army aided in the bloody fighting around Monte Cassino in March 1944. The Allies relentlessly bombed the mountaintop monastery, but the rubble and ruins only formed built-in fortifications for the defenders, who spent months tying up the Army's advance. The Army then moved to the Adriatic coast. The detachment's missions followed the Eighth Army as it fought up the entire eastern side of Italy into the mouth of the strategic Po Valley. Italy's terrain made it particularly easy for the Germans to defend. The mountains running down the center of the country gave them plenty of access to high ground. To get to their enemy, the Allies had to cross numerous rivers, making them

---

*For over fifteen years the author has been friends with Monteleone, whom his daughter fondly calls "Uncle Frank." Every day the author wears a very special gift from Monteleone: an eighty-five-year old scapula that the former OSS spy wore around his neck throughout all of his missions behind the lines in World War II. Monteleone sent the scapula to the author just before he accompanied the Marines of Lima Company 3/1 into the Battle of Fallujah. While in Fallujah, the author barely escaped death on several occasions; he remains convinced that the amulet played a powerful role in helping him survive.

easy targets. In this environment it was nearly impossible to overcome the Germans without solid, actionable intelligence. For that,
the Brits turned to the OSS.

Like most OSS groups in Italy, Thiele's group improvised and
learned to be very resourceful, eventually gaining four Italian air
force planes that were manned by Italian personnel. As the Allies
progressed further and further up the spine of Italy, it became
more difficult to insert agents because the coastline was strongly
held by the Germans and laden with mines. Richard Kelly's San
Marco men worked closely with Thiele's Eighth Army Detachment to insert agents by parachute or maritime landing. The
OSS operatives came to respect these former enemies and highly
valued their work. "The San Marco guys had balls," explained
Monteleone. "They were tough sons of bitches. They were like
our paratroopers or Rangers. These commandos did everything
and were extremely reliable. We trained them, but they hardly
needed to be trained."

At first the Eighth Army Detachment sent in single operatives
without any radio equipment. As soon as they obtained operational intelligence, the agents would make their way back across
the enemy lines to give the information to the Army. Although it
looked good on paper, this plan had major flaws when put into
practice. "The men would be infiltrated all right but 90% of the
time would be picked up by the enemy." Thanks to good cover
stories and documentation, the agents were eventually released,
but "the information would be received too late by the parties
concerned."

To avoid such delays, the detachment developed an alternate,
innovative plan: teams would be sent in behind the lines with
radio gear "so that their information would be immediately acted
upon and questions asked and answered. They would prepare
their intelligence system with a view of the area's becoming a
tactical zone. Meanwhile, they would report troop movements,
targets, defenses, etc."

This new strategy proved "highly successful." One of their most successful missions was called "Bionda." The goal of the operation was twofold: "to secure data on German mission and supply dumps in the Ravenna and Porto Corsini area for the Desert Air Force, and [then] initiate sabotage measures against the German shipping in the Ravenna-Porto Corsini Canal."

The daring mission began on September 17, 1944. Three Italian operatives from the Maritime Unit's San Marco Battalion— Lieutenant Anelo Garrone, NCO Giuseppe Montanino, and Private Antonio Maletto—were transported by boat deep into German-held northern Italy, landing them on the beach around one in the morning. From the beginning the perilous nature of the mission was clear. Monteleone recalled, "We landed the San Marco guys after seeing the flashlight signal. As we were landing these guys, we could hear German boats in the distance and voices. Voices carry on the water; they were German voices."

The OSS men spent the night hiding in the woods. The next morning Garrone sent the men out to explore their surroundings. "As soon as they returned it was ascertained that [the men] were at about one kilometer north of Porto Corsini and only 300 meters away from a German battery."

In this precarious position, the San Marco team didn't dare set up their radio and report in. Those back at the Eighth Army Detachment base became increasingly uneasy. Monteleone recalled, "We didn't hear from them for a couple of days, and we began to worry. With the German voices and boats we figured maybe the jig was up and they got captured."

Given their limited options, Lieutenant Garrone decided to take a risk. He approached a farmer working in his fields and told him they had escaped from the Germans and needed a place to hide. The farmer turned out to be an enthusiastic anti-Fascist and eagerly agreed to help. Because the Germans visited the farmhouse nearly every day, he suggested the men stay in a shed, where they soon set up their radio and began communicating with their base.

The operatives quickly discovered that anti-German sentiment was strong in the region. They requested that the OSS send in supplies for the partisans in the area and arranged to meet a supply boat on September 23. Unfortunately, German activity in the area made the rendezvous impossible that night and for several successive nights. "Since the last night we awaited the landing an armed encounter occurred with a German patrol, we decided to leave the zone for a Partisan area before the Germans started to mop up the region," reported Garrone.

Deprived of their resupply, the former Axis commandos suffered through the next couple of weeks. The men reported that they were "scarce in clothing, many times suffering from malaria fever." Despite the cold and sickness, the men "continued in [their] work until 12 October," when Garrone and Maletto returned to the OSS base in a boat a partisan sympathizer provided. Montanino remained behind to continue the mission. Less than a week later Maletto returned to the area with a full load of weapons and other supplies for the partisans in the region. For several months the San Marco men served as intermediaries between the Allies and the partisans to coordinate attacks on German targets. Although the poor winter weather conditions canceled many planned supply runs, the mission provided critical resources to the Italians fighting the Germans.

The Bionda Mission also enabled the team to carry out important espionage missions, including the destruction of key bridges and roads used by the enemy. During one such incident Montanino received intelligence that three German armored cars would be traveling down the road to Porto Corsini. He recalled, "I immediately reached the road and mined it with German mines, then I watched if the charges would have done their work; a few minutes after a truck loaded with German troops coming from Porto Corsini was blown to bits by an explosion."

All in all the Bionda Mission was considered highly successful. "During the time of the mission 339 cables concerning military intelligence were sent to the Base for the Command of the Eighth Army. Furthermore, three groups of OSS agents, three Allied Fliers, and two Allied soldiers who had escaped from concentration camps were recovered" behind enemy lines. Garrone added, "During those days all Allied Commands praised us in any possible way for our excellent work."

★ ★ ★

A HALLMARK OF MODERN American special operations forces involves killing or capturing high-value targets. On the Gina Mission, OSS agents from the Eighth Army Detachment, working closely with Italian partisans, managed to blow up a staff car and kill the commanding general of a German division on the Vergate front. OSS teams also destroyed a crucial supply depot, causing 60 million lire worth of damage to the enemy. They captured thousands of Germans and helped exfiltrate dozens of downed Allied airmen and former POWs.

Most importantly, the OSS agents also transmitted highly valuable information. They scoped out the defenses of the Gothic Line. In fact, the detailed data, plans, drawings, and photographs they obtained from the Gothic Line were considered "the best piece of ground-intelligence work that has come out of Italy." This team was also the first to employ a newly developed miniature box camera in the field, paving the way for the use of numerous such devices in the decades to come. Much of the intelligence the Eighth Army Detachment missions obtained helped the Allies track troop movements and identify supply lines and other targets for attack.

★ ★ ★

OVER TIME, THE SIZE of the Eighth Army Detachment grew significantly from the original single officer and four men to four officers and fifteen OSS men working with fifty-three agents and five members of the Italian air force. The detachment and Dick Kelly's Maritime Unit successfully conducted over a dozen missions in key occupied areas of northern Italy, with as many as thirty-five agents behind enemy lines at one time. Their close cooperation with the Italians also meant that they had four airplanes to use. They were essential in resupplying teams behind enemy lines, especially when the moon was bright, precluding the use of boats. "One cannot overstress the importance of having an airplane completely at one's disposal," noted an operative. One plane, the *Savoia,* was particularly successful, even attempting missions in broad daylight while under heavy enemy fire. "This was the only airplane in Italy which would attempt to drop in heavy flak area. The record proves that every time it went out, flak was encountered. It is a tribute to the skills of the pilots and to the crew as a whole that the airplane always returned safely."

When the moon was dark the Eighth Army Detachment were able to employ their PT boats to ferry in supplies and personnel. "In all, fifteen sea operations were attempted by this Detachment and nine proved successful. The PT boats always had on board members of the Detachment who personally went ashore every time to insure success and to talk to the people on shore."

Throughout this period, the British Eighth Army leadership was so impressed with the work of the OSS and MU that they relied on the organization to handle all clandestine operations in the area instead of their own SOE, which was also in the theater. At one point the Brits even recommended that Thiele "be incorporated into the Eighth Army G3 as Special Ops Officer." Such accolades were largely unheard of. OSS records drily note, "It is gratifying to note that [the British] preferred an American organization to their own."

23

STELLA

NOT ALL OF THE MISSIONS CONDUCTED by the MU or Eighth
Army Detachment were a success; many were miserable failures.
Infiltrating behind enemy lines was incredibly dangerous, and
agents faced brutal torture and near-certain death if captured. One
OSS operative, a macho Italian who improbably went by the code
name "Stella," recalled meeting a beautiful woman in a bar while
on a mission in the Udine region deep in enemy-held northern
Italy. The seductive, blue-eyed blond sat near him and struck up a
conversation by asking for a match. She flirted openly with Agent
Stella, eventually asking him, "Are you Roman?"

Stella confirmed that he was. The woman whispered to him that
"she knew a very easy way to cross the line . . . 'for a nominal
fee.'" Stella erred on the side of caution, replying that "it wasn't
my intention to put my life in jeopardy and I preferred to await
developments."

After leaving the bar, he soon met up with an undercover resistance officer named Captain Martellini, whom he decided to use
as a shield. "I mentioned the fact that I had met a young lady there
who could arrange for a person to cross the lines for a certain sum,
and the captain begged me to introduce him to the young lady as
one wanting to go to a certain city in 'invaded Italy.'"

Stella met the young woman again a few days later and informed
her that he had a friend who wished to cross the lines. Thereafter

Stella realized he was being followed, but "due to the bizarre layout of the city, it was not too difficult to elude his shadow." However, within days Stella's shadow reappeared. Identifying himself as German police, he arrested Stella and dragged him into Gestapo headquarters for questioning. "We know who you are," they began. The Gestapo inquisitors informed Stella he would only be freed if he answered their questions, saying, "We also know that you have asked to cross the front lines for your own personal reason." The gorgeous Axis counterintelligence agent at the bar had done her job. Understanding the Germans didn't really know who he was at all but had merely taken the bait according to his plan, the OSS agent refuted their claims and added, "In regard to crossing the lines, it is necessary that I clarify the fact that not I, but the GNR Captain Martellini had expressed that desire."

A quick telephone call brought Martellini to the office. The captain assured the questioners that he had, in fact, been the one interested in crossing the lines. Martellini went even further, saying that Stella had never made any anti-Fascist remarks and adding, "As far as I am concerned, this man is to be excluded from any suspicion whatsoever."

Despite the officer's assertions, the Germans continued to interrogate Stella, repeatedly asking him where he lived. Knowing that he had a potentially damning letter in his room, Stella attempted to put them off. But the interrogators began their "sweet tortures." After many rounds of brutality, Stella eventually passed out. They revived him with a bucket of cold water and carried him away to a temporary cell. Stella recounted what happened next:

> The following afternoon a stinking-drunk sailor was thrown into the same room. He had scabs over his face, and on his front gums he had only three teeth. The lackey who accompanied him shoved him inside, saying (from what I could get), that I was a partisan. The drunken sailor grunted something, then threw himself at me, sinking those three lurid teeth into my neck; I fought him off with all my

strength, and a few moments later he fell asleep. I soaked up the blood and tied a handkerchief about my neck.

When Stella next went in for questioning, one of the Germans asked about the handkerchief. Stella "told him of the incident and that vampirish individual." In response, the German grinned. "You are in a fine fix!" he exclaimed. "That man is venereally [*sic*] diseased. If you behave yourself we will see that you are taken care of and that you are given the first treatments to kill the bacilli."

Faced with this new horror and knowing that his landlady—an Allied sympathizer—had likely destroyed the evidence in his room by this time, Stella told the Germans where he lived and agreed to take them there the next day. He remembered, "When we arrived, the landlady gave me a slight nod, and I understood that everything had been taken care of. My spirits rose." Despite searching for several hours, the Germans found nothing incriminating. Stella began to hope that he would soon be released when disaster struck. An old friend saw him on the street and greeted him by name. Stella, who had been using a false name, couldn't explain the incident away. The Germans took him away for weeks of "indescribable torture." Stella fell severely ill and remained imprisoned until the Allies liberated the city.

24

INDIANA JONES

"THIS COAST IS HOT," MORDE NOTED. "There are minefields all the way. A PT boat hit one two or three weeks ago and blew up, losing ten men."

Despite the treacherous nature of the Italian coast, Lieutenant Ted Morde, the archaeologist who found the Lost Temple of the Monkey God, traveled to Ravenna for the purpose of exploring what the OSS, MU of Company D in particular, could do to further support British actions on the northern Italian front. The Brits "showed an appreciation" for MU's work, but it was difficult to see how the unit's boats could be brought into service in the area. MU and the Eighth Army Detachment in particular had been very effective on the eastern coast of Italy on the Adriatic Sea because that side of the country had a coastal road that was easy to access by water, providing plenty of targets for the frogmen. The northwestern shoreline, known as the Ligurian Coast, didn't have a similar coastal roadway. Instead, the roads in the area head "inland, supplying the Germans in the mountains," explained Morde. "Thus, with no coastal road at that point, meaning no culverts, bridges, tunnels, etc., there are no suitable targets for sabotage of the type Kelly's outfit, the San Marco group, pulled on the Adriatic side." In addition, the Germans had excellent radar coverage of the Ligurian coastline extending as far as fifteen miles out to sea, as well as a fleet of warships in the region. And they had constructed an extensive minefield that covered a similar range of the water and the beach as well. The mines came in "all types: magnetic, acoustic, contact, and a new kind of the 'trip' variety, a mine from which extends snag lines on floats to catch any vessel that trips a line, these extending for as much as 100 to 300 meters. There are thousands of them." The British believed it would be impossible to clear the mines, and Morde agreed: "For a one-time venture, no attempt could be made to clear the mines without costly losses. And not a damned thing, other than a seagull, could get over them, not even a canoe drawing three inches of water. Certainly not a PT, or our ARBs, or even a mattress, meaning electric surfboard." The days of easy infiltrations were gone.

With the waters heavily mined, the OSS called on Italian fishermen for help. In late January and early February, the MU hired several of these anglers to make a reconnaissance of a projected base. They did so and located a man who owned a great deal of property in the area. "This man agreed to organize partisans if MU would supply the arms." MU, of course, agreed. The fishermen carried the landowner and two San Marco men back to the area. The two successfully relayed information about German patrols and helped organize the partisans. When the Germans closed in on their positions, it was again the local fishermen who were able to exfiltrate the agents successfully.

The OSS continued relying on these locals for some time and outfitted four fishing boats with machine guns. The hazardous conditions meant that the British were unwilling to put vessels in the water, even though Italians were willing to make the runs. A report noted, "They rely on their shallow draft and good fortune" to avoid the mines.

In spite of the hazards, the OSS had moved Company D and two PT boats into the region, stationing them in the city of Livorno. "It was agreed that it would be best and wise to keep the boats here to stand in case there *were* any change."

However, the MU suffered a devastating setback that deprived it of the use of one of its PT boats and one of its best operatives.

On the morning of Saturday, January 13, Morde and another OSS operative climbed on board P-584 to meet with Ward Ellen, who skippered the craft. They met and discussed trivial matters from 8:30 a.m. until just before 9:30, when Morde went back to shore. He later recalled what happened next: "I had gone about 100 yards when I heard an explosion, but thought it came from another direction, since the sound was muffled by the wind, and a pile of bombed out buildings separated me from the pier near where Ellen's boat was tied up." Morde went aboard the other OSS boat, P-568 and was speaking with its captain when a crewman burst in.

"Come quick," the sailor shouted. "There's been an explosion on the other boat!"

Morde took off running and reached the scene "in two minutes flat, in time to see the crew of a U.S. salvage ship nearby pouring fire extinguisher fluid into the still burning interior of the P-584." Taking charge, Morde ordered everyone off the craft, knowing that it had thousands of gallons of high-octane gas on board that had not yet exploded. "Had that 3,800 gallons gone up, so would half of the harbor and at least six large ships nearby."

Still, the damage done by the smaller explosion was extensive. Although conscious, Ward Ellen was in shock and "badly burned about the face, head, hands, and feet. The skin hung in shreds." Despite his injuries, "before Lieutenant Ellen would allow himself to be taken to the hospital, he insisted on personally seeing that every member of his crew had reached safety." That task accomplished, a Jeep whisked the officer and the other agent who had been meeting with Morde to the nearby hospital as quickly as possible. There the pair "were swathed in facial and hand [bandages] for nine days, while their burned portions swelled, as all burns do. They were kept drugged for much of the time. Hair such as eyebrows had been singed off, and their faces with closed eyes for a time looked like two brown and red cabbages."

* * *

AROUND THE SAME TIME, the OSS shipped Sterling Hayden back home for some R&R. The movie star-turned-operator met briefly with the vice president of the United States. After a short rest, Hayden headed back to Europe, this time assigned to work with the First Army outside Germany. There Hayden felt that he came face to face with the real war for the first time. "For three and a half years I had managed to sidestep the war," he wrote. "War in the sense it is known only to the man in the line who fights—with no real knowledge of why it has to be, no commitment beyond his conditioned response to military discipline and love of country. That and the lack of any practical alternative."

Once an idealistic believer, Hayden was becoming disillusioned with war. He added, "The horror of war was finally clear as it swallowed men whole, rejected their identities, dulled their senses, lashed them with terror, then spewed them into this raid or that patrol, any time of day or night. . . . The average citizen hated military service, not so much because of the dislocation of his life and the sacrifice it involved, but simply because suddenly he was booted about, ordered around, and slammed up into the line because 'they' said so."

The First Army assignment also brought him into contact with members of other military branches who had little use for the OSS. Reporting for duty, he met with Colonel B. A. Dixon, the G-2 of the First Army, in Dixon's office trailer located outside Spa, Belgium. When Hayden entered, the colonel was meeting with several of his officers, and all were smoking and drinking cognac.

"I don't mean to be impertinent," began the colonel, "but what in hell is a Marine captain doing up here tonight?"

"Well, sir, I—," stammered Hayden.

"Ah ah," Dixon stopped him, raising a hand. "Don't tell me. You're OSS—ten thousand dollars says you're one of Donovan's beagles. Right?"

Hayden confirmed the colonel's suspicion.

"Well, if you're looking for Hitler, he's not here," joked Dixon, pouring Hayden a drink. "Gentlemen, I am going to tell you about the OSS. The OSS is the most fantastic damned organization in all of our armed forces. Its people do incredible things. They seduce German spies; they parachute into Sicily one day and two days later they're dancing on the St. Regis roof. They dynamite aqueducts, urinate in Luftwaffe gas tanks, and play games with I.G. Farben and Krupp, but ninety percent of this has not a goddamned thing to do with the war."

Hayden conducted several missions during his time with the First Army and later was assigned to do some mundane port inspections. He would survive the war and return to Hollywood to star in several infamous roles.

Meanwhile, deep in Austria, Jack Taylor doubted he would ever return to Hollywood.

25

SURVIVING

JACK TAYLOR WAS TRANSFERRED back to Morzinplatz and assigned a cell with several other prisoners. As in Taylor's first stay at the prison, the Germans dealt brutality to the inmates. He later recalled,

Toward the end of March, a woman doctor (M.D.) [taken prisoner by the Germans] was brought into Cell 3 and as was the custom, every personal article including eye glasses was withheld. After several days, another woman prisoner was placed in her cell who had better eyes and discovered that the doctor had lice. The doctor was horrified and begged for her glasses so that she could pick them from her garments, but her pleadings were unheeded. There was no opportunity to bathe or wash clothes. About the same time, another woman, Martha Russ, was brought in and had to have her wrists chained behind her back to the bars so high that she could barely touch the floor. In the night, through exhaustion, her feet slipped out from under and she was left hanging. Her screams were horrible. Later, I got possession of the order for the mistreatment of Martha Russ signed by her *Kriminalrat.* [Investigator] . . . Toilet paper was non-existent and we were rationed to three small pieces of newspaper or scrap-paper. I always read the scrap paper first and to my surprise found the above order torn in two. It had been written on the back of a useless mimeographed sheet to save paper and when the Meister handed it to me, he saw only the one original mimeographed side. The order directed the Meister to hang Martha Russ by her wrists backwards every night, no food for three days and not to bother the Referrent with any requests.

On March 31, 1945, Taylor and the other prisoners in the Morzinplatz were awakened at 3:00 a.m. and informed they would be leaving immediately. The Russians were just fifty kilometers away, and the Germans were evacuating the prisoners before the invading army could free them. Taylor and thirty-seven others were taken to the train station. The former dentist recalled, "I was terribly surprised to see the West railroad station absolutely untouched by bombs and everything functioning normally, also the yards were full of coal cars. Farther out, in the yards there were evidences of heavy bombing but all tracks were intact and functioning."

Taylor and his comrades were loaded onto a train filled with refugees. He and one of his Austrian companions, Schmeisser, plotted a night escape attempt, but "at the last moment Schmeisser backed out saying his wife and child would be murdered if he escaped." Taylor later regretted that he didn't flee without his friend, writing, "I had the windows partially open and blamed myself a thousand times later for not going ahead alone but, due to American bombings [of Austria], the entire civilian attitude towards Americans had changed so that it was questionable whether anyone would take one in alone. With an Austrian speaking that particular dialect it was a 50–50 chance."

While Taylor's train was steaming deeper into the Austrian countryside, the rest of his Dupont team was also devising a plan to escape captivity. Considered traitors to the German army, Grant, Perkins, and Underwood faced beheading. Held in a temporary prisoner cage, a bowling alley in Austria, they tunneled out of the compound. Once outside, the men split up. After weeks of avoiding partisans and evading German patrols, all three miraculously made their way back to OSS headquarters in Italy.

On the train, Taylor saw a glimpse of the horrors that were to come at his final destination: Mauthausen. One of the other prisoners had previously been incarcerated at Mauthausen and warned that the conditions were even worse than at Dachau, where this same prisoner had also been held. Soon Taylor and the other captives would experience the horrors of the camp firsthand: "We arrived at Enns at 0400 and marched 8 km to Mauthausen, crossing the Danube by ferry just at dawn," he remembered. "We could see, on the hill, the lights of the most terrible Lager in all Germany which was to become our home until execution."

26

MAUTHAUSEN

The rusty barge pulled up to a small wooden dock on the Danube, and the SS guards pushed the thirty-eight prisoners off the craft. Freely using the sticks they carried, the Germans prodded the condemned men up a steep hill. Jack Taylor paused briefly, turning his head for a last glance of the dark waters of the Danube, now far behind him. To the side of the hill he noticed a massive rock quarry and a long stone stairway descending into its depths. He observed sickly looking, painfully thin men methodically hauling massive rocks step over step. The stream of skeletal inmates fed the line like a conveyor belt in a factory. "They were the most terrible looking half-dead creatures in filthy ragged stripes and heavy wooden shoes," reported Taylor. "And as they clanked and shuffled along the cobblestones, they reminded me of a group of Frankensteins. We kidded ourselves saying we would look the same in a few days, but we were all struck with cold, dread terror."

As the thirty-eight men trudged forward to what would be for most their final destination, they saw a high wall topped with an electric barbed-wire fence that guarded the camp. The group of prisoners didn't know it yet, but the guards often maniacally tossed inmates onto the fence, electrocuting them to death as a twisted form of entertainment.

To their left, below the main camp, they saw a line of squat, windowless buildings. Originally built as stables for horses, the low sheds were first repurposed to house POWs and then later converted into a "hospital," a place that no one would ever willingly enter for treatment.

The maniacal SS Officer Hans Prellberg was waiting outside the entrance to receive Taylor and the group as they approached the gates. Mauthausen was the epicenter of a constellation of approximately twenty-six satellite camps administered by the SS. In total they held over 91,000 prisoners. The work camps primarily furnished slave labor for various German war industries. Prellberg worked over the prisoners and was "particularly brutal as he slapped, punched, kicked and beat most of us over the head with a cane belonging to a crippled Slovak in our group," recalled Taylor. "Two young Russians and a Hungarian were unmercifully beaten because they did not understand German. All commands were given in German and I had to keep extremely alert to save myself similar beatings."

Taylor's group was forced to join a larger group of prisoners. The guards reiterated the camp rules and regulations. "If you attempt to escape and are recaptured, you will be shot immediately, like this," announced one officer. He pulled out his pistol and shot a prisoner standing nearby who had recently attempted escape.

The officers then marched the prisoners into an open area and lined them up outside the showers. They were stripped, shaved of all body hair, showered, and deloused. The guards issued them threadbare striped prison garb. For three hours they mercilessly questioned each individual, beating, slapping, slugging, and spitting upon the men. "You American swine!" SS officer Hans Bruckner repeatedly shouted as he used the cane taken from the disabled Slovak to strike Taylor's back again and again.

Several noncommissioned SS officers, working in "relays," intimidated the prisoners and ruthlessly interrogated them. "Where are you from? Who are you? Why are you here?" Every time the SS guard would ask a question, "Whatever the answer was, he would hit you over the head."

When the initial interrogation finally ended, Taylor and the rest of the men marched through the main gate at Mauthausen. A heavy iron sign, which proclaimed in German, "Work will set you free," hung over the entrance.

The guards led the newly arrived inmates into a courtyard and forced them to stand at attention barefooted for over an hour in the freezing cold. "This S.O.P. (standard operating procedure) was not changed even during the most severe part of the winter when men stood barefooted in the snow," wrote Taylor.

Over the next forty-eight hours, the prisoners received no food. However, they did receive prison numbers stamped on cloth next to a colored triangle designating their status. The original prisoners from the camp wore green triangles, and all political prisoners wore red triangles. "Each contained letters abbreviating his nation in the red triangle. [For instance,] F for France and B for Belgium." The guards then issued the inmates a wrist bracelet with the same number stamped in metal. Taylor's number was 138070.

The SS marched the men to Block 13, their crude barracks. Taylor explained, "There were 25 prisoner barracks each normally designed for 220 men, i.e., 70 triple-decker single bunks plus 5 double-decker singles, but at this time holding nearly 400 each. This was increased to almost 600, which made it necessary for three to 'sleep' in each single bunk. Toilet and hygienic facilities were proportionately inadequate."

The men slept in their clothes for warmth—and to keep them from being stolen. Taylor recalled, "After two days, we began by devious means to get wooden shoes and old trousers or shirts; until then we walked around in the cold and mud barefooted and clad only in ragged underwear. Within a week I had, through friends, collected a full compl[e]ment of assorted rags for clothes." The barracks were unheated. Thin blankets provided the only source of warmth for the men. "On unusually cold nights, there was heavy nocturnal traffic in blankets. The blankets, incidentally, were collected each morning and redistributed at random each night, thereby spreading lice and fleas from a few to all," recalled Taylor.

Life in Mauthausen degenerated as the Germans' inhumane, brutal treatment of the prisoners turned many into animals. The men had to survive not only the SS but also danger from within the prison population. The SS assigned many convicted German criminals, inmates who were murderous thieves and forgers, as the barracks heads (*Blockeldesters*), who ruthlessly supervised their fellow prisoners "with a heavy hand." The barracks heads "used their fists, blackjacks, sticks, rubber hoses and razor straps to maintain 'order.'"

The prisoner population shifted between ten and fifteen thousand inmates who were literally worked to death or, later, exterminated in gas chambers. At the time Taylor was one of a few Americans in Mauthausen. He learned of only three others: a woman named Isabella or Carlotta Dien; Sergeant Louis Biagioni, an OSS Secret Intelligence agent; and Lionel Romney, an African American of the U.S. Merchant Marine who had been captured when the Italians sunk his ship. Mauthausen consisted of a diverse population, which included intelligentsia and artists of Third Reich–occupied countries. In Taylor's bunkhouse were Frenchmen, Germans, Russians, and many inmates from Central and Eastern European countries. One of the most notable was Vojtech Krajcovic, a renowned Slovakian economist who had also served as governor of the National Bank Bratislava and head of the Economic Institute of Bratislava.

Taylor reported, "We were all forced to work as soon as we got something approaching shoes and many of our group were assigned to the Kommando repairing the railroad and highway around Enns. This was heavy and continuous pick and shovel work for 12 hours with ½ hour off for lunch . . . and included a 16 km round-trip march to and from work. Most of our group were high class professional men and the strain and misery of this type of work at first, can be imagined."

Gradually, even the most upstanding men transformed into thieves and savages. Stealing was "practiced on a scale that can't be imagined." Taylor recalled, "One had to carry with him at all times his total belongings. Stealing became a matter of life and death" because "one could not support life on the regular prison food." Mauthausen rations would starve a gerbil. As Taylor recalled, "Food consisted of flavored hot water (very dilute unsweetened ersatz coffee) at five for breakfast. Lunch was one liter of erpsin (beet) soup, much thicker but less palatable than in Vienna. Supper was 1/10 to 1/17 kilo of black bread. The bread was composed of wheat flour, ground potato peelings, sawdust, and straw. On Sunday, in addition we received a slice of margarine or a tablespoon of cottage cheese."

Mauthausen was both a slave labor camp and a death factory. Once a human being was used up, he or she was exterminated. Germans gassed prisoners, shot them, beat them to death, or killed them by various other means. To attempt to hide their crimes, the Germans cremated the bodies. One of the first work details to which Taylor was assigned was the construction of a crematorium. Taylor and his work party knew completion of the facility meant the deaths of more inmates—including themselves. "We dawdled at our work to delay completion of the crematorium because we knew that the number of executions would double when cremation facilities were available."

But the Germans knew Taylor and his comrades were stalling. "One Saturday morning, Prellberg and SS *Hauptscharführer* Martin Roth (head of the crematorium) belabored *Kapo* Jacinto for his failure to finish the work quickly and informed him that it must be finished and ready for operation on the following day or we (workers) would be the first occupants of the new ovens." The death threat was serious, and Taylor and his fellow inmates "finished the job in the allotted time."

According to Taylor, "The crematoriums were large brick structures containing a firebox for burning wood and coal and over this were the ovens fitted with rounded supports at intervals for the bodies. The bodies were carried into the ovens on steel stretchers and with a quarter turn were rolled out. The new crematorium with two ovens could handle twelve bodies at a time, 160 a day and with the old ovens a total of 250 a day. Insufficient cremating facilities held down the number of executions as all bodies showing signs of violent death could not be buried. Gassed bodies were often disfigured from clawing, biting, etc. and chemical analysis of the tissues would show cyanide. All 'violent-death' bodies had this stamp on their paper: *Die leiche muss aus hygienischen grunden gefert verbreannt werden* [sic] which says, 'The corpse must for hygienic reasons be cremated.'"

With the crematorium finished, the Mauthausen death factory went into full swing. "The next day, Sunday April 10th, 367 new Czech prisoners, including 40 women, arrived from Czechoslovakia and were marched through the gate straight to the gas chamber and christened the new ovens. Black oily smoke and flames shot out the top of the stacks as healthy flesh and fat was burned as compared to the normal pale yellow smoke from old emaciated prisoners. This yellow smoke and heavy sickening smell of flesh and hair was blown over our barrack 24 hours a day and as hungry as we were, we could not always eat," recalled Taylor. He continued:

The gas used was Zyklon B cyanide a granular powder, contained in pint-sized cans and the same used for infection of clothing. In a small room, adjacent to the gas chamber, was a steel box connected immediately to a blower, which was in turn connected to the shower system. While wearing a gas mask, the operator bashed in the ends of two cans of powder (one can will kill 100 people) with a hammer and after placing them in the box, clamped the lid on hermetically tight and started the blower. (In winter, when the gas would not evaporate fast enough from the powder, steam was introduced into the box from the other end.) After two hours, the intake blower was stopped and the larger exhaust blower was turned on for about two hours. Wearing gas masks, the prisoner operators removed the bodies to the cold room (capacity 500) where they were stacked like cordwood awaiting cremation. See enclosure 'Instructions for the service of Pourric [*sic*] Acid Delousing Chambers in K.L.M', by the Chief doctor. It is worded for delousing but the instructions were especially for gas chamber operators. The blowers and gas receptacle were removed by the SS and attempts made to destroy them. In March 1945, Ziereis and Bachmayer (see protocol) ordered all ventilation sealed in the police wagon and a small trapdoor installed. A group of 30 to 40 prisoners were told that they were being transported to Gusen, a subsidiary camp about 8 km away, were crammed into the wagon, the door locked and a bottle of poison gas dropped through the trapdoor on an angle iron specially placed to break the bottle. The 'police wagon' was immediately driven to Gusen and after parking for an hour the prisoners were delivered to the crematorium. The same numbers of Gusen prisoners were then loaded into the 'police wagon' for transport to Mauthausen with identical results. From March to October 1945 the car circulated 47 times with an average of 35 victims each way on the round trip, making a total of approximately 3,300. In October, ventilation was installed again, and the police-wagon resumed its original function.

Whereas many prisoners were gassed, others were simply shot to death. Taylor reported, "Until 1943, daily executions by rifle or tommy-gun were done openly back of Block 15 where those waiting to be executed were forced to watch their comrades, three at a time, being mowed down. When gas and injection deaths practically replaced shooting, all shooting was done individually in another small room adjacent to the gas-chamber. The victim was told that he was to have his picture taken and was led into this room where a camera was set up on a tripod. He was told to face the corner with his back to the camera and immediately he assumed this position, he was shot in the back of the neck with a small carbine by an SS man standing to his left and slightly behind. Prisoner operators stood behind a door looking through a peephole so as to know when to drag the body out. SS *Standartenführer* Ziereis, commandant of Mauthausen, personally executed three hundred to four hundred men here in the above-mentioned manner during ten shooting 'expeditions' over a period of four months."

After finishing work on the crematorium, Taylor was transferred to cell block 10, which was occupied by a cosmopolitan group of prisoners, including Czechs, Poles, Russians, Germans, and Austrians. They were "old-timers," survivors who, through "devious means," consistently obtained the extra food necessary to stay alive. "Bread, margarine, potatoes and occasionally horsemeat, cereal, and schnapps were obtainable through the black market. Czechs, Austrians and Hungarians were allowed a few packages from home until March of 1945. The two French Lieutenants (Maurice and Albert), Krajcovic and I had received bread and margarine for our watches and ring at the rate of two loaves of bread and 1/2 kilo margarine for each Swiss watch. Divided four ways, this food lasted a week. In Block 10, I collected and boiled potatoes peelings and scraps from the more fortunate prisoners but our bread ration was reduced daily."

Before arriving at Mauthausen, Taylor's weight had already dwindled to just 130 pounds due to the harsh conditions in Vienna. His stay at the execution camp only increased his emaciation. He reported, "I had terrible dysentery and innumerable small sores on my legs and back, but I continued to work as best I could to prevent being put on the sick-list and transferred to the 'hospital' (*Sanitatslager*) where, believe it or not, five sick people were assigned to each single bunk, rations were half 'normal' and infinitesimal amounts of medicine were supplied. Very few ever returned alive from this 'hospital,' and the daily death toll at this time from starvation was 400 to 500."

The conditions and deaths at Mauthausen were unimaginable and largely unknown to most of the world, including the United States. Many of his fellow prisoners approached Taylor, saying, "We're sorry you're here, but, IF you live, it will be a very fortunate thing," they said. "For you can tell Americans and they will believe you, but if we try to tell them, they will say it is propaganda."

Every nationality "trusted me because I was an American," wrote Taylor. "Consequently, I was the recipient of hundreds of eyewitness atrocity accounts with first hand evidence in many cases." He risked his life to bury American GI dog tags as well as the epaulet of a fellow Navy officer from another OSS team, whom his German captors in Mauthausen executed in cold blood. It was too dangerous for Taylor to take notes, but he "kept a mental account of each story."

Later, he had the opportunity to write down some of the horrific details:

The following examples taken from the enclosed sworn statements are in addition to the normal methods of execution, i.e., gassing, shooting, hanging, etc.: clubbing to death with wooden or/iron sticks, shovels, pick-axes, hammer, etc; tearing to pieces by dogs trained especially for this purpose; injection into the heart or veins of magnesium-chlorate, benzene, etc.; exposure naked in sub-zero weather after a hot shower; scalding-water shower followed by cow-tail whipping to break blisters and tear flesh away; mashing in a concrete mixer; drowning; beating men over a 150 foot cliff to the rocks below; beating and driving men into the electric fence or guarded limits where they are shot; forcing to drink a great quantity of water then jumping on the stomach while the prisoner is lying on his back; freezing half-naked in sub-zero temperatures; buried alive; eyes gouged out with a stick, teeth knocked out and kicked in the genitals, red hot poker down the throat, etc., etc., etc.

In a bizarre twist of fate, some inmates of the camp had the opportunity to become part of the most diabolical part of the Third Reich that had enslaved them—the SS. "About the middle of April, a request was made to the prisoners for volunteers for the Waffen SS (Infantry). It was limited to Germans (Austrians included) and about 1000 volunteered, as they understood that the other alternative was execution (this was later disproved). Some also sought a chance to escape in this way. About 300 were selected from those volunteers, given regular SS rations, including cigarettes, outfitted in old *Afrika Korps* light khaki, drilled and trained for combat and assigned to minor policing tasks inside the camp. It was a very clear demonstration of the inherent German love for authority and the ruthlessness with which they automatically operate. From fellow prisoners, they overnight became our masters and did not spare the rod."

The desperation inside Mauthausen represented a microcosm of the entire Third Reich that was crumbling before the Allied offensives.

27

LAST ACTS

IN APRIL 1945, THE ALLIES UNLEASHED their last great offensive in northern Italy. The Eighth Army attacked in the east on April 9, and General Mark Clark's Fifth Army assaulted the center. To lay the foundation for this effort, seventy-five different OSS teams had been working behind the German lines on missions to sabotage German operations and support the partisan resistance. Many of the most successful operations came from the Eighth Army Detachment and the Maritime Unit of Company D.

The OSS played a key role in the final Allied offensive, supplying weapons, food, and equipment to tens of thousands of Italian partisans; helping tie up countless German troops; and even clearing the Axis forces out of entire regions throughout northern Italy. Agents also continued to provide the Allies with a consistent stream of actionable intelligence, particularly bombing targets. They also conducted hit-and-run raids and ambushed German convoys. As a result, movement of Axis troops became nearly "impossible." Partisans accomplished "not only the immobilization of enemy columns, but the cutting of potential enemy escape routes to the north and the prevention of demolitions particularly of the municipal, industrial, and transport organizations."

German Field Marshal Albert Kesselring, commander of all Axis forces in Italy, took note of the damage the OSS-supported Italian resistance caused and saw the need for a strong response. "Activity of partisan bands . . . has spread like lighting in the last ten days . . . and is beginning to show clear results," he wrote. "Speedy and radical counter measures must anticipate this development."

Throughout the waning months of the war, the MU and the Eighth Army Detachment units continued operating in the Adriatic. One of the more successful MU/Eighth Army efforts to enter northern Italy around this time was the PIA mission. Known as the Fabulous Five, the PIA operatives' code names were Rolando, Buffalo Bill, Red, Stalin, and Potato. In addition to gathering key intelligence and locating bombing targets, in one of the Five's great coups involved the capture of a Fascist police department "right under the eyes of the Gestapo."

Despite the intensity and successes of the operations, OSS headquarters was in the midst of deactivating MU. Lieutenant Kelly and Captain Thiele had to make do with fewer Americans, as several men were already being called home. A month earlier the wounded, badly burned Ward Ellen had returned to the United States for treatment. The OSS was considering plans for the use of MU personnel in the Pacific. However, the war in that theater ended before many of the MU men from the Mediterranean could redeploy.

* * *

DURING THE CLOSING WEEKS of the war, the OSS coordinated a general uprising to liberate a heavily defended stretch of fifty miles of Italian coast. Operating with a team of San Marco commandos in a mission near the Po Delta region of the Adriatic Coast, Marine Lieutenant George Hearn, assigned to the MU, led a band of partisans in heavy fighting. It "resulted in the killing of twenty-three enemy and the capturing of 436 prisoners, with a loss of one man killed and twenty-two wounded." He also forced the surrender of Germans controlling the city of Chiogga, near Venice. "The German city garrison of thirty, though heavily fortified and reinforced by more than one thousand men in the surrounding area, surrendered without firing a shot."

In yet another operation, the MU planned a special project to capture valuable German technology. "[MU will] move as quickly as possible into enemy-occupied Italy to seize the newest German maritime sabotage equipment for use in some other theater [PTO]. Plans are being drawn up with special teams to rush to the German operational bases, training and experimental areas, to seize this material," noted one OSS planning document. James Angleton, from X-2 in Rome, the OSS resident expert on Italian underwater operations who had vetted the San Marco men, would assist in capturing high-value targets from *Decima MAS*.

* * *

THE OSS PLAYED THE CRUCIAL role in the surrender of all German forces in Italy. During the final months of the war in Europe, the American intelligence agency engaged in intense negotiations with the SS. In the stunningly successful Operation Sunrise, SS *Obergruppenführer und General* Karl Wolff der Waffen, commander of the SS troops in Italy, covertly sent word to the Allies in early 1945 that he desired to facilitate a German surrender in the country. In Zurich, he secretly met with Allen W. Dulles, head of the OSS station in Switzerland (and a future director of the Central Intelligence Agency), and offered the surrender of all German and Italian troops in Italy.* As a result of these clandestine discussions, the Germans fighting on the Italian front surrendered on May 2. World War II in Italy ended six days before the capitulation of the remainder of the German armed forces in Europe.

---

*Shortly thereafter U.S. troops arrested General Wolff at his private villa in Bolzano, Italy, and took him into captivity.

28

GOD BLESS AMERICA

LIEUTENANT JACK TAYLOR WAS SO SICK with dysentery that he could hardly walk. From his normal weight of 165 pounds he was down to about 114. He recalled, "I was so weak that I could not stand at attention . . . for roll call for any length of time without fainting." Even in his weakened condition Taylor grabbed on to the hope drifting throughout Mauthausen:

Terribly optimistic rumors had been circulated regarding the position of the Russians and we had expected to be over-run by 20 April but, either the Russians turned north from Vienna to Czechoslovakia or they were stopped by superior German forces at the mouth of the Danube valley at St. Polten about 60 km away. About this time the first contact with the International Red Cross was made and all women from the western nations including the American Miss Dien were evacuated to Switzerland. These times became very dangerous as certain streets were walled off with barbed wire and we feared a mass execution. At certain unpredictable times, all prisoners were isolated in their blocks and a general tenseness gripped the whole camp, SS included. We heard rumors that the Commandant and other high ranking officers were discussing our futures as a mass wherein we would all be executed or transported to another area, or left in the lager which would be defended using us for hostages.

Food became impossible to obtain. Our daily 'bread' was cut to practically nothing and [inmates] in prominent positions who had not eaten 'prisoner food' for two years were at this time forced to. In the *Sanitatteslager* (hospital) the starving were cannibalizing their own dead comrades, cutting out the heart, liver and muscles. Jews in the tent camp (*Zelt lager*) were paying a $20 gold piece for two loaves of bread and half kilo of margarine, and two wagonloads of dead were hauled away each day to the mass grave on the hill. Gold, diamonds and jewelry were being accumulated by the SS from the Jews, and our bread was being used for this purpose. One night a lone plane came over and dropped one bomb (some said up to three bombs) in the adjacent Jew tent camp. We all then expected a mass bombing of the whole lager, but it never materialized. In the morning, I saw the upper half of a body, which had been blown from the Jew camp 200 yards and landed on the eaves of one of the bar barracks. About fifteen were killed and forty-seven injured most of whom probably eventually died.

The Red Cross arrived at Mauthausen on April 25 and "started the evacuation of Frenchmen, Dutch, and Belgians." At least one British officer spoke French well enough that he was able to get in on the evacuation efforts. "The Frenchmen departed singing the Marseillaise, and many were overcome with tears," recalled Taylor. "Despite their successful efforts to remove some of the prisoners from the prison, the Red Cross workers weren't allowed within the camp itself, and thus didn't witness the true atrocities occurring there." Later Taylor and the others saw evidence that the Red Cross had also delivered packages that the prisoners had never received. "SS troops were noticed eating bars of chocolate and smoking American cigarettes," wrote Taylor. "Several empty cartons were picked up by prisoners and brought to me." The SS had stolen all the American goods, and they also pilfered most of the things sent to the Frenchmen, giving each of them only one bar of chocolate. Eventually Taylor received a package meant for Hungarian prisoners that contained Ovaltine, cheese, and sugar. He recalled, "My system was so deteriorated that I could not 'keep down' this real food. My Czech and Pole friends did everything they could to help me and with the aid of some opium, I was able to get started again on the cheese and later the Ovaltine and sugar."

But just as the Red Cross was bringing hope to some of the Mauthausen inmates, the Germans were cruelly ending the dreams of those who were left behind. On April 26, 1945, the day after Red Cross evacuations began, the Germans killed more than a thousand prisoners at the camp. With the Allies marching ever closer, the Reich increased executions and cremations, essentially covering up the evidence of the atrocities they had committed.

Unbeknownst to Taylor until much later, he narrowly escaped execution at that time. Taylor knew that he toiled under a death sentence—he had been in line, a dead man walking, three times before. But Russian soldiers who pushed him out of the way, taking his place, ultimately saved him from death on each of the previous occasions. The Russians sacrificed their lives for Taylor because they wanted the lone American officer to survive. They needed his position and his voice to bear witness to the horrors and atrocities the Nazis committed in the camps. However, Taylor was unaware that camp officials had once again drafted orders for his termination. A fellow inmate and friend of Taylor's named Dr. Stransky Milos worked in the political department. Seeing Taylor's name on the list of people to be executed, Milos erased his name as well as that of another friend on April 26. The rest of the people on the list, many of them prisoners transported from Vienna along with Taylor, were executed on April 28.

In the late spring, "American P-38s came over at about 100 feet and really gave us a thrill," said Taylor. "We never dreamed that Americans would ever be near, but now we heard rumors that they were in Regensburg and coming fast." At the beginning of May, the SS officers abruptly departed from the camp, bringing an end to the daily executions. On May 4 the prisoners began to hear the sound of battle in the distance, and Taylor began to hope against hope that the Americans would finally arrive and set the camp free.

* * *

THE DISTANT SOUND OF an engine put Staff Sergeant Albert J. Kosiek and the rest of his reconnaissance team on high alert. The group had set out before dawn that morning, ordered to scout the bridges in the area, and had no idea what they might find this deep in German territory. Peering through his binoculars, the sergeant saw a white car with a red cross painted on its hood headed right for their position.

Cautious that this might be a trick, the entire group trained their weapons on the vehicle as it slowed to a stop. Two men got out of the car and explained that they were looking for a general because they wanted to surrender a large concentration camp to the Americans. Although taken by surprise, Kosiek immediately determined that liberating the camp should be his next priority. He radioed his CO and requested permission to approach the camp. He "stressed the fact that 1,600 prisoners were depending upon us for fast liberation"* and talked the officer into authorizing the team to go to the camp.

Still on the lookout for a trap, Kosiek first reached the camp at Gusen and then headed for Mauthausen. Along the way he received new orders to return to his original reconnaissance mission. *Fat chance!* thought Kosiek. He later wrote, "From beginning to

---

*In actuality there were tens of thousands of prisoners at the two camps Kosiek's team liberated.

end I had to explain the situation impressing my superiors that to return now would possibly be more dangerous than to continue. They realized it was no longer a matter of choice and that the inevitable would have to be."

At first glance, Kosiek thought Mauthausen looked like a factory, but soon the electric fence came into view and behind it he saw "hundreds of people who went wild with joy when they first sighted us," said the sergeant. "It's a sight I'll never forget. Some had just blankets covering them and others were completely nude, men and women combined, making the most emaciated looking mob I have ever had the displeasure to look upon. I still shake my head in disbelief when that picture comes before me, for they hardly resembled human beings. Some couldn't have weighed over forty pounds." The German prison guards greeted the newcomers with an American salute, and the crowd of prisoners went wild. "Never before have I felt such a sensation running through me as I did at that moment," recalled Kosiek. "I felt like some celebrity being cheered at Soldiers Field in Chicago. That was the first time I have had people so overjoyed at seeing me. As I stood there looking out at the mob I realized what this meant to them and I was glad we had made the effort to free the camp." Kosiek had the former inmates gather in the courtyard of the prison. From somewhere the prisoners found instruments and started playing "The Star Spangled Banner." Kosiek recalled, "My emotions were so great that the song suddenly meant more to me than it ever did before. Many of the refugees were crying as they watched our platoon standing at attention presenting arms."

Taylor felt elated when fellow prisoners excitedly broke the news "that an American Jeep and halftrack were at the entrance" of Mauthausen. Though weak with malnutrition and barely ambulatory, Taylor was determined to walk on his own two feet toward his liberators. The OSS operative staggered toward the gates of Mauthausen, where he encountered a crowd of "frenzied" prisoners gathering in front of the fence. Though he could hardly make any headway through the mob, the spectacle gave him hope that the prisoners' stories might actually be true. He continued to doggedly push and navigate his way through the cheering, emaciated group of inmates until he found himself standing before a tall, burly soldier wearing the uniform and stripes of an American sergeant. The newcomer identified himself as "Albert Kosiek, Troop D, 11th Armored Division, Third U.S. Army."

With a quivering hand, Taylor held up his dog tags and whispered the words that first came to mind:

"God Bless America."

29

SUNSET

"Artifice" entered the posh Milanese residence. James Angleton, Rome's X-2 counterintelligence chief, had previously vetted the *Decima MAS* agents who joined the Allied side, and now he would be called upon to capture their leader, infamously known as the Black Prince. Junio Valerio Borghese had been hiding in the home of a friend for several days following the surrender of the German forces in Italy. By this time the Allies had captured most of the Axis-aligned *Decima MAS* operatives, but Borghese remained at large. The new, forward-thinking X-2 counterintelligence chief saw how useful a man like Borghese could be to the United States against a new potential adversary—the Russians. Angleton was determined to bring the Black Prince safely into American custody.

The OSS intended to capture Borghese and squeeze him for as much information as possible. However, the British and the Italian partisans had different plans for the Black Prince: both groups intended to execute him without a trial. At his first meeting with Borghese, Angleton offered the *Decima MAS* leader a fair trial if he would cooperate. However, Borghese was suspicious of the OSS's true intentions and declined his offer.

Yet, when Borghese learned the partisans had discovered his whereabouts and were en route to claim their prize, the Black Prince quickly turned himself over to Angleton. Concerned for his captive's safety, Angleton dressed Borghese in an American military uniform and drove him to an apartment in Rome, where the Americans arrested him on May 19. For several months the former Italian special operations chief provided invaluable intelligence to the Allies. His working relationship with Western intelligence agencies would continue after the war. Some have alleged that the Black Prince may also have helped plan a Cold War underwater sabotage operation. The Allies had promised the Russians a particular Italian battleship, the *Giulio Cesare*, as a war prize. They turned it over to the Soviets in 1949. It was commissioned in the Soviet navy as *Novorossiysk* and became the flagship of the Black Sea fleet. In what is considered the worst Soviet naval disaster in history, the prized vessel sank after a mysterious massive explosion tore a 150-meter hole in her bow, killing more than six hundred sailors. Multiple theories as to the cause of the explosion persist to this day, including a mine and possible underwater sabotage linked to former *Decima MAS* operatives.

Despite Borghese's assistance, the Italians pressed for his prosecution, and a lengthy trial began in the fall of 1945. The court convicted him of collaborating with the Germans and sentenced him to nine years in prison, of which he served four. Upon his release the neo-Fascist Black Prince became heavily involved in the postwar Italian political landscape—a Cold War crossroad between the East and the West.

* * *

MAY 8, 1945, MARKED the end of the war in Europe. Thereafter the Allies focused almost entirely on the war in the Pacific. Many MU agents in Europe transferred to the Pacific, including Ted Morde. In late July 1945, Morde led a mission to conduct an intelligence survey of an island off the coast of China. When his team was still yards from shore, they came under heavy fire from twenty-four Japanese-crewed junks moored near the beach. According to the official records, "Throughout the running battle which ensued he directed the action of his group with coolness though continuously exposed to enemy fire." Morde and his men managed to evade the Japanese, allowing them to thoroughly explore and map the island. During a heavy monsoon storm that threatened to capsize his vessel, Morde himself used a small oar-driven boat called a sampan to take soundings of the beaches in "an operation taken at great risk and accomplished with great difficulty." Later, he recruited approximately seven hundred workers who helped the team repair the air strip, which allowed the U.S. Army Air Corps to land planes on the island.*

* * *

AS THE WAR IN THE PACIFIC came to a close, the OSS deactivated the MU in June 1945. Many MU operatives transferred into the special operations branch and received parachute training and continued to conduct maritime missions, despite the disbandment of the MU. The final OSS combat swimming mission of World War II, dubbed "Caprice V," took place in August 1945. A rescue team was tasked with finding the agents from an earlier submarine-launched Caprice mission which had conducted reconnaissance of a small group of occupied Batu Islands off the west coast of Sumatra. Two OSS swimmers, including Gordon Soltau, future all-pro

---

*Morde was also likely briefed on OSS plans to target Japanese shipping on China's Yangtze River. An MU officer in China proposed outfitting swimmers with "non-magnetic limpets and dependable incendiaries." In typical OSS fashion, the MU found an expert on the area in Lt. Commander Richard Otter of the Norwegian navy. Otter spent "many years as a piloting officer in Chinese Coastal waters and interior waters, including the Yangtze." OSS sent Otter to the Bahamas for a crash course in combat swimming and then on to China, but the war ended before the swimmer commandos could be unleashed against the Japanese river vessels.

football player for the San Francisco 49ers, were part of the mission to recover the lost men. On the first beach the Caprice team attempted to infiltrate, they received automatic weapons fire from Japanese sentries. The men retreated and successfully infiltrated a neighboring island a short distance away. In a dramatic fashion, Soltau was "dispatched upstream, swimming to reconnoiter along the way" to ensure the rescue team didn't get ambushed by the Japanese. Soltau and the men got into several other fire fights while leaving no stone unturned in their quest to find the agents of the original Caprice mission. However, their valiant efforts were in vain; they never located the missing men.

* * *

DURING THE LAST FEW months of the war in the Pacific, the U.S. Navy grew increasingly concerned about the prospect of underwater commando attacks as the Allied fleets approached the Japanese home islands. For help in gauging and responding to this threat, they turned to America's experts on underwater commando operations: the OSS and Commander Woolley.

At the Navy's request, Woolley embarked on a mission to create a "comprehensive film report" detailing enemy equipment and tactics. In Europe, he began procuring enemy submersibles and equipment. To complete the study, he conducted interrogations of former enemy underwater combat operatives. According to Donovan, "Commander Woolley was imminently successful on this mission and has been highly commended by the Navy Department for this work."

Woolley continued to work closely with the Navy, forging the path from World War II's Maritime Unit to the future SEALs program. He "was frequently in consultation with [the] Navy Department" about underwater combat swimming and pioneered the development of innovative equipment, including a "wooden craft submersible." Woolley's valuable contributions and the technology, tactics, sources, and methods the MU developed would become crucially important in the years to follow.

30

"THIS IS THE FIRST TIME
I'VE EVER BEEN IN THE MOVIES"

AS THE AMERICAN TROOPS MARCHED into Mauthausen, an embedded film crew from the Army Signal Corps rolled their cameras, capturing the shocking images of emaciated prisoners, huddled for warmth in their ragged coats and threadbare striped prison garb. Despite his ordeal and deteriorated condition, Jack Taylor spoke lucidly about all the suffering he had seen and endured, when questioned by the film crew:

I'm lieutenant senior grade, Jack H. Taylor, U.S. Navy. I'm from Hollywood, California, and believe it or not, this is the first time I've ever been in the movies. I've been working overseas in occupied countries in the Balkans for eighteen months. In October '44, I was the first Allied officer to drop into Austria. I was captured December 1 by the Gestapo, severely beaten—even though I was in uniform—severely beaten and considered as a non-prisoner-of-war. I was taken to [a] Vienna prison, where I was held for four months. When the Russians neared Vienna, I was taken to the Mauthausen Concentration Lager, an extermination camp, the worst in Germany, where we have been starving and beaten and killed and, fortunately, my turn hadn't come. Two American officers at least have been executed here. Here is the insignia on one, a U.S. Naval officer, and here is his dog tag. And here is the Army officer's. They were executed by gas in this lager.

When one of the film crew off-camera asked how many ways the prisoners were executed at Mauthausen, Taylor flatly replied, "Five or six ways: by gas; by shooting; by beating, beating with clubs; by exposure, that is standing outside naked for forty-eight hours and having cold water thrown on them in the middle of winter; dogs; and pushing over a hundred-foot cliff. This is all true. It has been seen and is now being recorded." He noted that he had been sentenced to death and added with a wry smile that "fortunately, the 11th Armored Division has come through and saved us in time."*

The U.S. troops transported Taylor out of the camp on May 5, less than twenty-four hours after liberating the camp. He spent his first night of freedom in a house with Sergeant Kosiek and his men. Kosiek recalled, "The boys rustled up some food; [Taylor] enjoyed his meal. He told us that he would never forget our platoon of twenty-three men as long as he lives. He told us he never expected to see Americans again. He was sentenced to death four times while at the camp, but was spared by the refugees. He was to go to the gas chamber on May 6. . . . We sat and talked with him until 3 o'clock in the morning."

Freed at last, many of the former inmates turned aggressively against prisoners who had aided their captors. As he was riding away from the iron gates of Mauthausen toward the hospital for recovery from an unimaginably horrific incarceration, Taylor witnessed his fellow inmates impaling those who had served as block leaders and Kapos, brutal enforcers for the Germans, on the barbed wire that surrounded Mauthausen. When Taylor later returned to the concentration camp after having regained some of his strength, many of the Communists who had been inmates had taken control of the facility. They were holding trials and executions of the

---

*Remarkably, this film can be accessed on the Internet today.

vicious block leaders and others who had mistreated prisoners. Eventually the Americans put an end to the practice.

* * *

THE INCOMPREHENSIBLE DEATH toll at Mauthausen continued to climb even after the liberation of the camp. Former prisoners were dying at an appalling rate—more than fifty per day from disease and malnutrition. Even the most advanced American medical care and food could not undo the damage inflicted by their barbarous imprisonment. Galvanized by the ongoing suffering he witnessed all around him, Taylor, though still weak, chose to return to duty, even though he could have gone home. He did this not to aid the war effort, but to fulfill a promise he made to many of his former inmates, living and dead, and the countless others he did not know: he would gather evidence against the Germans who ruled the concentration camps to prepare the prosecution for the war crimes trials that he hoped would follow. Lieutenant Taylor returned to the Mauthausen Concentration Camp and, with former prisoners, collected testimony, documents, and other evidence of the Germans' crimes against humanity, and along the way he had the satisfaction of "running down SS men hiding in the area." He also took time to catch up on all the meals he had missed, gaining thirty pounds in just two weeks.

One of the most important documents he collected was a set of thirteen "death books" kept by prisoners who acted as camp secretaries at Mauthausen. These recorded the "official" cause of death for everyone who perished at the camp, but unbeknownst to their German captors, the inmate secretaries devised a secret code to document the actual causes of death, such as gas chamber or lethal injection. These records would prove crucial in the Nazi trials at Nuremberg. Military lawyers would call Taylor's report "outstanding" and some of "the best war-crimes evidence" ever produced for the trials.

During the autumn of 1945, Taylor was honorably discharged from the OSS and returned home to California. Never one to remain idle for long, he actually reapplied to the OSS, pestering his case officer for an assignment. The OSS operations were winding down in Europe, but the agency saw indications of looming hostilities with the Russians and began to mount intelligence operations. Despite his vast intelligence expertise and knowledge, Taylor was not fluent in any foreign languages and had limited understanding of Russian or Eastern European culture. Therefore, much to his disappointment, the OSS declined to assign him on any future missions.

Though the bitter winds of the Cold War were beginning to blow, on October 1, 1945, President Truman prematurely disbanded the OSS for a multitude of political and budgetary reasons. The importance of intelligence operations would once again come to the forefront, but the United States now lacked a national intelligence agency. All the incredibly pioneering special operations forces the OSS created were dissolved, including Operational Groups, Jedburghs, SO, and the Maritime Unit. After completing the high-priority underwater warfare study for the U.S. Navy, Commander Woolley was ordered to close down the MU. Like most of his colleagues in the Maritime Unit, he returned to civilian life and became an American citizen. Practically the only evidence of the MU's existence lay in Top Secret records locked away in government safes and in the minds of veterans sworn to secrecy. The stories of the contributions and sacrifices made by the heroic men and women who served in the OSS were largely left untold.

But Taylor would serve one final mission; arguably his most important. In March of 1946, Jack Taylor was called out of retirement and returned to active duty. Promoted to lieutenant commander, he traveled to Germany to serve as a star witness for the prosecution at the Mauthausen-Gusen Camp Trials held at the Dachau Concentration Camp.

EPILOGUE

DACHAU CONCENTRATION CAMP, SPRING 1946

"Will you describe the type of flames and smoke that emanated from the crematory when an old prisoner was cremated?" asked the prosecutor.

Taylor matter of factly responded, "Ordinarily it was a pale brown, acrid smoke, heavy with the smell of burnt hair, and this was wafted over the camp, particularly block thirteen. It seemed to go up and then settle down."

Jack Taylor was the prosecution's star witness at the Mauthausen-Gusen Camp Trials, a set of subsidiary trials tied to the Nuremberg Trials. Nuremberg included a series of military tribunals to bring to justice the most notable members of the Nazi Party. "Dubbed the greatest trial in history," Nuremberg called to account a "who's who" of the surviving members of the German war machine: Alfred Jodl, Albert Speer, and Hermann Goering, among others. American authorities conducted the Mauthausen-Gusen Trials to try officers and camp guards from Mauthausen in the occupied American Zone of Germany at the site of some of Germany's greatest atrocities: the Dachau Concentration Camp.

For days, Taylor stoically kept his emotions in check as he re-counted his experiences at Mauthausen in excruciating detail to the court. He began his testimony by stating, "I have tried to forget most of these things for the past year."

In his training as an OSS operative, Taylor had learned to pay attention to numbers, quantities, dates, sights, sounds, and smells that might provide clues about enemy movements and intentions. Now those same skills proved invaluable in his testimony against the Germans who had immorally enslaved and killed thousands in violation of international law.

The prosecutor pressed for details on the restrooms, asking Tay-lor to describe the "sanitary facilities" the Germans claimed to have furnished the inmates. Taylor shot back "I don't remember the number of toilets, but it was, I would say, enough for a normal complement of two hundred (200) prisoners, possibly ten (10) toi-lets. However, it was so bad, and so many of us had dysentery, that in the daytime they would open up the manholes and the sewer out in the street, and most everyone used the manholes."

Taylor also faced intense questioning about the number and manner of executions. He described one group:

They were three hundred and sixty-seven (367) new Czech prisoners, including forty (40) women, arrived straight from Czechoslovakia. They had been marched overland, and were marched straight through the gate to the gas chamber without any preliminary which the usual transports received, that is, the bathing, stripping, and new clothes. They were taken right down and disposed of. . . . They were taken in to the crematorium, as all executed prisoners were, but this particular group—we knew from witnesses and the fact that they weren't old prisoners and the fat—there was so much fat on them, or more fat than there would be on an ordinary prisoner that the flames from the crematorium were going out straight—were going out the top of the smoke stack—which was different from the average prisoner.

In great detail, he also described the lethal gas chambers to which unsuspecting inmates were often subjected: "It was rigged up like a shower room, regular shower nozzles in the roof. In fact, new prisoners, like the group of Czechs who came in, thought that they were going in to have their bath. They were stripped, they were put in this room naked, and then supposedly got a shower, and then the gas came out the nozzle, shower nozzles in the roof."

The men against whom Taylor testified were found guilty and sentenced to death by hanging or, in some cases, given life sentences.

After the trial, Taylor returned home to California and was awarded the Navy Cross. Racked with PTSD and haunted by life changing experiences seared in his mind, he was determined to integrate into postwar American normalcy. He married and started a family. Taylor's love for the sea compelled him to try his hand at "Taylor Products," a "marine specialists" firm. Sadly, the business did not succeed, and he was forced to return to his dental practice. But the war never left Jack Taylor.

* * *

ON A SHELF IN A DUSTY NAVY warehouse in Honolulu, workmen carefully stowed heavy wooden crates containing the last of the LARUs. The Sleeping Beauties and other gear went to similar storage facilities. The war was over, and the Navy saw no further need to employ the pioneering underwater equipment. With the OSS disbanded, the U.S. underwater combat training program came to a standstill and, along with MU men like Taylor and Lambertsen, was effectively put into mothballs.

But in 1947, Lieutenant Commander Douglas "Red Dog" Fane (so known for his titian hair), who had command of an Underwater Demolition Team (UDT) unit, sought out LARU inventor Dr. Christian Lambertsen, by then a professor at the University of Pennsylvania. Recognizing the value of Lambertsen's breakthrough technology, Fane pulled the rebreathers out of retirement and located two Sleeping Beauty submersibles in a California warehouse. He wanted to test out new ways to deploy the underwater craft from submerged submarines. Improvements in radar meant that swimmer teams could no longer be launched from surfaced subs. As one naval commander explained, "For the safety of your men, if for no other reason, you will have to go underwater. Operations from the submarines are the only possible way of conducting secret UDT missions."

Fane began extensive testing of the submersibles with swimmers using the LARUs. Because of Lambertsen's experience with both devices, he asked him to pilot the Sleeping Beauty in a test that attempted to launch and recover the submersible from the deck of a moving submarine. Fane, Lambertsen, and another frogman observed and photographed the mission. Wearing LARUs, the men exited the submerged sub and stood on the deck while the sub was moving. Fane's cohort recalled, "It had been proven that a speed of two knots would not tear off our face masks if we kept facing the current, but no one knew whether they would tear off or flood if we turned." Fortunately the LARUs functioned well. "There was a sensation of tremendous speed," he noted. "I gingerly experimented with turning my head a little to one side. The downstream edge of the mask began to vibrate, but no water leaked in, so I was able to see Fane. His red hair was streamed back, his ears were flapping in the submarine breeze, his trunks and lung were bellied out behind and whipping about. I could think of no better simile than Ben Hur driving his chariot in his race around the Roman Coliseum."

The tests were successful, leading to the conclusion that, "The day when diver fights diver undersea, and raiding parties march out of the sea to attack beaches, and divers in submersible craft will reconnoiter coasts and harbors, is not far off." The UDTs successfully performed exercises the OSS had spent most of World War II perfecting.

Based on this compelling evidence and firsthand experience, Fane oversaw the creation of a "Submersible Operations" platoon, the first unit of its kind in the U.S. Navy. The UDTs undertook numerous combat missions in the Korean War. During these operations, many of the men were trained by former MU combat swimmer John Booth, now working with the Central Intelligence Agency. Throughout the Korean War, the UDTs would maintain a close working relationship with the agency. In the early 1960s, the American military once again became very interested in the use of special operations units. The earlier experiences of the OSS MU and the UDTs led some to contemplate the creation of a special operations unit comprised of underwater swimming specialists. The Green Berets or U.S. Army Special Forces, founded on the principles of the OSS Operational Groups and Jedburghs and led by OSS veteran Colonel Aaron Bank, also followed suit and created a combat swimmer program.

On March 10, 1961, in a memo submitted to Admiral Arleigh Burke, Chief of Naval Operations, a naval group examining special operations and amphibious landings advocated the creation of a new unit that would provide "additional unconventional warfare capabilities within, or as an extension of our amphibious forces." The memo added, "An appropriate name for such units could be 'SEAL' units, SEAL being a contraction of SEA, AIR, LAND, and thereby, indicating an all-around, universal capability." Burke approved the proposal, and soon two new units would be activated.

A few months later, in his speech before a special joint session of Congress in which he outlined the dramatic and ambitious goal of sending Americans safely to the moon, President John F. Kennedy also supported the expansion of special operations units, saying, "I am directing the Secretary of Defense to expand rapidly and substantially, in cooperation with our Allies, the orientation of existing forces for the conduct of non-nuclear war, paramilitary operations and sub-limited or unconventional wars. In addition, our special forces and unconventional warfare units will be increased and reoriented."

In January 1962, SEAL Teams One and Two officially became operational.

★ ★ ★

DR. JACK HENDRICK TAYLOR, Hollywood dentist, global adventurer, world-class sailor, and First SEAL, would not live long enough to witness the modern SEAL Teams. He and other members of the Maritime Unit risked their lives—with some of them making the ultimate sacrifice. Their pioneering efforts helped forge the U.S. Navy SEALs—their legacy would culminate in operations such as the daring raid that resulted in the death of Osama Bin Laden. Tragically, in May 1959 at the age of fifty, Taylor was killed in a fiery crash while piloting a plane near his home in El Centro, California. Jack took his story to the grave, as did most of the men of the Maritime Unit. Dutiful to the end, the men of the Maritime Unit maintained their vows of silence, but their spirits and accomplishments live on today.

THE FIRST SEALS AFTER
THE WAR

Jack Taylor—For his actions during the war Taylor received the Navy Cross. His citation reads as follows:

> For extraordinary heroism in connection with military operations against an armed enemy of the United States; as chief of the Maritime Unit, Office of Strategic Services Detachment, United States Armed Forces, in the Middle East, from September 1943 to March 1944, Lieutenant Jack Taylor, USNR, personally commanded fourteen separate sorties to the Greek and Balkan enemy-occupied coasts. This activity was carried out despite intense enemy efforts to prevent any kind of coastal traffic whatsoever. Lieutenant Taylor, through clandestine operations, deserving of the highest commendation and careful planning and skillful navigation effected numerous evacuations of intelligence agents, doctors, nurses, and downed airmen. Tons of arms, ammunition, explosives, and other military supplies were delivered to Marshal Tito and other resistance forces through the efforts of Lieutenant Taylor. For three months, at all times surrounded by enemy forces, and on three occasions forced to flee from enemy searching parties, Lieutenant Taylor and his intelligence team operated in Central Albania and transmitted by clandestine radio important information regarding enemy troop movements, supply dumps, coastal fortifications, anti-aircraft installations and other military intelligence of great value to the Allied

forces. Parachuting into enemy territory on the night of 13 October 1944, with a team of three Austrian deserter-volunteers, he had personally trained and briefed, he began a secret intelligence mission to Austria. Handicapped from the very start by failure of their plane to drop radio equipment, living in constant danger of capture, and the physical and mental strain on his men, the courage and energy of Lieutenant Taylor prevailed and throughout the remainder of October and November, the mission collected target intelligence of the highest value to the Allies. On 30 November, the eve of their departure for Italy, the party was captured by the Gestapo. Through four months of imprisonment in Vienna and one month in Mauthausen prison camp, he was subjected to the customary interrogation methods of the Gestapo. During his capture, Lieutenant Taylor injured his left arm seriously. With this handicap and also being forced to exist on starvation rations and work at hard labor, he resisted all attempts to force him to divulge security . . . the brilliant results of his operations have been an essential aid to the victory of Allied Arms.

Following his testimony at the war trials, Taylor returned to civilian life. He started a company that sold maritime specialty items, but when that venture failed, he returned to his dental practice full time.

Reports indicate that Taylor, like many who have served in wartime, found it difficult to return home and exhibited some symptoms of PTSD. Fourteen years after his return home, he died in a plane crash in California. He left behind a wife and a daughter.

STERLING HAYDEN—The tall, handsome leading man returned to his movie career although he always maintained that he disliked acting and only did it because it paid for his boats and voyages. He appeared in dozens of movies, including many westerns released in the 1950s. In *Dr. Strangelove* he was General Jack Ripper, renowned for the infamous lines, "I can no longer sit back and allow Communist infiltration, Communist indoctrination, Communist subversion and the international Communist conspiracy to sap and impurify [*sic*] all of our precious bodily fluids." He also appeared in *The Godfather, The Long Goodbye, 1900, Nine to Five,* and many other films. He wrote two books: an autobiography titled *Wanderer* and *Voyage: A Novel of 1896.*

His marriage to Madeleine Carroll, his wife at the time he joined the OSS, barely survived the war. They divorced in 1946, and the next year Hayden married Betty Ann de Noon. Over the course of an eleven-year marriage they had four children together, and Hayden was awarded custody when their marriage ended in 1958. He married for the last time in 1960. He and his third wife, Catherine Devine McConnell, had two children together, and they remained married until Hayden's death from prostate cancer in 1986. Throughout his life he remained a wanderer, skipping around from city to city and spending as much time as possible at sea.

ALPHONSE THIELE—Thiele returned to New Jersey and the gas station business he had left behind. He married Walkiria Terradura, the beautiful partisan he had met in Italy, and they started a family. Later they moved back to Italy.

RICHARD KELLY—Kelly returned to his prewar career on Madison Avenue. He started a family and also wrote adventure stories in the 1940s and '50s for a popular magazine known as *The Blue Book.*

TED MORDE—Morde never did return to Honduras or provide verifiable details about the Lost City of the Monkey God. After the war he continued working for the U.S. government for a time as a special adviser to the Egyptian premier and ambassador. Never one to settle for the boring life of a bureaucrat, Morde later got involved in the television and film news industry, serving as the president of Spot News Productions and founding his own production company called Ted Morde, Inc. Morde married a model named Gloria E. Gustafson, and the couple had a son and a daughter.

He was found hanging in his parents' shower on June 26, 1954. Although the medical examiner said he had committed suicide, others theorized that he may have been murdered.

CHRISTIAN LAMBERTSEN—After the war, Dr. Lambertsen continued his work with the U.S. Navy, resuming his pioneering development of the LARU. He established the crucial link between the Maritime Unit and the Navy's UDT program and became known as the father of combat swimming and diving. For the rest of his life he would continue advising the U.S. government on various scientific matters. He held positions on a wide variety of boards and committees, including several run by the National Research Council's Committee, the National Academy of Sciences' Space Science Board, the Office of the Secretary of the Navy's Oceanographic Advisory Committee, the Smithsonian Advisory Board, NOAA's National Undersea Research Center Advisory Board, and NASA's Environmental Sciences Review Committee, Lunar Base Planning Group, Radiation and Environmental Health Working Group, and several others. At the same time, he pursued a career as a professor at the University of Pennsylvania School of Medicine and also founded the Environmental Biomedical Stress Data Center at the same institution. The university continues to hold an annual Christian J. Lambertsen Honorary Lecture each year.

Lambertsen's list of awards is nearly as long as his résumé and includes military recognition, such as the U.S. Army Legion of Merit, the Meritorious Civilian Service Award and Military Oceanography Award from the Secretary of the Navy, the Department of Defense Distinguished Public Service Award, the U.S. Coast Guard Distinguished Public Service Award, the U.S Special Forces Green Beret Award, the U.S. Special Operations Command Medal, and the U.S. Chief of Naval Operations Citation. The U.S. Army Special Forces Diving Center in Key West, Florida, is named after Dr. Lambertsen.

In his civilian life, he received the Pennsylvania Alumni Award of Merit, the Lindback Award for Distinguished Teaching, the UDT-SEAL Association Lifetime Achievement Award, and various awards from NASA, the Aerospace Medical Association, the Undersea Medical Society, the Marine Technology Society, the Underwater Society of America, the New York Academy of Sciences, and the Navy Historical Society.

After a long and full life committed to science, medicine, and public service, he died in 2011 at the age of ninety-three.

H. G. A. WOOLLEY—Commander Woolley had a profound impact on America's underwater activities after World War II when he consulted with the U.S. Navy. In June of 1945, General Donovan personally recommended Woolley for the Legion of Merit in a letter that read as follows:

> It is recommended that the Legion of Merit, in appropriate degree, be awarded to Commander H. G. A. Woolley, D.S.C., Royal Navy, for exceptionally meritorious conduct in the performance of outstanding services to the United States.
>
> Prior to July 1941, Commander Woolley arrived in the United States for services with the British Admiralty Delegation. As the result of cables exchanged between this country and our Ambassador in London, the latter advised that a Presidential representative should confer with Commander Woolley who would be able to inform him of British plans and forces available in the event of operations being necessary to seize the Atlantic Islands. Commander Woolley was interviewed by the Representative and subsequently by the President.
>
> At the suggestion of the President, it was requested that Commander Woolley might be appointed officially to advise United States Service Departments on British Combined Operations questions. This was approved by the British Chiefs of Staff in Washington and London and the United States Chiefs of Staff were informed officially of his appointment and availability on 23 July 1941.

From this date until February 1942, Commander Woolley was in close touch with the United States Marine Corps (particularly with officers of USMC Headquarters and with the Fleet Readiness Section) and was able to provide considerable information regarding British plans, operational technique, equipment, etc. on matters with which the United States amphibious forces were currently equally concerned. He also was sole alien observer at the large scale amphibious landing exercise at New River in August 1941 and attended many discussions and represented the British view on technical and organization problems which arose in the exercise. Subsequently, he attended a large scale landing exercise at Virginia Beach in January 1942 and took part in the ensuing discussions. These included an address before the staff of the Ground Forces.

In connection with Army forces, Commander Woolley was consulted regarding possible future operations against Dakar and was specially commended for an address on Combined Operations to Military Intelligence Divisions in November 1941.

In February 1942, Commander Woolley was replaced by a British Inter-Services Committee of which he was to have been a member. However, at this time he was borrowed by the COI, from the British at the consent of Field Marshall Dill, to brief the former on British Combined Operations organization and particularly British small raiding forces (Commandos) in connection with discussions on this subject between COI, the President, and the Secretaries of War and Navy.

On completion of the foregoing work, in May 1942, at the request of COI, he was placed under the orders of Colonel Goodfellow, chief of Secret Operations, and directed to establish and conduct a base for training of agents in clandestine maritime operations (infiltration by sea, sabotage of shipping, etc.). This work was carried out very successfully. When the Colonel commanding the British para-military school subsequently visited the United States at my request, he ment [sic] and gave a most favorable report in comparison with the similar British school.

Commander Woolley originated the idea of the development of

underwater swimming apparatus for use in sabotage operations and supervised the development of the Browne and Lambertson [*sic*] apparati. The Browne apparatus was subsequently adopted for use by the Navy Department. He also originated and supervised development of new type 2 man and 8 man folbots which have been of considerable value to OSS and of which some 300–400 have been ordered and delivered for British use because they were much better suited for operations than any similar material developed in England.

He also originated the idea of the use of an inflatable paddle board. This and the first flying mattress were developed under his supervision. The latter was further developed under his successor and has also been adopted and used by the Navy Department.

At the end of 1942, he was sent on a tour of Marine Corps and Army Training Camps to study new training methods and equipment with a view to his appointment as Training Instructor of OSS Operational Groups.

At my direction, he then formed the Maritime Unit of OSS on the basis of an operating, planning, training and supply Branch to meet OSS Maritime requirements in the Field. Detailed plans were prepared for all theatres and the first unit was selected, trained and dispatched to the Eastern Mediterranean and carried out valuable service in establishment of caïque and similar services.

Commander Woolley proposed and was given permission to [organize] the first OSS Special Commando Swimming Unit. This was subsequently transferred to the United States Navy in the Pacific and has performed valuable operational services. He also arranged with the Navy Department for three Sub chasers for OSS in London for use by Norwegians in Norway Ferry Service. These were instrumental in the accomplishment of most valuable service. He also recommended use of fast surface craft to facilitate OSS operations and obtained approval for the inclusion of 12 such craft for OSS use.

Commander Woolley arranged for training of the first operational groups at Camp Edwards. [Liaison] was affected between Commander Woolley and the Naval Combat Demolition Unit. He visited

Fort Pierce in this unit's initial stages and assisted in the preparation of training programs and in advice on equipment and procedure.

During the whole period February 1942 to September 1943, Commander Woolley's services were devoted entirely to the C.O.I., subsequently the Office of Strategic Services. He was unsparing in effort and highly commended by his associates from time to time for the many successful results obtained.

It should be remembered that Commander Woolley selected camp and training sites in California and Nassau and advised on training programs for swimmers at these locations. In the case of Nassau he made all arrangements with British authorities and was of great value in liaison. On behalf of OSS, at their direction, he took charge of a British Small Raiding forces mission and rendered valuable service in the demonstration of their equipment and technique to OSS, War and Navy Departments. The Navy Department has since ordered quantities of the equipment demonstrated.

At Commander Woolley's suggestion, the Navy Department became interested in the possibilities of attacks by swimmers against harbour defenses and requested the use of OSS swimming groups for experimental tests and exercises. The swimmers were successful and the exercises were of considerable value. The Navy Department especially expressed thanks for Commander Woolley's work in this connection (op 30–3N 4 Serial 005930 of 8 January 1945).

Commander Woolley also supervised development of a wooden surface craft submersible. He made himself familiar with intelligence on enemy sneak craft and was frequently in consultation with Navy Department on such matters.

In May 1945, when the Navy became seriously concerned regarding Japanese attacks with sneak craft, OSS was asked to make a comprehensive film report on this subject for use in the field to aid in defensive measures. At the request of the Navy Department, Commander Woolley was appointed to the project and on the 11th of May loaned to the Navy Department to proceed to Europe to obtain specimen enemy craft, operators, etc., so that they could be closely studied. This project has been given high priority by the Navy Department. Commander Woolley was imminently successful on this mission and has been highly commended by the Navy Department for this work.

It is considered that Commander Woolley has rendered unusually meritorious service of an exceptional nature to the United States Government and that he merits consideration for a suitable award in appreciation of his services.

The entire service of Commander Woolley, both prior to and since the service upon which this recommendation is based, has been honorable.

This recommendation is based upon my personal knowledge and from official records on file in this agency.

The recommendation was approved.

After the war, Commander Woolley decided to become an American citizen and returned to Hollywood, where he resumed his screenwriting career. He also started a family.

WARD ELLEN—After sustaining serious burns while serving his country in Italy and providing crucially important service to the Maritime Unit, Ellen was mustered out of the OSS. There is no record of his postwar activities.

FRED WADLEY—He initially returned to the California Beach Patrol and then moved to the Santa Monica Police Department. He passed away in the 1960s of a heart condition.

HANS TOFTE—The Copenhagen native continued his work for the U.S. intelligence community for many years, serving first as a troubleshooter for CIA Director General Walter Bedell Smith. He later collected intelligence and supported guerrilla activities for the United States in the Korean War and then accepted several missions to Latin America. After years of valuable service to his country, in 1966 he was dismissed from the agency for keeping classified documents in his apartment, something Tofte said was "customary." He died of heart failure in 1987.

LLOYD SMITH—For his heroic efforts behind enemy lines, Smith earned the Distinguished Service Cross in acknowledgement of his role in rescuing the nurses from Albania. He was also decorated for his activities on the "Eagle" mission, also known as "The Brenner Assignment," which is also the title of another book by Patrick K. O'Donnell.

After the war, Smith hung up his cloak and dagger and became an accountant. He settled in northern Virginia and started a family.

JOHN BOOTH—After the war, Booth worked with the CIA training underwater operatives and was involved in the Korean War. Booth had charm and a glint in his eye and remained a ladies' man until the day he died. He often said, "I screwed my money away on women, but I wouldn't change a thing."

At age ninety, he regularly swam five miles out to a reef in Key West, Florida, where he would spear and catch lobsters for food. This was his way to save money so he could purchase cigars and scotch and pick up "senior hotties at the DAV [Division of American Veterans]."

He remained active into his nineties. When camping outside became difficult, he tied a rope to a tree so he could pull himself off the air mattress when he got up in the morning. Uncle John, as the author's daughter called him when he stayed with them, is greatly missed.

GORDON "GORDY" SOLTAU—Soltau left the Navy in 1945 and then attended the University of Minnesota, where he excelled as a football player. In 1950, he joined the San Francisco 49ers as a place kicker and wide receiver. He was the NFL's top scorer in

1952 and 1953, and he was the 49ers top scorer for the nine seasons he played, with a total of 644 points. He was also very active in starting the NFL Players Association. At the time NFL players didn't receive the huge salaries they earn today, and Gordy, like most of his fellow players, had a day job. He worked at a printing and office supply shop that was purchased by Diamond International, and he worked his way up to executive vice president of the company.

After his football career, Soltau remained active in sports as a broadcaster. He is a member of the Bay Area Sports Hall of Fame, and in San Francisco June 16, 2008, was declared Gordy Soltau Day. Gordy and his wife, Nancy, had one daughter and two sons. Now eighty-nine years old, Soltau continues to live in the Bay Area.

FRANK MONTELEONE— Uncle Frank, as he is known to the author's daughter, is a good friend to the author and considered part of the family. After the war he married his sweetheart and started a family. He became an expert tailor, specializing in high-end luxury apparel, often custom making suits for celebrities. In 2004, Frank sent the author the scapula he wore around his neck on his most dangerous missions behind the lines in World War II. The author wore it during the Battle of Fallujah and continues to wear it proudly every day.

JOHN P. SPENCE—Spence remained in the Navy after the war, serving as a chief gunner's mate and master chief gunner's mate until his retirement in 1961. He and his wife and children then settled in California, where he worked for various military subcontractors. He later moved to Oregon, where he remained active with veterans groups until he died in his sleep at the age of ninety-five.

JUNIO VALERIO BORGHESE—The end of the war did not put an end to the Black Prince's Fascist political leanings. He associated with several Italian neo-Fascist organizations, gradually becoming

more and more extreme in his beliefs. In December 1970, he participated in an aborted coup attempt and then fled the country to avoid
arrest. He died in Spain in 1974 under suspicious circumstances.

"WILD BILL" DONOVAN—At the close of the war Donovan
served as special assistant to the chief prosecutor at the war trials, a
role for which he was uniquely suited given his experience as a lawyer and the head of the OSS. After the trials he returned to his law
practice, Donovan, Leisure, Newton & Irvine, but continued to
advise U.S. presidents and accept assignments for the government.
He and the firm helped buy the land for Walt Disney to create the
theme park Disney World. He served as U.S. ambassador to Thai-
land from 1953 to 1954.

He lived to the age of seventy-six, when he passed away due to
complications of vascular dementia. After his death the International Rescue Committee awarded him the Freedom Award. As
befits the man President Eisenhower called "the Last Hero," he
is buried at Arlington. Donovan's legacy and vision lives on in all
modern special operations, psychological operations, and intelligence. The past is present as the very agencies and organizations he
pioneered are looking back to tackle the present and future.

ACKNOWLEDGMENTS

Over the past twenty-two years, I have interviewed thousands of World War II veterans. In my prior books, the beginning of the thank you section always began with the veterans, and this one does as well. This is their story that they have entrusted to me. Sadly, this year has been a watershed, as many of my friends have passed. Of the scores of men from the Maritime Unit that I interviewed, I only know of two who are still living: combat swimmer and NFL All-Pro football player Gordon Soltau and Frank Monteleone.

I have many other people to thank, including my longtime friend Cyndy Harvey for her excellent editorial advice throughout the entire process. In addition, I'm very grateful to Brian Danis, who has spent many years following the men and researching the Maritime Unit. Thanks also to my research assistant Daniel Hamilton.

I'd also like to thank the innumerable staff at the National Archives in College Park, Maryland, who have come and gone during the last twelve years, including the late John Taylor. I am also grateful to OSS Society President Charles Pinck for his unconditional support over the years, including presenting me with the 2012 Waller Award for my body of work related to intelligence and special operations history. It was a great honor to receive the award in front of the current leadership of America's intelligence and special operations community.

Great thanks go to my editor and very good friend Robert Pigeon for his vision, belief in the project, and skillful shaping of the draft. Also, thanks to Lissa Warren, the best publicist in the world, and Sean Maher and Kevin Hanover from Da Capo's marketing department for always doing an excellent job.

I also want to thank several of my good friends and readers: Justin Oldham for his great advice and reading of drafts; my good friend David Mitchell, who offered invaluable suggestions; Ben Ibach, a dear friend and one of the smartest guys I know; Theana Kastens, whose keen eye improved the book; and former photo editor and superb artist, James Noel Smith.

Finally, I'd like to thank Dawn Hamilton, an extraordinary woman, who freely gave her time, input, and editorial advice to this project because of her love for history and heartfelt desire to have the veterans' story finally told.

NOTES

Back in 2001, I began interviewing the veterans of the Office of Strategic Services. I traveled to their homes and was welcomed to their reunions. Out of the five thousand veterans I have interviewed over the course of twenty-two years, I found them to be some of the most compelling, interesting, and extraordinary individuals I ever had the opportunity to meet and befriend.

They were also the most secretive. The men and women of the OSS remained silent about their war. When I gained their trust, it came with a powerful feeling of responsibility that I took very seriously. I was deeply honored to be named a member of the OSS Society, a postwar association of OSS veterans, and even more grateful when I was awarded the 2013 Waller Award for scholarship into Special Operations History.

I first found a tiny portion of Jack Taylor's amazing story in the National Archives in 2002. I was drawn in and became obsessed. I wanted to write a book about Taylor and attempted to weave in part of his story in the book *They Dared Return*; however, it was so vast that it demanded its own treatment. This book focuses on Jack and the core group of men around him. The Maritime Unit is an extensive subject and could easily span multiple volumes, and the book does not attempt to capture MU's back story in its entirety. In fact, additional treatments are required, especially with respect to OSS operations in the Adriatic and in the Pacific.

This book took more than a decade to produce. Many of the veterans in it are among my dearest friends. Sadly, only a few of them are still alive. Their story resides in millions of documents located in 3.5 cubic miles of records in the National Archives in College Park,

Maryland. I have dedicated years of research in these archives. The vast majority of the material quoted in this book comes from record group 226, the Office of Strategic Services, and entries dedicated to the Maritime Unit. In the notes it will be referred to as "NARA." The records were miscategorized, sometimes misfiled, and extremely complex. I often felt like an archaeologist sifting through a dig and trying to reconstruct a mosaic from the documents that were scattered about in different record groups and entries.

First SEALs tells a portion of this significant story and attempts to honor the renaissance men of the OSS.

* * *

PROLOGUE

1   Details on the Shoreham Hotel from the Omni Hotels website: www.omnihotels.com/FindAHotel/WashingtonDCShoreham.aspx.

2–3   Scene in Shoreham Hotel pool comes from Woolley's letter to Huntington, dated November 1942. NARA.

2   SCUBA Lambertsen filed the original patent for the LARU in 1940. He later outlined his invention in the *Journal of the American Medical Association*. I interviewed Dr. Lambertsen extensively in 2003 regarding the development of the LARU and his experiences within the Maritime Unit. In 1942–1943, Lambertsen makes reference to SCUBA and changed the name of the LARU to SCUBA in 1952. Jacques Cousteau is sometimes credited with the invention of the term SCUBA, but he invented his open-circuit diving regulator in 1943.

3   "assist in the . . . and raiding forces." Dennis J. Roberts, "History of the Maritime Unit." This is an unpublished report largely cowritten by Theodore Morde and Roberts that resides in NARA.

CHAPTER 1:
"CAVITIES IN THE LION'S MOUTH":
THE BIRTH OF UNDERWATER COMBAT SWIMMING

6   Scene in Alexandria Harbor comes from Jack Greene and
         Alessandro Massignani, *The Black Prince and the Sea Devils: The
         Story of Valerio Borghese and the Elite Units of the Decima Mas*
         (New York: Da Capo Press, 2004), 91–106.

6   "painfully constricting [their] legs." Ibid., 91–106.

7   "[I had] to drag . . . to avoid drowning." Ibid., 91–106.

8   "Overnight, [the eastern Mediterranean] . . . the dominating
         power." William Schofield, P. J. Carisella, and Adolph Caso,
         Frogmen: First Battles (Wellesley, MA: Branden Books, 2014),
         143.

9   "Our intelligence organization . . . Spanish-American War."
         Michael Warner, *The Office of Strategic Services: America's First
         Intelligence Agency* (Central Intelligence Agency, 2000), www.cia
         .gov/library/center-for-the-study-of-intelligence/csi-publications
         /books-and-monographs/oss/art02.htm.

9   "through COI and . . . a centralized intelligence agency." *War
         Report of the OSS (Office of Strategic Services)*, introduction
         by Kermit Roosevelt (New York: Walker and Company and
         Washington, DC: Carrollton Press, Inc., 1976), 5.

9   "the significance of . . . in modern warfare." Ibid., 5.

9   "knew everybody." Author interview with an OSS veteran who
         was one of Donovan's aides.

10   "accepted [the mission] . . . in World War II." Ibid., 7.

10   "It is essential . . . pertinent information." Ibid., 7.

10   "specialized trained research . . . and psychological scholars."
         Ibid., 7.

10   "that he should . . . securing of information." Ibid., 8.

11   "modern counterparts of . . . of former days." *OSS Morale
         Operations Branch Propaganda Branch, 1943–1945*, NARA.

11   "big league professionals . . . bush league club." Patrick K.
         O'Donnell, *Operatives, Spies, and Saboteurs: The Unknown Story
         of the Men and Women of World War II's OSS* (New York: Free
         Press, 2004), xvi.

11   "they were making . . . of faith and hope." *War Report*, 6.

11   "kill the umpire and steal the ball." O'Donnell, *Operatives, Spies,
        and Saboteurs*, xvi.

12   "Ph.D. who could win a bar fight." From author's discussions
        with various OSS veterans and the president of the OSS society.

12   "The OSS undertook . . . history of our country." Richard
        Harris Smith, *OSS: The Secret History of America's First Central
        Intelligence Agency* (Berkeley: University of California Press,
        1972), 3.

12   "All the services . . . turned semi-guerrillas." Sterling Hayden,
        Wanderer (Dobbs Ferry, Sheridan House Inc., 1998), 310.

12   "To get from . . . disguised fishing vessels." Dennis J. Roberts,
        "History of the Maritime Unit," NARA.

14   "a daredevil, bent . . . his own show." Joseph E. Persico, *Piercing
        the Reich: The Penetration of Nazi Germany by American Secret
        Agents During World War II* (New York: Barnes & Noble Books,
        1997), 124.

14   "[He was] perpetually tense . . . over dry lips." Ibid.

CHAPTER 2:
AREA D

15   "She is, of . . . condition reflects this." NARA.

16   "General appearance and . . . port side amidships." NARA.

16   "blacked out . . . submarines." "History of the Maritime Unit,"
        NARA.

16   "It was necessary . . . and almost steal." Ibid.

17   "Area D." Ibid.

17   "The barracks were . . . they sit outdoors." Lt. JH Glenn to
        McDonnell, letter dated July 3, 1943, NARA.

17   "There is an . . . are fighting for." Ibid.

17   "[f]our elderly and . . . out mess duties." "History of the
        Maritime Unit."

19   "I can't recall . . . for the *Maribel*." Handwritten note by Lt. Jack
        Taylor, NARA.

19   "average Joe." OSS Evaluation for Ward Ellen, NARA.

19   "picturesque language." Ibid.

19   "Considerably disgruntled by . . . inactivity too frequent." Ibid.
20   "to teach each . . . territory by sea." Lt. Jack Taylor, *Report on
            Maritime School Training*, NARA.
20   "Under the direction . . . half mile inland." "History of the
            Maritime Unit."
20   "killing the enemy . . . raised the alarm." Ibid.
20   "The students got . . . were poor shots." Ibid.
21   "1) You are . . . your boat effectively" Ibid.
21   "the instructors encouraged students to take risks." Ibid.
21   "of a daring type." Ibid.
21   "rendezvous at an . . . bearing 152°." "Training Problem No. 4,"
            NARA.
21   "POSITION OF . . . east of beach." Ibid.

CHAPTER 3:
THE RACE TO DESIGN A REBREATHER

23   "Almost weekly reports . . . Maritime Unit." "History of the
            Maritime Unit."
23   "With the possibilities . . . the harbor." Woolley memo, dated
            1942, NARA.
25   "Soon after I . . . mock-up unit." Commander H. Woolley
            to Colonel M. Preston Goodfellow, "Underwater Swimming
            Units," November 23, 1942, NARA.
25   "for thirty minutes . . . ten feet." Commander H. Woolley,
            "Using Self-Contained Breathing Apparatus," October 25, 1942,
            NARA. The memo is significant because it is one of the first
            times a near version of the term "SCUBA" is used.
26   "might possibly be . . . apparatus." Ibid.
26   "appeared to have . . . underwater swimming." Ibid.
27   "To learn about . . . hypercapnia." R. D. Vann "Lambertsen
            and O_2: Beginnings of operational physiology," UHM 2004,
            Vol. 31, No. 1—Lambertsen and O_2. Also from author
            interviews.
27   "Chris was impressed . . . of ventilation." Ibid.
27   "The demonstration was . . . done that." Ibid.
28   "My pressure tests went . . . a goner." Ibid.

28   "As one of my professors . . . my education." Ibid.

28   "tests were carried out . . . with it." Woolley memo, NARA.

29   "apparatus in a proper . . . by the diver." "History of the
            Maritime Unit;" also various OSS technical memos by Woolley,
            Taylor, and Duncan, dated 1942, NARA.

29   "The Diving Unit . . . with respiration." Ibid.

29   "[When Frank] had heard about this . . . as possible." Woolley
            memo, 1942, NARA.

29   "that cash would be paid for them." Ibid.

30   Early OSS documents referred to the LARU as the Browne-
            Lambertsen rebreather.

CHAPTER 4:
COMBAT SWIMMERS

31   "made it impossible to stay in longer." Jack Taylor, "Report on
            Ocean Trials of Browne Lung," 1943, NARA.

32   "the regulator in the oxygen . . . to burst." Ibid.

34   "coach and advisor . . . Navy Dep," Lt. Robert Duncan to
            Commander Woolley, letter, May 19, 1943, NARA.

34   "We will need . . . that time." Ibid.

34   "specially trained force . . . trench mortars," Lt. Robert Duncan
            to Commander H. Woolley, interoffice memo, May 8, 1943,
            NARA.

35   "the boards can . . . chambers." Ibid.

35   "there is no question . . . at sea." Ibid.

35   "In general, I . . . the beach." Lt. Jack Taylor, "Comments on
            Aqua-Marines," May 13, 1943, NARA.

36   "With reference to . . . one assignment." Lt. J. H. Duncan to
            Taylor via Commander Woolley, memo, July 1, 1943, NARA.

36   "a good man . . . the game." Maritime Unit Assessments, Area D,
            1943, NARA.

36   "A very good . . . the average." Ibid.

37   "enough wind to . . . folbots." Area D training memos, 1943,
            NARA.

37   "I believe that . . . very little." Commander H. Woolley, memo,
            "OSS Surfboards," 1943, NARA.

38   John P. Spence's description of the origin of the term "frogman"
            comes from Patrick Kiger, "John Spence: Fighting Frogman,"

AARP blog, posted November 5, 2013, http://blog.aarp.org
/2013/11/05/john-spence-fighting-frogman/. The author also
interviewed Spence in 2003. (Over the course of twenty-two years,
he has conducted more than four thousand interviews with World
War II veterans, including interviews with five hundred operational
members of the OSS. The interviews were cross-checked with
the documents in the National Archives. He has spent more than
a decade researching hundreds of thousands of records for the
OSS and has written four books on the subject. Thousands of
documents were used to write this book.)

38   "shape . . . vertical fins." "History of the Maritime Unit."

38   "transferred in great secrecy." Ibid.

38   "other flaws developed." Ibid.; also from other OSS internal
        documents at NARA.

39   "both hand and foot." Ibid.

39   "The significance of the order . . . the field." Ibid.

40   "if he was not . . . the U.S. Navy." Taylor to Woolley, 1943,
        NARA.

CHAPTER 5:
SILVER SPRINGS

41   "The Champ." The opening scene comes from an interoffice
        memo from Duncan to Sexton, "Trips to Florida," September 7,
        1943," NARA.

42   "I remember showing him . . . favorite things!" KTVZ.com
        news sources, "'America's first frogman' dies in Bend at 95,"
        KTVZ.com, October 30, 2013, www.ktvz.com/news/americas
        -first-frogman-dies-in-bend-at-95/22721664.

42   "exchanged ideas with . . . underwater equipment." Lt. Duncan
        to Lt. Com. Sexton, letter, October 2, 1943, NARA; also,
        "COMBAT DEMOLITION UNIT (U.S. NAVY) Proposed
        Joint Action with MARITIME UNIT," September 2, 1943,
        NARA.

42   "Every man . . . potential use." Ibid.

43   "a discussion with . . . demolition unit." Ibid.

43   "the training of . . . duplicating effort." Ibid.

43   Additional detail on the trip to Silver Springs comes from several
        memos located in the NARA: Duncan to Woolley, August 23,
        1943; Sexton to Woolley, August 26, 1943; Sexton to Duncan,

September 7, 1943; Sexton to Lichtman, September 14, 1943.

43   "I received one . . . useless orders." Lt. Duncan to Lt. Com.
        Sexton, "Report on Trip to Ft. Pierce, FL. and Silver Springs,
        FL," October 2, 1943, NARA.

44   "As I have discussed . . . under guard." Captain Alfred Lichtman
        to Lt. Commander Sexton, "Work at Silver Springs," September
        17, 1943, NARA.

44   "Experimentation under Lt. Alexander . . . all matters." Ibid.

CHAPTER 6:
CRAZY YANKS: THE MARITIME UNIT'S
BEACHHEAD IN EGYPT

47   Opening scene comes from author interview with Lloyd Smith
        and internal OSS memos.

48   "six foot five . . . his thigh." Hayden, *Wanderer*, 312.

49   "Haven't [I] seen . . . Oh." Ibid., 310

49   "the chiefs of . . . hair." Ibid.

49   "oddly chilling guy." Persico, *Piercing the Reich*, 124.

49   "To be truly challenging . . . of life" Hayden, *Wanderer*, 23–24.

50   "like a duck to water." OSS training memo, Hayden personnel
        file, NARA.

51   "To complete my . . . John Hamilton." Hayden, *Wanderer*, 310.

52   "I developed a system . . . be killed." O'Donnell, *Operatives,
        Spies, and Saboteurs*, 4.

52   "To break a bear hug . . . Ruin him." Ibid., 5.

52   "Unfortunately, his insults . . . his arms." Henrik Kruger, *Hans V.
        Tofte Den Danske Krikshelt* (Aschehoug Danish Publisher, 2005),
        from Clint Sporman, who provided translation.

53   "In a sense . . . out alive." *Operatives, Spies, and Saboteurs*, 5

53   "every bit as . . . a bayonet." Author interview.

54   "means of a piratical war." Wilson to Churchill, September 9,
        1943, NARA; also, author interview.

55   "protection from the . . . base camp." Taylor to HQ, memo,
        August 1943, NARA.

55   "it was absolutely . . . Middle East." Taylor to Woolley, cable,
        August 1943, NARA.

56   "Daffy intolerable. . . . hasn't heard." "History of Maritime Unit

in Cairo," NARA.

56   "was completed two . . . exasperating delays." Jack Taylor,
        memos on *Samothrace*, September 1943, NARA.

56   "borrowed a Jeep . . . some sailing." Hayden, *Wanderer*, 310.

56   "Some of these . . . and goldbricking." "History of the Maritime
        Unit in Cairo," NARA.

57   "they were wasting . . . maritime matters." Ibid.

CHAPTER 7:
PIRATE YACHTS AND SPIES OF THE CLOTH

60   "urgently needed medical . . . from Cairo." Taylor to Deputy
        Director of ME, "Maritime Ferrying Service—Report on Trip to
        Samos and Turkey," October 13, 1943, NARA.

60   "Samos being dead . . . impossible situation." Ibid.

60   "grab any fast . . . and speed." Ibid.

60   "good use." Ibid.

60   "blew a fuse." Ibid.

60   "U.S. was not . . . very unappreciative." Ibid.

62   "dive-bombed and strafed . . . starboard." Ibid.

62   "Nine Junkers circling . . . debris column." Ibid.

CHAPTER 8:
"HAGGLING, BRIBING, FINES, DELAYS,
INSPECTIONS, BULLSHIT"

65   "If that crazy . . . take you." Taylor to Deputy Director of ME,
        "Maritime Ferrying Service—Report on Trip to Samos and
        Turkey," October 13, 1943, NARA.

65   "three hours of . . . plain uncooperativeness." Ibid.

66   "checked with the . . . British hands." Ibid.

66   "he had thought . . . was gone." Ibid.

66   "The operator assured . . . could get." Ibid.

66   "We prepared to . . . to go." Ibid.

66   "It seemed all . . . them short." Ibid.

67   "Departing, we were . . . the island." Ibid.

67   "more knots than . . . and sail." Ibid.

67   "Bomb burst and . . . Turkish coast." Ibid.

68   "Lieutenant Taylor has . . . to Maritime." Acting Chief,
        Maritime Unit, to Lt. Col. William P. Davis, III, "Background

Report as of September 30, 1943," November 29, 1943, NARA.

68   "Provisionally tried underwater . . . destruction." Jack Taylor, "Outline of Maritime Operations Proposed by Maritime Unit of OSS," September 10, 1943, NARA.

69   "Underwater operatives and . . . enemy defenses." Ibid.

70   "his appreciation for . . . medical supplies." Taylor, "Maritime Ferrying Service."

70   "It was experience . . . Yugoslav partisans." "History of the Maritime Unit."

70   "sign for it . . . their mind." Taylor, memo to OSS HQ, October 1943, NARA.

70   "a formidable sheaf . . . complex situation." Hayden, *Wanderer*, 310.

70   "a group of escapees . . . Greek Islands." Ibid., 311.

70   "The British . . . fistful of orders," Ibid.

CHAPTER 9:
TREASURE ISLAND

74   "I was a lifeguard . . . I volunteered." Author interview.

75   "who was jokingly . . . his tail." Ibid.

75   "a certain amount of consternation." Ibid.

75   "ideal for planting . . . underwater demolitions." "History of the Maritime Unit."

77   "The first few . . . being detected." Author interview and John Booth, "*Report on Operation Cincinnati*," NARA.

78   "In these tests . . . underwater swimmers." Roosevelt, *War Report of the OSS*, 227.

78   "The exercise was . . . terrorist attacks." LCDR Michael Bennett, USCG, "The US Coast Guard and OSS Maritime Operations During World War II," last updated January 8, 2009, www.cia .gov/library/center-for-the-study-of-intelligence/csi-publications /csi-studies/studies/vol-52-no-4/guardian-spies.html.

CHAPTER 10:
THE *YANKEE*, OPERATION AUDREY, AND THE BOOT

81   Opening scene from author interview with Lloyd Smith.

82   "everything was in . . . first impossible," Carl Hoffmann, Chief
      SO, *OSS Partisan Supply Operations*, 1944, NARA; numerous
      internal documents on the operation were also sourced.

83   "It has simply . . . vessels running." Ward Ellen, "Report on
      'Audrey'," March 25, 1944, NARA.

83   "virtually without a rest." *OSS Partisan Supply Operations*, 1944,
      NARA.

83   "Within the next . . . boats arrived." Ibid.

83   "Within three weeks . . . to receive." Ibid.

85   "battered, leaking fishing schooners." Ibid.

85   "quite remarkable since . . . not risk." Ibid.

85   "responsible for the . . . except communications." Ibid.; also *War
      Report of the OSS.*

85   "By plunging through . . . weather served." Hayden, *Wanderer*,
      313–314.

86   "repeatedly asked the . . . surface craft." "History of the Maritime
      Unit."

CHAPTER 11:
"THE LITTLE PEARL HARBOR"

87   "A mob of . . . ran madly." Hayden, *Wanderer*, 312.

87   "pumped tracers over . . . effect whatever." Ibid.

88   Scene of Hayden's interaction with the Yugoslav partisans. Ibid.,
      312–313.

CHAPTER 12:
THE ULTIMATE RESCUE

91   The scene on the C-53 comes from various excellent survivor
      accounts, including Lawrence O. Abbott and Clinton W.
      Abbott, *Out of Albania: A True Account of a WWII Underground
      Rescue Mission*, and Agnes Jensen Mangerich, *Albanian Escape:
      The True Story of U.S. Army Nurses Behind Enemy Lines*. The
      author also wrote about the escape in *Operatives, Spies, and
      Saboteurs* and conducted interviews with their rescuer, Lloyd
      Smith.

93   "It was learned . . . in Albania." OSS Memo on Stranded Nurses,
      1943, NARA.

94   "When the brass . . . the States." Hayden, *Wanderer*, 312.

94   "like we were . . . a bank." Ibid.

95   "I arrived at . . . partisan territory." Lloyd Smith, "Report
        on Rescue of Nurses," Smith Personnel File and Albanian
        operations, NARA.

96   "We have people . . . your help." Ibid.

96   "It was still . . . out again." Ibid.

97   "Crawl up. . . . rope tight!" Lawrence O. Abbott and Clinton
        W. Abbott, *Out of Albania: A True Account of a WWII
        Underground Rescue Mission* (Lulu Press, 2010), 173–176.

97   "to find out . . . landing forces." Hayden's Silver Star Award and
        memo from Tofte, NARA.

97   "Captain [Hayden] managed . . . the 25th." Ibid.

98   "However, Captain [Hayden] . . . the Jeep." Ibid.

98   "After a hazardous . . . 27 December." Ibid.

98   "No Allied aircraft . . . by hand." Hayden, *Wanderer*, 316.

98   "On the way . . . to be." Ibid.

99   "immediate steps were . . . temporary standstill." Hans Tofte,
        Hayden's Silver Star Commendation, NARA.

99   Scene with British general and Yugoslav partisans. Hayden,
        Wanderer, 315–316.

CHAPTER 13:
BACK TO ALBANIA

101   "We're sending you back in." Author interview with Smith.

102   "This cousin was . . . entirely theirs." Lloyd Smith to Chief,
        Special Operations, Cairo Section, "Evacuation of Three
        American Nurses from Albania," March 29, 1944, NARA.

102   "We always tell . . . to do." Ibid.

103   "We waited in . . . just shivering." Ibid.

103   "If my cousin . . . on him." Ibid.

103   "was awakened . . . bring them." Ibid.

104   "in the best . . . had received." Ibid.

104   "The coast was . . . German-held shore." Ward Ellen memo and
        commendation, NARA.

104   "about thirty of . . . in circles." Hayden, *Wanderer*, 316–317.

105   "No one said . . . a time." Ibid., 317.

105   "I had agreed . . . We go!" Ibid., 325.

106   "were suddenly relieved . . . figure heads," Ellen memo on MU
        Italy, 1944, NARA; also "History of the Maritime Unit."

106   "Since the British . . . to them." Ellen memo on MU Italy, 1944,
        NARA.

106   "18,932 rifles, . . . American divisions." Hoffmann, *OSS Partisan
        Supply Operations.*

107   "the cost of . . . of OSS." Ibid.

CHAPTER 14:
NO PICNIC

109   "supplying ten tons . . . starving islanders." Taylor, résumé of
        activities, 1944, NARA.

109   "using British pinpoints . . . greater independence."
        Commanding Officer, Hq. SBS to Operations Officer, OSS
        Algiers, "Report on 'Picnic' Operation," April 5, 1944, NARA.

109   "strongly recommended that . . . practically over." Ibid.

110   "because he had . . . and judgment." Ibid.

110   "We discovered that . . . yards apart." J. H. Taylor, "Outline
        of Duties with Office of Strategic Services," October 4, 1945,
        NARA.

110   "Since the sector . . . everything possible." "Report on 'Picnic'
        Operation," NARA.

111   "pyrotechnic signal flare . . . port side." A. C. Young to the
        Commanding Officer, "Report on Picnic II," April 4, 1944,
        NARA.

111   "The vessel returning . . . without water." Taylor, "Outline of
        Duties."

111   "At all times . . . radio transmitter." "Report on 'Picnic'
        Operation"; also documents relating to Taylor's Navy Cross
        commendation, Taylor personnel file, NARA.

112   "dodging Germans and unfriendly Albanians." Taylor, "Outline
        of Duties."

112   "The enclosed communications . . . in advance." Taylor, Mission
        Report, 1944, the cover letter from Donovan is also included in
        the report, NARA.

113   "Full political . . . into consideration." Ibid.

CHAPTER 15:
THE KELLY PLAN

116   "Realizing: (a) The superb . . . Italian personnel." Richard M.
       Kelly, "Kelly Project," NARA.

116   "MU-OSS is the . . . the British." Ibid.

116   "would in a . . . any theater." Ibid.

117   "suggesting methods not . . . Majesty's Navy" "History of the
       Maritime Unit."

117   "the sinking or . . . temperature, etc." Ibid.

117   "a large swimming . . . an hour." OSS Documents on Decima
       MAS, NARA.

118   The operators intensely trained for a year. Greene and
       Massignani, *The Black Prince*, 26.

118   "Thus, by proper . . . by sabotage." "History of the Maritime
       Unit."

118   "1. A close-fitting rubber . . . to swimming." Ibid.

119   "Italian divers and . . . while closed." Ibid.

120   "make available the . . . Marco Battalion." Ibid.; also various
       documents associated with MU and the Mediterranean theater.

120   "about fifty years . . . the Allies." Morde letter, NARA.

120   "fanatic in the . . . mysterious guile." Doug Henwood, "Spooks
       in Blue," in Namebase.org., accessed March 2014, www.
       namebase.org/campus/henwood.html.

121   "take over the . . . the Pacific." MU memo dated 1944, NARA.

121   The OSS cataloged . . . the Pacific. Frank J. Rafalko, ed. *Counter
       Intelligence in World War II, A Counterintelligence Reader, Vol. 2.*
       (National Counterintelligence Center), www.fas.org/irp/ops/ci
       /docs/ci2/.

122   "It was the . . . valuable work." "History of the Maritime Unit."

122   "lack of German . . . sabotage activities." Ibid.

122   "rough but accurate . . . German fortifications." *War Report of the
       OSS*, II:70.

122   "take charge of . . . and demolitions equipment." "History of the
       Maritime Unit."

123   "The duke and . . . could operate." Morde letter, NARA.

123   "The main charge . . . the stern." Washington to Algiers,
       Incoming message/cable, June 9, 1944, NARA.

124   "because of commitments . . . this matter." Washington to
       Algiers, Incoming message/cable, May 1, 1944, NARA.

124   "Lt. Kelly immediately . . . of Italy." "History of the Maritime Unit."

CHAPTER 16:
OSSINING

125   "Considerable [enemy] personnel . . . at traffic." "History of the Maritime Unit."
126   "intelligence information, which . . . high priority." Ibid.
126   "not adept at . . . up bridges." Morde letter, NARA.
126   "They are cocky . . . and gratitude." Ibid.
127   "Handling other trainees, . . . field man." Training records, NARA.
127   "to destroy two . . . of Pesaro." "History of the Maritime Unit."
128   "four Nazi armored . . . several days." Ibid.
128   "A seven hundred . . . downed airmen." Ibid.
128   "all personnel escaped without injury," Ibid.
128   "Although the Maritime . . . in Italy." Ibid.
129   "excellent point to land." Packard Mission Report, NARA; also after-action debriefing, NARA.
129   "The region was very . . . natural hiding-place." Ibid.
129   "[Crossing the highway] . . . stopped us." Ibid.
130   "was of the . . . and urgency." Ibid.
130   "were of tremendous help . . . their breakthrough." Ibid.

CHAPTER 17:
SWIMMER COMMANDOS

131   Opening scene from author interview with Gordon Soltau and various memos on Operation Betty.
131   "reduce the striking power." "History of L-Unit," NARA.
132   "Right before D-Day, . . . was scrubbed." Ibid.
132   "The most conspicuous . . . definite missions." "History of the Maritime Unit."
133   "It was obvious . . . than this." Ibid.
133   "when he became . . . Lambertsen unit." Ibid.
133   "Dampness and cool . . . of depth." "History of L-Unit."
134   The acronym SDV can refer to "swimmer delivery vehicle" or "SEAL delivery vehicle."
134   "whenever a particular . . . never materialized." Ibid.

136   "the [OSS swimmers] . . . by then." Edwin P. Hoyt, *SEALs at War* (New York: Dell Publishing, 1993), no page number available.

137   "in distress and . . . swim further." *Operatives, Spies, and Saboteurs*; also "Report on Burrfish" and "Report on Mission to Yap," NARA.

137   "they abandoned all . . . no success." Ibid.

139   "I jumped up . . . get closer." Author interview.

139   "perfectly at home . . . very nice." Ibid.

139   "Just remembering it . . . around us." Ibid.

139   "Get your goddamn . . . of there!" Ibid.

140   "I held my . . . the charge." Ibid.

140   "Boom!" Ibid.

140   "It was sickening . . . little bellies." Ibid.

140   "This was a . . . your life." Ibid.

141   "As we swam . . . cannon fire." Ibid.

141   "When you get . . . back in." Ibid.

141   "We had a . . . went by." Ibid.

142   "Why didn't you . . . clandestine mean?" Ibid.

142   "We weren't there . . . the bushel." Ibid.

142   "It ran pretty . . . underwater demolition." Ibid.

143   "Where are the . . . Forces refined." Ibid.

143   "Shooting wasn't our . . . their fires." Ibid.

144   "If we were . . . a hook." Ibid.

144   "several wires and old wreckage." Ibid.

145   "expressed a desire . . . [OSS] again." "History of the Maritime Unit."

145   "expressed his appreciation and satisfaction." Ibid.

145   "obtained hydrographic and . . . of chaungs." Ibid.

146   "This area abounds . . . possibilities." Ibid.

146   "a siege of . . . training course." Ibid.

146   "Johnny . . . paddy [rice] farmer." "Methods of identifying members of the Caprice Party," August 17, 1945, NARA.

147   "You are not . . . my life." Author interview.

CHAPTER 18:
THE DUPONT MISSION

152   "I am an . . . help you." Persico, *Piercing the Reich*, 120.

154   "refresher course." Taylor, résumé of activities, NARA.

CHAPTER 19:
"I WAS PROMISED THIS MISSION,
AND I WANT IT"

156   "a flat cultivated . . . excellent cover." Jack Taylor, "Dupont Mission Report," May 30, 1945, NARA.

158   "I was promised . . . want it." Persico, *Piercing the Reich*, 125.

158   "were in their . . . their integrity." Taylor, "Dupont Mission Report."

158   "could be depended . . . an emergency." Ibid.

158   "entirely abnormal . . . four bodies." Ibid.

159   "I pulled down . . . front yard." Ibid.

159   "To our amazement . . . previous run." Ibid.

159   "To our utter . . . an investigation." Ibid.

159   "I stepped in . . . containers." Ibid.

160   "a medium-sized marsh . . . sleeping bag." Ibid.

160   "continued past Nougledel . . . Leithe Geb." Ibid.

161   "As it was . . . the hayloft." Ibid.

161   "Buchleitner and family . . . by others." Ibid.

162   "a locomotive factory . . . January [1945]." Ibid.

162   "housed several hundred . . . ever seen." Ibid.

162   "two trains of . . . human beings." Ibid.

162   "was being widened . . . themselves working." Ibid.

163   "Political information showed . . . (people's army)." Ibid.

164   "would go to . . . as machinery." Ibid.

164   Living up to . . . his girlfriend. "The Overseas Target," *OSS History Vol II*, 318.

165   "Suddenly, the door . . . his head." Taylor, "Dupont Mission Report."

CHAPTER 20:
VIENNA CAPTIVITY

169   Quotes in this chapter come from Jack Taylor, "Dupont Mission Report Part II: Capture, Gestapo and Vienna Prison."

CHAPTER 21:
DECIMA MAS STRIKES BACK

175   Unless otherwise specified, quotes in this chapter come from Staff Officer (Intelligence) Leghorn, "Unsuccessful Limpeteer Attack on Leghorn. 18th–19th November, 1944," Report, November 25, 1944, NARA.

178   "Explorer Theodore . . . without saying." Theodore Morde, "In the Lost City of Ancient America's Monkey God," *Milwaukee Sentinel,* September 22, 1940, 28–29, news.google.com/ newspapers
?nid=1368&dat=19400922&id=yjBQAAAAIBAJ&sjid=Nw 0EAAAAIBAJ&pg=6930,4275460.

179   "Frankly I am . . . this war." Morde to Lichtman, letter, January 22, 1945, NARA.

179   "Mines go off . . . the harbor." Ibid.

179   "ten Lambertsen Diving . . . each unit." Lt. G. M. Kaydouh, USNR to Col. Edward J. G. Glavin, letter, October 4, 1944, NARA.

180   "boatman . . . chests." Lupo Team Report, NARA.

180   "[One agent] lost . . . genital organs." Ibid.

CHAPTER 22:
THE EIGHTH ARMY DETACHMENT

183   "Captain Thiele personally . . . serious damage." Captain Thiele's Citation for Legion of Merit, NARA.

184   "flair for handling . . . and airplanes." Ibid.

184   Walkiria Terradura, a . . . years to come. "Walkiria's War: The True Story of Walkiria Terradura," www.walkiriaswar.com/ story4.html.

185   "unusually frank and . . . highly reliable" Monteleone Personnel File, NARA.

186   "The San Marco . . . be trained." Author interview and
       Operatives, Spies, and Saboteurs, 132.
186   "The men would . . . Corsini Canal." Robert Young, "The
       OSS's Eighth Army Detachment in Italy: A Few Men and Their
       Radio," *The OSS Society Journal*, Summer/Fall 2010.
187   "We landed the . . . German voices." Author interview.
187   "As soon as . . . German battery." Bionda Mission Report,
       Bionda Radio File, and reports related to the operation, NARA.
187   "We didn't hear . . . got captured." Author interview.
188   "Since the last . . . the region." Bionda Mission Report; author
       interview.
188   "scarce in clothing . . . 12 October." Bionda Mission Report.
188   "I immediately reached . . . an explosion." Ibid.
188   "During the time . . . excellent work." Ibid.
189   "the best piece . . . of Italy." Alphonse Thiele, *History of the
       Eighth Army Detachment*, 1945, NARA.
190   "One cannot overstress . . . one's disposal." Ibid.
190   "This was the . . . returned safely." Ibid.
190   "In all, fifteen . . . on shore." Ibid.
190   "be incorporated into . . . Ops Officer." *War Report of the OSS*,
       Vol II, 102.
190   "It is gratifying . . . their own." Thiele, *History of the Eighth Army
       Detachment*.

CHAPTER 23:
STELLA

Quotes in this chapter come from the Stella Mission Report, NARA.

CHAPTER 24:
INDIANA JONES

195   "This coast is . . . ten men." Morde to Lee, letter, January 1945,
       NARA.
195   "showed an appreciation." Thiele, *History of the Eighth Army
       Detachment*; *War Report of the OSS*, Vol. II, 102.
195   "inland, supplying the . . . red cabbages." Morde to Lichtman,
       letter, January 22, 1945, NARA; also "Full Report on
       Destruction of P-584," NARA.

198   "For three and . . . said so." Hayden, *Wanderer*, 330.
199   "I don't mean . . . the war." Ibid., 229.

CHAPTER 25:
SURVIVING

Quotes in this chapter come from the Dupont Mission Report.

CHAPTER 26:
MAUTHAUSEN

Quotes in this chapter come from the Dupont Mission Report.

CHAPTER 27:
LAST ACTS

215   To lay the foundation . . . partisan resistance. *War Report of the OSS*, 115.
215   "impossible . . . transport organizations." Thiele, *History of the Eighth Army Detachment*; other reports on the Eighth Army Detachment and Company D, NARA.
215   "Activity of partisan . . . this development." Kesselring to subordinates, telegram, February 26, 1945, in *War Report of the OSS*, Vol. II, 114.
216   "resulted in the . . . firing a shot." Hearn's Citation for Bronze Star Medal, NARA.
217   "[MU will] move . . . this material." Kelly, "Operational Report, Company D 1–15 March, 1945," March 18, 1945, NARA.

CHAPTER 28:
GOD BLESS AMERICA

219   "I was so . . . without fainting." Taylor, Dupont Mission Report.
219   "Terribly optimistic rumors . . . eventually died." Ibid.
220–221 "started the evacuation . . . and sugar." Ibid.
221   Unbeknownst to Taylor . . . the camps. Ibid.
221   The rest of . . . April 28. Transcripts of Mauthausen-Gusen Camp Trials, NARA.

222   "American P-38s came . . . coming fast." Taylor, Dupont
        Mission Report.

222   "stressed the fact . . . liberation." Former Staff Sgt. Albert J.
        Kosiek, "Liberation of Mauthausen (and KZ Gusen I, II & III),"
        THUNDERBOLT—The 11th Ard. Div. Association, Vol. 8, No.
        7, May–June 1955, webcache.googleusercontent.com/search?q
        =cache:http://www.nizkor.org/hweb/camps/gusen/kosiek1x.htm.

223   "From beginning to . . . presenting arms." Ibid.

223   "that an American . . . Bless America." Taylor, Dupont Mission
        Report.

CHAPTER 29:
SUNSET

228   "dispatched upstream, swimming . . . the way." Operation
        Caprice V reports and memos, August 1945, NARA.

228   "comprehensive film report . . . wooden craft submersible."
        Donovan, Commendation recommendation, NARA.

CHAPTER 30:
"THIS IS THE FIRST TIME
I'VE EVER BEEN IN THE MOVIES"

229   "I'm lieutenant senior . . . this lager." The original version of
        the film resides in NARA. An online version of the film can be
        found at www.jewishvirtuallibrary.org/jsource/Holocaust/mauth
        film.html.

230   "Five or six . . . in time." Ibid.

230   "The boys rustled . . . the morning." Kosiek, "Liberation of
        Mauthausen."

231   "running down SS . . . the area." Taylor, Dupont Mission
        Report.

231   "death books." Ibid.

231   "outstanding . . . the best war-crimes evidence." Persico,
        Piercing the Reich, 312, and Harry Cimring, American Dental
        Association, "In Memoriam" article; various documents related
        to the trial located in NARA.

EPILOGUE

233   "Will you describe . . . eating." Transcripts of Mauthausen-
       Gusen Camp Trials, NARA.
234   All quotes are from the transcripts of Mauthausen-Gusen Camp
       Trials, NARA.
235   All quotes are from the transcripts of Mauthausen-Gusen Camp
       Trials, NARA.
236   "For the safety . . . UDT missions." Francis D. Fane, *The Naked
       Warriors: The Elite Fighting Force That Became the Navy Seals*
       (Annapolis, MD: Naval Institute Press, 1995), 279.
236   "It had been . . . we turned." Ibid., 290–291.
236   "There was a . . . Roman Coliseum." Ibid., 291.
237   "The day . . . far off." Ibid., 293.
237   "additional unconventional warfare . . . universal capability."
       Rear Adm. William E. Gentner, memorandum, March 10, 1961.
237   "I am directing . . . and reoriented." John F. Kennedy, "Special
       Message to the Congress on Urgent National Needs," speech
       delivered May 25, 1961.

THE FIRST SEALS AFTER THE WAR

239   "For extraordinary heroism . . . Allied Arms." Jack Taylor's Navy
       Cross Citation, NARA.
240   Details on Jack Taylor's death from an ADA "In Memoriam"
       article written by Taylor's dental partner, Harry Cimring.
240   "I can no . . . bodily fluids." *Dr. Strangelove or: How I Learned to
       Stop Worrying and Love the Bomb*, directed by Stanley Kubrick,
       1964.
243   "It is recommended . . . this agency." William Donovan to the
       Adjutant General of the War Department, "Recommendation
       for the Award of the Legion of Merit to Commander H.G.A.
       Woolley, D.S.C., Royal Navy," letter, June 21, 1945, NARA.
247   Information on Hans Tofte from James Barron, "Hans Tofte,
       World War II Spy Later Dismissed by the C.I.A.," *New York
       Times*, August 28, 1987, www.nytimes.com/1987/08/28/
       obituaries/hans-tofte-world-war-ii-spy-later-dismissed-by-the
       -cia.html.
248   "I screwed my . . . a thing." Author interview.
248   "senior hotties at . . . American Veterans]." Ibid.

INDEX

Combat historian, bestselling author, and renowned leadership speaker Patrick K. O'Donnell has written nine critically acclaimed books that recount the epic stories of America's wars.

His books include *Dog Company: The Boys of Pointe du Hoc—The Rangers who Accomplished D-Day's Toughest Mission and Led the Way across Europe; Give Me Tomorrow: The Korean War's Greatest Untold Story–The Epic Stand Of The Marines Of George Company; Beyond Valor; Into the Rising Sun; Operatives, Spies, and Saboteurs;* and *The Brenner Assignment.* He also wrote *They Dared Return,* which provided the inspiration for the film *The Real Inglorious Bastards.* In addition, his book *We Were One: Shoulder to Shoulder With the Marines Who Took Fallujah* was selected for the USMC Commandant's Professional Reading List, and all of his books have been selections of the History, Military, and/or Book-of-the-Month Clubs.

A frequent contributor to the *National Review* and other major publications, O'Donnell has provided historical consultation for Dreamworks' award-winning miniseries *Band of Brothers* and for scores of documentaries produced by the BBC, History Channel, and Discovery Channel.

During the Battle of Fallujah, he served as a combat historian and war correspondent in a Marine rifle platoon. He is also an expert on WWII espionage, special operations, and counterinsurgency on the modern battlefield.

He is a recipient of the Colby Award, which is awarded to non-fiction "that has made a major contribution to the understanding of intelligence operations, military history, or international affairs," and he received the 2012 OSS Society's Waller Award for outstanding scholarship in special operations and espionage.

He is also the founder of The Drop Zone, the first online oral history website for WWII veterans. Over the past twenty years, O'Donnell has interviewed over 4,000 veterans who fought in America's wars, from WWI to Afghanistan.

www.facebook.com/patrickkodonnell
www.thedropzone.org
www.patrickkodonnell.com